100 THINGS BRONCOS FANS SHOULD KNOW & DO BEFORE THEY DIE

100 THINGS BRONCOS FANS SHOULD KNOW & DO BEFORE THEY DIE

Brian Howell

The Library of Congress has catalogued the previous edition as follows:
Howell, Brian, 1974–
100 things Broncos fans should know & do before they die / Brian Howell.
p. cm.
Includes bibliographical references.
ISBN 978-1-60078-732-4
1. Denver Broncos (Football team)—Miscellanea. I. Title. II. Title: One hundred things Broncos fans should know and do before they die.
GV958.D37H68 2012
796.332'640978883—dc23
2012017040

This book is available in quantity at special discounts for your group or organization. For further information, contact:

Triumph Books LLC
814 North Franklin Street
Chicago, Illinois 60610
(312) 337-0747
www.triumphbooks.com

Printed in U.S.A.
ISBN: 978-1-62937-316-4
Design by Patricia Frey

For Melissa, Connor, Isabel, Lucas, and Mason

Contents

Acknowledgments

There was a time when professional football in Denver wasn't so popular, wasn't so lucrative, and wasn't so fun to watch. When Austin "Goose" Gonsoulin joined the Broncos as a rookie in 1960, he seriously wondered whether there would even be a team in 1961.

Nearly 60 years later, the Broncos have become one of the model franchises in the National Football League. Although it took a while for them to learn to win, the Broncos eventually figured it out and haven't really stopped. They've won three Super Bowls and played in eight. They have produced four Hall of Fame players (with many more to come). For me, a lifelong fan of the franchise, researching and writing about some of the most memorable players, coaches, games, and seasons in team history was a pure joy.

Many individuals contributed to this book. I am grateful for the insights, stories, and memories provided by former Broncos greats Billy Thompson, Tom Jackson, Floyd Little, Shannon Sharpe, Goose Gonsoulin, Karl Mecklenburg, Craig Morton, Steve Atwater, Marlin Briscoe, Alfred Williams, and Sammy Winder and former head coach Dan Reeves. Recent players Elvis Dumervil, Eric Decker, and David Bruton were gracious with their time as well.

In addition, the memories and opinions of longtime Denver sports talk host Sandy Clough, former Broncos radio broadcaster Larry Zimmer, and *Denver Post* writer Terry Frei assisted me greatly. The stories of former Denver Gold running back Harry Sydney and Robert Howsam, the son of the Broncos' original owner Bob Howsam, helped make this book come alive even more.

Thanks to Broncos public-relations guru Jim Saccomano, whose knowledge of the team is unsurpassed. Thanks also to Broncos executive director of media relations Patrick Smyth and

Denver radio personalities Andy Lindahl and Brandon Krisztal, whose assistance in contacting former players was invaluable.

Finally, thanks to my wife, Melissa, and our children, Connor, Isabel, Lucas, and Mason, who put up with my long hours and late nights at the computer and the library.

Introduction

I was nine years old the first time I walked into Mile High Stadium to watch the Denver Broncos play a football game. It was only the preseason, the lowly Indianapolis Colts were in town, and I was sick the whole night. Yet I still remember it being my introduction to Broncomania. Even in the preseason, Mile High Stadium was a loud place. Of course, it helped that we were sitting in the ever-rowdy south stands.

John Elway was just beginning his second year, and as he grew up as an NFL player, I grew up as a Broncos fan. Tickets were tough to come by, but every once in a while my dad and I found a way to get in. We sat through a 14–7 Broncos loss to the New York Giants on a frigid and snowy day in 1989. We were on our way out of the stadium during a preseason game against the Dallas Cowboys when the thunder inside the stadium began to rumble; we went back to our seats to watch the Broncos win an overtime thriller. We were there during one of Elway's greatest comebacks: against the Houston Oilers in the 1991 playoffs. And I sat through the final, miserable game of the Wade Phillips era.

I still remember the corny parody songs that local radio stations cooked up before the Broncos' trip to the Super Bowl in 1986. I'll never forget watching Gerald Willhite's backflips, Sammy Winder's "Mississippi Mud Walk," Karl Mecklenburg and Rulon Jones terrorizing quarterbacks—and, of course, Elway, the king of them all.

As I got older, my journalism career allowed me to see the Broncos in a different light. I wrote about Terrell Davis the first time he ran for 100 yards, against the Arizona Cardinals in 1995. I covered training camp in Greeley. I sat in the press box during impressive wins and mindboggling losses. I covered the team during the brief Jay Cutler era, the final two years of the Mike

Shanahan era, and the first season of Josh McDaniels' forgettable tenure as head coach.

Through it all, one thing has never changed: the passion for the Broncos is unmatched by any other team in the city, and I doubt it can be matched by most teams around the country.

Looking back, it's amazing to consider that Denver was never supposed to be a football town. Baseball was always pegged to be king in the Mile High City. The Denver Bears were a fixture in town years before football came on the scene. In fact, Denver fielded minor league teams throughout the 20th century and even as far back as the 1800s. Even Mile High Stadium, the original home of the Broncos, was built for baseball; it was originally called Bears Stadium, named for the popular baseball team.

Before the Broncos arrived in 1960, numerous efforts were made to bring Major League Baseball to Denver. All those efforts failed, including a plan that involved the Broncos. Robert Howsam figured that, by founding the football team, he might one day be able to lure an MLB franchise to the city, too.

It took more than three decades, but Major League Baseball did eventually find its way to Denver. But it was football that put Denver on the map as a sports town. It's highly likely that the tremendous success of the Broncos was the pull that eventually led to the Colorado Rockies and Colorado Avalanche NHL team.

To see how far Denver has come as a sports town is remarkable but not nearly as remarkable as how far the Broncos have come. From the start, the Broncos had the look of a franchise doomed to fail—and they almost did. The local media didn't pay much attention to them. Neither did the fans. On more than one occasion, the team nearly left Denver.

Somehow they made it through the rough 1960s and became a significant part of Denver's fabric. Every home game since 1970—when the AFL and NFL announced their blockbuster merger—has been a sellout. "Broncomania" was alive and well in the 1970s, when the Broncos made it to the Super Bowl, throughout the glorious 1980s, and into the championship years in the late 1990s. It continues today, with the city seemingly covered in orange and blue on Sundays in the fall. Media outlets now send teams of journalists to cover the Broncos every week.

Under the direction of owner Pat Bowlen, the Broncos have become an elite franchise in the NFL. Through 2015, the Broncos had been to a NFL record–tying eight Super Bowls (all but one of their appearances coming under Bowlen's watch).

For me, working on this book was not only a trip down memory lane; it was an awesome opportunity to get to know more about the team I grew up with. This book takes a look at the most important players, coaches, and executives in team history, as well

The symbol of Broncos pride, "Bucky the Bronco" adorned the south stands of Mile High Stadium and now looks over the new Sports Authority Field at Mile High. Photo courtesy of Getty Images

as the most significant events in the team's 50-plus years. It tells the story of how the Broncos began as ragtag nobodies and became a team that defines a city; how it became Elway's team; how a young, God-fearing quarterback with mechanical problems became the biggest sports story in the country; and how a Hall of Fame–bound quarterback played out his second act in the Mile High City. It also highlights many other aspects of Colorado that make the state what it is today.

Denver has a Major League Baseball team, a perennial playoff team in the National Basketball Association, a National Hockey League team, and a Major League Soccer champion. It has world-class ski trails just a short drive away. But make no mistake, Denver is—and always will be—a football town.

1 The Duke

The circus came to Denver in the spring of 1983.

People all around town wanted a front-row seat. The press analyzed it from every angle. Denver had never seen such a show, even if it was a one-man production.

May 2, 1983, was the day John Elway became a Denver Bronco. From that day forward, Denver and the Broncos haven't been the same.

"The team was fairly anonymous, and the No.1 overall pick in the NFL Draft decides that he will play for the Denver Broncos," said Tom Jackson, a former teammate and current analyst at ESPN. "He comes to the Broncos and he brings legitimacy."

As a franchise, the Broncos were already 23 years old when Elway arrived. They had been to a Super Bowl. They had the Orange Crush defense. They had seen several great players don the orange and blue.

Elway's arrival was different.

"We had a lot of good things that had happened to us, but John legitimized us in many, many ways," Jackson said. "Making us legit as a football team and as an organization probably meant more than any other one thing that happened to us."

Now, more than 30 years after Elway's arrival in Denver and nearly 20 years after he threw his last pass, nobody disputes that Elway was the best player in franchise history and the greatest athlete in the history of Colorado sports. "The Duke of Denver," as he became known, played his last game on January 31, 1999, yet he is still the most recognizable and beloved athlete in Colorado. His No. 7 jersey is worn all around the state, no matter the time of year.

"John Elway is the greatest of us all," said former Broncos great Floyd Little, who, like Elway, is a member of the Pro Football Hall of Fame.

During Elway's career, from 1983 to 1998, he led the Broncos to two Super Bowl wins, became the first quarterback to start in five Super Bowls, made the Pro Bowl nine times, won an NFL Most Valuable Player award (in 1987), and engineered 47 game-winning or game-tying drives. He also set an NFL record with 148 wins as a starting quarterback (a record which has since been broken). Through the 2015 season, he still ranked among the top 10 in NFL history in completions (4,123), passing attempts (7,250), passing yards (51,475), and touchdown passes (300). Elway was the first starting quarterback in league history to win the Super Bowl in his final game.

"It culminates with back-to-back Super Bowl wins, which really put an exclamation mark behind everything that he did," Jackson said. "But there's nothing more important that ever happened to this organization than John Elway coming and playing for the Broncos."

It all started in 1983. He was the No. 1 pick in the NFL Draft that season—but many forget that he was taken by the Baltimore Colts. After refusing to play for the Colts, Elway was traded to Denver (more on that deal later).

More than 30 quarterbacks have been taken with the No. 1 overall pick in the history of the NFL Draft. Few ever came into the league with as much hype as Elway. He always seemed destined for greatness. Born in Port Angeles, Washington, his father, Jack, was a football coach who made a name for himself at the high school level before a successful career as a college head coach, most notably at San Jose State and Stanford University. Elway was a star baseball player and quarterback at Granada Hills (California) High School and was the most highly recruited prep quarterback in the country in 1979.

He went on to Stanford, where he became an All-American and etched his name all over the NCAA and Pac–10/12 Conference record books. He threw for 9,349 yards and 77 touchdowns for the Cardinal, finishing second in the 1982 Heisman Trophy race (Georgia running back Herschel Walker won the award). In 2015, the Pac-12 Conference celebrated its 100th anniversary and named Elway as its offensive player of the century.

Elway was also a star on the baseball diamond and actually earned his first money as a pro athlete in baseball. Out of high school, he was selected in the 18th round of the draft by the Kansas City Royals but chose not to sign. In 1981, he was a second-round pick of the New York Yankees (selected ahead of future baseball Hall of Famer Tony Gwynn). Elway signed with the Yankees and, in 1982, played for their Single A team in Oneonta, New York.

Despite his prowess on the baseball diamond, there was no question Elway's future was in football.

"All you had to do was watch the film on him and you could tell he was going to be a great quarterback," said Dan Reeves, the Broncos head coach from 1981 to 1992. "What you didn't know was what kind of work ethic he had and everything else, and that showed up very quickly."

The Denver faithful knew something special was on the horizon when the Elway trade was announced. For a franchise and a city that had to live through the not-so-memorable quarterbacking of Mickey Slaughter, Jacky Lee, John McCormick, Max Choboian, Steve Tensi, and more, Elway was an instant celebrity. Even his veteran teammates took notice.

"We went out to watch him throw mini camp probably a couple weeks after that," Jackson said. "We all came to watch him throw, and I know that somewhere in the conversation was, 'We're going to the Super Bowl. We're going to be going to multiple Super Bowls.' The kid could throw like nobody's business. I had just never seen anything like it."

Sammy Winder, who was in his second year as a Broncos running back in 1983, said, "That was the first time I had ever been a part of anything on that level. He was in that fishbowl and everybody was watching him. The good thing about it, he turned out to be the quarterback that all the hype was about. But that first year, with the media and attention and all that he got, if you wanted to be in the paper, be somewhere with John."

For Denver fans, Elway was something they had never seen. To that point, the best quarterbacks in franchise history—Frank Tripucka, Charley Johnson, and Craig Morton—all came to the Broncos as veterans with only a few years left in their tanks. Elway was young, supertalented and, God willing, he would be there a while. Denver's media rode the wave of the hype. During training camp, both Denver newspapers, the *Denver Post* and *Rocky Mountain News*, ran daily updates on what Elway was doing—on the field and off.

Veteran Steve DeBerg was the incumbent starter and he had five years of NFL experience under his belt. He wasn't Elway, though, and when DeBerg was introduced as the starter for the preseason—yes *preseason!*—opener against Seattle on August 5, 1983, the 53,887 fans at Mile High Stadium actually booed. When Elway came into the game in the second half, he executed a 10-play touchdown march on his first drive, completing five of six passes along the way.

Elway's accomplishments in college and his tremendous skill earned him instant respect from his teammates. That preseason opener aside, though, it took a little while for the results to show up.

Reeves named Elway the starter coming out of training camp, but Elway wasn't ready. He completed one of eight passes for 14 yards and an interception in the opener at Pittsburgh before being pulled for DeBerg. Elway started the first five games, but in four of them he was relieved by DeBerg. Through those five games, Elway threw one touchdown pass and five interceptions. "He struggled early because I really started him probably before he was comfortable with the terminology [of the offense]," Reeves said.

Reeves benched Elway for several games, just so his young quarterback could sit back and observe. "When he came back after I had let Steve DeBerg play, John kind of had time to learn the offense," Reeves said. When all was said and done, Elway's rookie year was certainly nothing to brag about. He completed just 47.5 percent of his passes, with seven touchdowns and 14 interceptions. On one play that year, he lined up behind left guard Tom Glassic to take the snap; after a few seconds, Glassic turned around and motioned Elway toward the center. Elway took a lot of heat for his troubles, but former Broncos quarterback Craig Morton, who retired before the 1983 season, said it made Elway better.

"He had to go through all the learning steps," Morton said. "He paid he price. It did not come easy for him. He took all the shit that he could take. When you're that great, you just tone it out. You don't read what your critics are saying. He was destined to be the greatest. If you come out of it, you're going to be great. If you don't, you'll be like a lot of them that can't do it, and you're not going to win anything. You've got to take a lot of crap to be successful."

As disappointing as Elway's rookie year turned out to be, that season also provided the first glimpse into what was to come. In Game 15 of that season, the Broncos played host to the Colts. The team that Elway spurned jumped to a 19–0 lead after three quarters. In the fourth quarter, Elway threw salt on the wound by tossing three touchdown passes, the last with just 44 seconds left, to lead the Broncos to a 21–19 win. It was the first of his legendary comeback wins. "That's when you knew you had something special," Reeves said. "It didn't take long to figure out you were going to have a chance in every ballgame you were in."

In 1984, the Broncos went 13–3, including 12–2 in Elway's starts. He led them to three fourth-quarter comebacks as they won the AFC West division. Then he started all 16 games in 1985, going 11–5 with six more comebacks.

"That first year, he just wasn't sure what he was going to call and what he was going to do at times," Winder said. "To a certain degree, he had to earn some respect. As an athlete and as a passer, he got that respect from the first day of camp. After that, becoming a team leader and someone we looked up to, certainly he had to go out and produce and earn that. It took him a couple years before he really got it down, before he stepped into the huddle with confidence, in my opinion. I think at that time is when he started telling people what they do on this play and things of that nature. He gained more and more respect."

With each win, the Broncos could tell Elway was a special player. He led them to a Super Bowl in his fourth year and again in his fifth. Then he took them to another in his seventh season. During those years, he never had a star running back or a Pro Bowl receiver on his side, but he willed the Broncos to success. During his career, he accomplished at least one fourth-quarter comeback in each of his 16 seasons.

"You never knew what was going to happen," said linebacker Karl Mecklenburg, who was a rookie with Elway in 1983 and played with him through 1994. "He would scramble around and throw the ball across the field and do some crazy stuff, but he was a special guy. He lived for that [final] two minutes. When you get in the two-minute drill, then John is calling the plays. Everything changed, and I know he lived for that. He loved that opportunity, and that's where his real competitive nature was able to come out. Those were huge.

"As a defensive player, it allowed us to do things we probably couldn't do either, normally. On a lot of teams if you get behind, it's over. With our team, we were able to take chances. We were able to overload situations, we were able to blitz more, we were able to do a lot of things that could come back and bite you, but with John there, we had a comfort level that as long as we kept it close [until] the end of the game, we had a chance."

What Elway did as a player was special. He had a rocket for an arm and still owns just about every significant passing record in Broncos history. He also had exceptional athletic ability that allowed him to get out of trouble and make plays with his feet. He rushed for 3,407 yards and 33 touchdowns.

In the postseason, he won 14 of his 21 starts, compiling 5,425 yards in total offense and accounting for 33 touchdowns in those games.

Through it all, Elway was a mega-star. Denver had never seen anything like him. Neither had the people of Tokyo. The Broncos played an exhibition game there one year, and Elway was *the* man.

"We arrived [for a practice] and I was on the team bus," said KOA Radio's Larry Zimmer, who called Broncos games for 26 seasons. "There were, I would say, 400 to 500 young little Japanese kids. When the buses pulled up they were just chanting, 'Elway! Elway! Elway! Elway!' John was just engulfed by these kids when he got off the bus."

By the time Elway arrived in Denver, Jackson had been with the Broncos for a decade, already helping them to a Super Bowl. Elway's arrival gave Jackson something he had never seen before, too.

"There was a point at which Elway was leaving the stadium after a game his rookie year, and he was surrounded by 10 or 12 police officers just getting out of the stadium and to his car," Jackson said. "I remember thinking at the time, *Oh my goodness, he's one of* those *athletes*. It's the moment I realized he truly is a superstar, even though to know John, I think the reason we all didn't realize it is that he was so unassuming in the role of superstardom. He probably handled it as well as anybody I've ever known. He really did make us feel like he was just another guy on the team doing his job, but his job obviously was more important than anybody else's."

His down-to-earth personality was a big part of what made Elway so popular among his teammates. Mecklenburg said Elway hated when the team was introduced as "John Elway and the

Broncos." Elway lifted weights with his offensive linemen and ran sprints with his wide receivers. On different days, he would eat lunch with different position groups, just to get to know the players on a personal level, including the names of their wives and kids. In turn, they got to know him.

"He wanted to be at everything," Mecklenburg said. "He's a superstar, and he didn't have to show up to everything. He showed up at every single team function and was as dedicated to winning as anybody I've ever met. He willed it to happen and really was a great leader in so many different ways. I've got great respect for John."

Fans embraced Elway for the same reasons. He was not only a great player, but he took time out for the fans when he could. Jim Saccomano, the Broncos' vice president of corporate communications, tells a story of the Broncos being on the road in New Jersey. Elway was riding in the elevator when the door opened and a new bride walked in. A wedding was going on at the hotel and the excited bride, recognizing Elway, told him how much her new husband would love to meet him. Elway politely declined, saying he had meetings to get to. After the bride got off the elevator, Elway felt regretful, and he went out of his way to find the wedding party and meet the groom.

Zimmer tells another story of a preseason game in Indianapolis. The rest of the team headed to the stadium for a walkthrough, but Elway and Zimmer stayed back to do a pregame interview. When they were done, they started to walk to the stadium together.

"We come out and there was a kid waiting on the loading dock," Zimmer said. "He had obviously watched all the players file out and he didn't see Elway, so he waited. He wanted John's autograph. John gives him the autograph and puts his arm around him and said, 'Do you want something to eat?' The kid hesitated and John said, 'Oh, come on with me. The team is going to have lunch. You can come have lunch with me.'

"He is a very humble person. He never did let celebrity go to his head."

Elway's life has been a remarkable journey since that day he became a Bronco in 1983. As a player, he enjoyed tremendous success and went through trials, including painful Super Bowl defeats and a well-publicized feud with Reeves.

His personal life has also included highs and lows. He and his wife, Janet, raised four children in Denver before divorcing after his playing days. His father, Jack, was by his side throughout his life and literally by his side at the end of his career. Jack worked as a Broncos scout from 1993 to 1999. Jack passed away at the age of 69 in 2001, shortly before John's twin sister, Jana, passed away from lung cancer in 2002.

The struggles he underwent made Elway perhaps more loved in retirement than he was as a player because fans could identify with his all-too-human trials. He is still the face of the Broncos, and on August 8, 2004, he became the first player in team history to be inducted into the Pro Football Hall of Fame.

"Someone asked me the other day if I had any regrets about my career," he said during his Hall of Fame speech. "There's only one, and that's that my father, Jack, and my sister, Jana, couldn't be here. My dad wasn't just my best friend. He was my hero, my mentor, and my inspiration. He was the keeper of my reality checklist and the compass that guided my life and my career. And he taught me the number one lesson of my life: always make your family proud."

John Elway provided a lifetime of thrills to Broncos fans during his 16 seasons as a player. He brought another level of excitement when, as owner of the Arena Football League's Colorado Crush, he delivered another championship to Denver in 2005. In 2011, another chapter in the Elway book began when he was named the Broncos' executive vice president of football operations and general manager—and then put together a squad that went to the playoffs for the first time in six years.

Elway's legend grew as the leader of the Broncos. During his first five years as an executive, the Broncos won five consecutive AFC West titles. They had never before won more than two division titles in a row. They also went to the Super Bowl twice, winning the championship in 2015. He was the architect of the NFL's No. 1 offense in 2013, and then he built the NFL's top defense in 2015.

From the day he became a Bronco, he did what his dad wanted by making the family proud—not just his own, but the entire Broncos family.

2 World Champs—Finally!

Elway had been to the Super Bowl three times and left as a loser three times. And as a team, the Broncos had been to the Super Bowl four times and left as a loser four times. Facing the defending world champion Green Bay Packers in Super Bowl XXXII on January 25, 1998, at San Diego's Qualcomm Stadium, many expected Denver to go home empty-handed again.

The Packers, led by three-time league MVP Brett Favre, were 11-point favorites. They also had a perfect 3–0 record in Super Bowls. On top of all that, the NFC had won 13 straight Super Bowls.

In the beginning, it looked grim. Green Bay took the opening kickoff and marched down the field, capping the drive with a 22-yard touchdown pass from Favre to Antonio Freeman.

This day, however, belonged to Elway and the Broncos.

"I never thought we could lose," tight end Shannon Sharpe said. "Obviously the oddsmakers didn't see it that way, but you don't play games on paper. You don't play games based on what somebody did the year before. You don't play games based on someone being the MVP. I felt confident in what our team had, what we could do."

The Broncos countered Green Bay's score with a touchdown drive of their own, capped by Terrell Davis taking the ball in from the 1-yard line to tie the game at 7–7.

On Green Bay's next possession, Favre threw an interception. That set up a go-ahead touchdown by the Broncos—a score that provided one of the signature moments of the game.

Migraine headaches had plagued Davis for years, and he got another one toward the end of the first quarter. The Broncos had the ball on the 1-yard line. On the sideline, Davis told Shanahan, "I can't see."

Shanahan looked at his star running back and told him, "Just do this: You don't worry about seeing on this play because we're going to fake it to you. But if you're not in there, they won't believe we're going to run the ball."

Davis pulled his helmet on and made his way to the huddle. After the snap, Elway faked a handoff to Davis, and while the Packers defense converged on the middle of the field to stop Davis, Elway rolled to the right and waltzed into the end zone untouched for a 14–7 lead.

Another Packers turnover led to a Jason Elam 51-yard field goal that put the Broncos ahead 17–7. Green Bay wasn't done, though.

Favre threw a six-yard touchdown pass to Mark Chmura just before halftime, and then the Packers tied the game with a field goal early in the third quarter.

Then came the defining moment of the game—and of Elway's career. Tied at 17 late in the third quarter, the Broncos had third-and-6 from the Packers 12. Elway dropped back to pass but quickly stepped up in the pocket and ran to his right. As he tucked the ball into his right arm, he glanced to his right at the first-down marker and dove headfirst. Three Packers defenders converged at the 5, hitting Elway and sending him spinning through the air.

"When Elway, instead of running out of bounds, turned it up and got spun around like a helicopter, it energized us beyond belief," defensive lineman Mike Lodish told *Sports Illustrated* after the game.

The decision gave the Broncos a first down at the Packers 4, and two plays later Davis, his migraine now gone, ran into the end zone to give the Broncos a 24–17 lead going into the fourth quarter.

On the next two plays, the teams traded turnovers, and then Green Bay seized momentum with a four-play, 85-yard touchdown drive capped by Favre's third touchdown pass of the day. Now the game was tied at 24–24.

With 3:27 to play, the Broncos took over at the Green Bay 49-yard line. A Packers penalty, three Davis rushes, and an Elway pass to fullback Howard Griffith put the ball at the 1-yard line with 1:47 to go.

Hoping to leave their own quarterback with enough time to pull out a win, the Packers defense pulled back and let Davis score a touchdown. It was the Super Bowl–record third rushing touchdown of the day for Davis, who ran for 157 yards and went on to earn game MVP honors.

Denver led 31–24, but Favre had the ball with 99 seconds on the clock. The Packers' first four plays netted 39 yards, putting them on the Broncos 31 with 42 seconds left. Green Bay never gained another yard. Favre threw back-to-back incomplete passes, leaving him with fourth-and-6 with 32 ticks left. Favre threw down the middle to Chmura, but Broncos linebacker John Mobley stepped in front of the pass and knocked it down.

The Broncos' sideline erupted.

"It was a bit surreal," safety Steve Atwater said, 14 years after that moment. "I can go back to the feeling we had during that game at any time. All I have to do is put myself right at the end of the game, when John Mobley knocked the pass down and we looked up at the clock and saw that, really, the game was over. When we realized that, we were just overcome with emotions."

Elway took one last snap, knelt down to run out the clock, and then leaped in the air, his arms raised and tears forming in his eyes.

March to the Dance

Many believe the 1996 Broncos were better than the 1997 Broncos. However, it was a stunning loss to Jacksonville in the 1996 playoffs that helped set up the subsequent championship season.

"I believe that it propelled us to the next two years," center Tom Nalen said years later on Denver sports radio 104.3 FM.

During the 1997 regular season, the Broncos started 6–0 and sat at 11–2 through 13 games, their two losses coming by a combined five points. Back-to-back losses at Pittsburgh and at San Francisco cost the Broncos the AFC West title, but they wrapped up the regular season with a 38–3 win at home against San Diego and went in as a wild-card team at 12–4. AFC West champ Kansas City, at 13–3, was the only team in the conference with a better record. "I felt very confident going into the playoffs," tight end Shannon Sharpe said. "We had felt we had been the best team in the AFC up until that stretch where we had lost [two] games in a row."

Denver had the top-rated offense in the NFL in 1997, led by Elway, who had one of his finest seasons. He threw for 3,635 yards, a career-high 27 touchdowns, and only 11 interceptions. Terrell Davis ran for 1,750 yards, and both Sharpe and Rod Smith had more than 1,100 yards in receptions. The Broncos also had a top-five defense, led by linemen Neil Smith and Alfred Williams, linebackers John Mobley and Bill Romanowski, and defensive backs Darrien Gordon, Steve Atwater, and Tyrone Braxton.

In the first round of the playoffs, the Broncos got revenge on Jacksonville, crushing the Jaguars 42–17. Next, the Broncos visited archrival Kansas City. A pair of Davis touchdown runs and a tremendous effort by the defense silenced the Chiefs 14–10. "It was the loudest game I've ever been involved with," Nalen said. "To hear the silence after the game, it was awesome."

The next week, in Pittsburgh, Davis ran for 139 yards, Elway threw for 210 and two touchdowns, and the defense forced four turnovers. The Broncos led 24–14 at the half and held on for a 24–21 win.

The second quarterback to lose three Super Bowls, Elway finally won one.

"It means the other three Super Bowls are all erased now," Elway said in *Sports Illustrated* after that game. "Those were the ultimate losses, but this is the ultimate win."

During the presentation ceremony of the Vince Lombardi Trophy, owner Pat Bowlen raised the trophy and proclaimed, "This one's for John!"

It was also for Austin "Goose" Gonsoulin, Floyd Little, Craig Morton, the Orange Crush defense, and the thousands of Broncos fans who had experienced highs and lows, but never the ultimate glory, through the first 38 years of franchise history.

"I was sitting in the stands in San Diego when they won," said Little, a running back who starred for the Broncos from 1967 to 1975. "For me to be there, actually seeing it and being in that stadium, I sat in the stands and I just didn't want to leave for a minute and savor the moment. We had finally arrived. God bless John Elway for making it happen for Denver and the fans, because they deserved a Super Bowl championship more than any other fans."

Defensive end Alfred Williams, who starred in college at the University of Colorado, didn't comprehend what a win would mean to the fans but said, "I know the devastation it would have caused if we had lost the game. I just didn't want to lose the game. That desire not to lose the game was stronger than the desire to win, in my eyes."

For the men on that team, that victory, along with another one a year later in Super Bowl XXXIII, altered the future.

"I believe it changed the lives of people and careers of a group of men that probably wouldn't be in that same position if we would have lost," said Williams, who spent more than a decade building a successful career in Denver sports radio. "We have a guy that became a head coach in Gary Kubiak, we have guys who are doing

TV and radio and various different opportunities. We have a guy who is now a president of the organization [Elway]. There were just so many opportunities that sprang up from winning that game for all the guys who were a part of the teams."

Following their Super Bowl victory, the Broncos returned to Denver. It was estimated that more than 600,000 fans attended the celebratory parade, which was about a mile long through downtown Denver.

"It was pretty wild," Atwater said. "Just to realize the magnitude of what we'd done and [that] we did it all together as a team, it really was a good time. I wish everybody in their NFL career could experience that at least once."

The Broncos weren't the first team to deliver a major championship to Denver. The Colorado Avalanche beat them to it by winning the National Hockey League's Stanley Cup in 1996. (The Avs added another Stanley Cup in 2001, and in 2007 baseball's Colorado Rockies captured the hearts of Denver fans with a run to the World Series.) But any Denver sports fan will be quick to tell you, winning the Super Bowl was different.

"When they cancel schools and you see 600,000 people out there for the parade and you go to city hall and you look out there and you see all those people, you know what it means," Sharpe said. "They had been wanting something of this magnitude for the longest time. Hey, winning the Stanley Cup is great. Winning the World Series would be fine. But Denver is a football town. For us to give the city what they had long longed for, so deservedly so, it was an unbelievable feeling. If you played on those Super Bowl teams in 1997 and 1998, you'll always hold a special place in the fans [of] Denver's heart."

3 Back-to-Back

The Broncos spent their first 38 years striving to be the best team in football. They spent their 39th season, in 1998, proving they were, without question, the top dogs.

"They were the king of the hill," Terry Frei of the *Denver Post* said. "They managed to live up to the billing."

From start to finish, there was never a doubt as to which team was the NFL's best, and the Broncos capped the season in Super Bowl XXXIII with a 34–19 rout of the Atlanta Falcons in a game that was never even close at Miami's Pro Player Stadium on January 31, 1999.

"That was our purpose—our sole purpose was to repeat," Sharpe said. "We didn't really care what our record was. The thought of being 13–0, 14–0, that was not even on the table for us. Win the division, have home field advantage, win another Super Bowl."

The Broncos started the 1998 season with a 27–21 win over New England and plowed through everyone on their schedule en route to a 13–0 start. Most of the games were blowouts, as the Broncos' average margin of victory that season was 12 points.

"We were pretty confident," Atwater said. "I don't recall us talking much stuff, in terms of in the newspaper saying, 'We're this, we're that.' But in practice we competed with each other and we all encouraged each other to give the best that each person could."

Davis was the NFL's most valuable player that season, as he became just the fourth player to rush for 2,000 yards in one season, finishing with 2,008. He also scored a team-record 21 rushing touchdowns.

Rod Smith and Ed McCaffrey both topped 1,000 yards in receiving, while Sharpe added 768 yards and 10 touchdowns.

Elway had another brilliant season—and when he missed four games with an injury, backup Bubby Brister came in to go 4–0 and put up remarkable numbers of his own.

The offensive line had three Pro Bowlers—Nalen, Mark Schlereth, and Tony Jones—and the defensive line got exceptional performances from Neil Smith, Trevor Pryce, and Maa Tanuvasa.

Linebacker Bill Romanowski went to the Pro Bowl, and fellow linebacker John Mobley was an All-Pro. Both starting cornerbacks, Ray Crockett and Darrien Gordon, returned interceptions for touchdowns. Safety Steve Atwater went to another Pro Bowl.

Even the specialists shined. Kicker Jason Elam tied the NFL record with a 63-yard field goal against Jacksonville and made another Pro Bowl, while punter Tom Rouen finished second in the NFL with 46.9 yards per kick, a team record that stood until Britton Colquitt broke it in 2011.

It seemed that everyone who stepped on the field for the Broncos in 1998 played with a confidence the team had never before displayed.

"The second year, it was just easy," Alfred Williams said. "Everything was just easy. It was, 'Okay, we've been there, we've

Where'd He Come From?

Howard Griffith may be the best fullback the Broncos have ever had. Signed as a free agent in 1997, Griffith was a fixture in the starting lineup from 1997 to 2000, paving the way for many of Terrell Davis' yards and touchdowns. During the two Super Bowl–winning seasons in 1997 and 1998, Griffith ran the ball a total of just 13 times for 47 yards and no touchdowns.

In fact, during his entire 121-game NFL career, Griffith ran for just three touchdowns. That made Super Bowl XXXIII a surprise to many. With Atlanta keying on Davis, the Broncos gave the ball to Griffith twice at the 1-yard line, and he scored two touchdowns in the game. "When you've got a 2,000-yard rusher in the backfield and he goes one way, they're going to go with him," Griffith said after the game.

done that,' so it was just easy to get focused, and we knew we had the right type of players. John [Elway] getting injured didn't really help things, but for the most part it really was easy to come to work, it was easy to understand the defenses, it was easy to figure out what teams wanted to do to us or against us, and it was easy to get motivated to play."

Throughout Super Bowl history, most champions have failed to get back to the big game the following year—let alone win it. Whether it's the pressure of being favored, lack of motivation, or something else, repeating as champion has proven over the years to be a difficult task. The 1998 Broncos, however, made it look easy.

"You get a bunch of stubborn veterans together, and you'll find out very quickly whether or not you have a good team," Williams said. "The stubborn veterans that want to win will make sure that everything in the organization will go towards winning. You have a bunch of stubborn veterans that don't care about winning, what you'll see is a sluggish team that really doesn't care about each other and will probably end up doing a lot of stupid things—penalties and turnovers."

As the season went on, it seemed the only question surrounding the Broncos was whether anyone would beat them. At 12–0, the Broncos faced the Chiefs at Mile High Stadium on December 6. Kansas City took a 31–21 lead in the fourth quarter, but Elway rallied the Broncos for 14 unanswered points, including a 24-yard touchdown pass to Sharpe with 3:34 to play for a 35–31 win.

Beating Kansas City put the Broncos at 13–0, making them, at that time, just the third team in NFL history to reach the mark. Their perfect run came to an unlikely end the next week at New York, as the 5–8 Giants stunned the Broncos 20–16. Denver had a 16–13 lead until the Giants scored on a 37-yard touchdown with 48 seconds to play.

"I was disappointed," Sharpe said. "I know if you win the Super Bowl and you're undefeated, that's special."

Victory may have been even sweeter the second time around, as John Elway celebrates the Broncos' victory over the Dan Reeves–coached Atlanta Falcons in Super Bowl XXXIII. Photo courtesy of Getty Images

In Miami the next week, the Broncos lost again, 31–21, which was less of a surprise considering the Broncos had never won a game in Miami. (Including the preseason, the Broncos fell to 0–8 all time in Miami. It wasn't until 2011 that the Broncos got their first-ever win against the Dolphins in Miami.)

They recovered to beat Seattle at home the next week and then went on a destructive tear through the playoffs. They crushed the Dolphins 38–3 in the divisional round, a game in which Davis ran for 199 yards. In the AFC Championship Game, the defense held future Hall of Fame running back Curtis Martin to 14 yards on 13 attempts in a 23–10 win over the New York Jets.

Then came Super Bowl XXXIII against the Reeves-coached Falcons. But Reeves wasn't the only familiar face on the other sideline. Atlanta's backup quarterback was Elway's former mentor, Steve DeBerg.

Elway showed both of them how far he'd come from the growing pains of 1983. He threw for 336 yards, including an 80-yard touchdown pass to Rod Smith, and ran for a touchdown to earn Super Bowl MVP honors.

"I never, ever thought I would be the Super Bowl MVP," Elway told *Sports Illustrated* after the win.

He earned it with one of the best postseason performances of his career.

"All week long, all the Falcons talked about was stopping our running game," he said. "I knew they were saying, 'Make Elway beat us.' My thought was, *Good, let's go.* I was so motivated, it wasn't even funny."

For the Broncos, it was the perfect end to the best season in franchise history.

"We've seen teams probably more talented than us that couldn't get it done," Sharpe said of winning back-to-back titles. "For us to go back and get it done, I think it says a lot about our team. It says a lot about our coaching staff that we were able to remain focused and not worry about who got the credit and just go out there and accomplish a goal that was hard-fought.

"When you look back now, you really appreciate what we were able to accomplish."

After the season, Elway retired. It was fitting that after being on the wrong side of three Super Bowl blowouts, he ended his career with a Super Bowl blowout victory.

4 Back on Top

At the conclusion of Super Bowl 50, quarterback Peyton Manning stood on the podium at Levi's Stadium in Santa Clara, California, and wrapped his hands around seven pounds of sterling silver.

One of the NFL's true all-time greats, Manning looked down at the Lombardi trophy in his hands and smiled like a proud father cradling a new infant.

For Manning and the Broncos, their 24–10 victory over the Carolina Panthers on February 7, 2016, was the culmination of a long, arduous quest to once again claim a world championship.

"It's a great sense of accomplishment for this team," Manning said. "We've been through a lot this year. This team has been unselfish, tough, resilient, and I think all that was on display tonight."

The journey throughout the 2015 season was tough enough, but this was the end of a much longer quest for both the Broncos and Manning.

It was the Broncos' third Super Bowl win, but their first since John Elway rode off into the sunset by beating the Atlanta Falcons 17 years earlier. Those 17 years included a few coaching changes, quite a few quarterbacks, and several heart-breaking defeats along the way.

The wait hadn't been as long for Manning, but it sure felt like it. The owner of most of the NFL's passing records, Manning's only previous Super Bowl win came nine years earlier, when he led the Indianapolis Colts to a victory in Super Bowl XLI.

Despite his one Super Bowl, Manning's reputation in big games had taken a hit. He lost Super Bowl XLIV with the Colts and then lost Super Bowl XLVIII with the Broncos. He had quarterbacked a few other crushing playoff defeats, too.

The Super Bowl droughts for both the Broncos and Manning came to head in 2015, when it was quite clear it was their last shot to try to win it together.

Manning and the Broncos had been knocking on the championship door since his arrival in Denver in 2012, but had always left the playoffs disappointed.

In 2012, the Broncos had a stunning 38–35 overtime loss at home to the Baltimore Ravens in the divisional round, despite holding a seven-point lead with less than a minute to play in regulation. The next year, they were crushed by Seattle, 43–8, in the Super Bowl. And, in 2014, the Broncos were stunned at home by Manning's former team, the Colts, 24–13, in the divisional round.

Two home playoff losses and an embarrassment in the Super Bowl led the Broncos to shake up the organization. Following the 2014 season, they fired coach John Fox and hired Gary Kubiak. A former Broncos quarterback and offensive coordinator, Kubiak came aboard with a whole new offensive and defensive scheme.

With a revamped plan and a 39-year-old quarterback leading the way, there were question marks about the Broncos going into the year. Manning had not played well late in the 2014 season, with injuries and age seemingly taking its toll on the legendary passer.

From the start, it was very clear that the Broncos had a stellar defense and they made game-winning and game-saving plays a routine.

Aqib Talib returned an interception for a touchdown to help the Broncos beat the Ravens 19–13 in the opener. The next week, Bradley Roby returned a Kansas City fumble 21 yards for a touchdown in the final 30 seconds to beat the Chiefs 31–24. In Week 3, the defense shut down the Detroit Lions in a 24–12 win.

Later in the season, a Chris Harris' 74-yard interception return keyed a win over the Oakland Raiders, a Talib pick-six sparked a win at Cleveland, and a DeMarcus Ware fumble recovery sealed a victory against Cincinnati.

"You know, we're arrogant, to be honest with you," Ware said. "We want to be the best and to lead...the NFL in sacks, to lead them in yards per rush on us—we want to have it all. At the end of the day, that's where greatness is bred. We take that tenacity out wherever we play, and that's what we want. We want to be the best."

They were the best, ranking No. 1 in the NFL in 2015. Most years, a No. 1 defense to go with a Manning-led offense would be downright scary for opponents. Manning had piloted a top-5 offense 12 times during his career.

This was not most years, however. Manning had his worst NFL season, and the Broncos' league rankings for yards (16th) and points (19th) were the lowest rankings ever for a Manning offense.

Despite Denver's 7–0 start, the season got awkward on November 15. That night, the Broncos lost their second in a row, 29–13 against the Chiefs. Manning completed just five of 20 passes and he was intercepted four times before getting benched for backup Brock Osweiler.

Manning's 17 interceptions led the NFL at the time, and there wasn't a close second. After the game, Kubiak said the reason for Manning's "benching" was health-related, citing shoulder, foot, and rib injuries that were bothering Manning.

"I'm disappointed in myself," Kubiak said. "This is on me. I probably should have made a decision not to play him in the game."

During the next six weeks, the quarterback situation overshadowed the defense. Manning spent those six weeks nursing his injuries, Osweiler took the reins of the offense, and Kubiak continued to answer questions about which one would play.

A fourth-year pro, Osweiler had done virtually nothing in his career to that point except watch Manning play. Prior to taking over in the Kansas City game, Osweiler had thrown 30 career passes.

The tallest Bronco ever, the 6'8" Osweiler made his first career start on November 22—his 25th birthday—at Chicago. It was the first of seven consecutive starts for Osweiler.

While he didn't exactly dominate, Osweiler played better than Manning. He led the team to a 5–2 record in his starts, threw 10 touchdown passes, and limited his turnovers. Considering Manning's age and injury status, it appeared this had become Osweiler's team.

"I'm not concerned with the quarterback situation," Osweiler said. "I'm going to show up whether I'm the starter or whether I'm the backup. I'm going to prepare the same exact way."

While Osweiler performed well, Manning wasn't about to go quietly.

In the regular season finale, Osweiler started, but the offense struggled and Osweiler was benched. Manning, now healthy, directed the Broncos to a come-from-behind 27–20 win at San Diego, capping a 12–4 season.

Adding just a little more awkwardness to the quarterback situation, Kubiak made the tough decision to name Manning the starter for the playoffs, despite Osweiler being the better quarterback during the regular season.

"It's best for our football team," Kubiak said. "It's taken all of us and I think it will continue to take all of us as we embark on this second season. We're excited about it."

Osweiler never took another snap in a Denver uniform. (After the season, Osweiler surprised many by bolting Denver to sign a lucrative free agent contract with the Houston Texans.) Once again, he was relegated to the sidelines to watch Manning run the offense, while the defense just kept doing its thing.

In the divisional playoffs, the Broncos and Steelers were tied at 13–13 in the fourth quarter. Roby caused a Pittsburgh fumble, which was recovered by Ware. Manning turned that into a 13-play,

Crushing Defeat

During the 2013 season, the Broncos had the most prolific offense in NFL history. Led by legendary quarterback Peyton Manning, the Broncos scored a record 606 points. Their average of 457.3 yards per game was the second-best average in league history. Manning, meanwhile, set NFL single-season records for passing yards (5,477) and touchdown passes (55).

Manning and the Broncos marched through the regular season and the AFC playoffs to reach Super Bowl XLVIII in East Rutherford, New Jersey. Once there, they faced a Seattle Seahawks team that boasted the league's best defense. That 2013 Seattle defense, in fact, is talked about as one of the best in history.

In the Super Bowl, it was no contest, with Seattle running away for a stunning 43–8 victory. The first play of the game was a snap that flew over Manning's right shoulder and into the end zone for a Seattle safety. The Denver offense was a disaster all night, with four turnovers and just 306 yards.

Manning's second interception was returned 69 yards for a touchdown by Malcolm Smith to give Seattle a 22–0 halftime lead. The Seahawks' Percy Harvin then returned the third quarter kickoff 87 yards for a touchdown and a 29–0 lead. Seattle would lead 36–0 before the Broncos finally got on the board on the final play of the third.

65-yard drive for what wound up being the winning touchdown in a 23–16 victory.

In the AFC championship game against New England, Manning threw a pair of touchdown passes to Owen Daniels and the Broncos' defense smothered Patriots quarterback Tom Brady all night. The Broncos survived with a 20–18 victory after Roby picked off a Brady pass on a potential game-tying two-point conversion with 12 seconds to play.

Despite struggling on the field, battling injuries, and getting benched for the first time in his career, Manning had found a way to help the Broncos return to the Super Bowl for the eighth time in franchise history.

"This was a sweet victory," Manning said after beating the Patriots. "To me, this victory is a great example of what this entire season has been like. It hasn't been easy. It's been a lot of different people stepping up and doing their parts at different times. It's been a unique season, there's no question about it."

The Broncos and Manning still had unfinished business, though. They had overcome a lot of adversity, but had yet to complete their Super Bowl quest.

Manning and the Broncos' offense struggled against the Panthers. Their 194 yards of total offense were the fewest by any Super Bowl winner. It didn't matter, though, because Denver's defense came to play. Again.

Led by league MVP Cam Newton, Carolina had the NFL's No. 1 offense in 2015, but the Broncos held them to a season-low 10 points, forced four turnovers, and racked up a Super Bowl–record seven sacks.

Linebacker Von Miller, who won Super Bowl MVP honors, had 2.5 sacks. On his first sack, he stripped the ball from Newton, and Malik Jackson recovered the fumble in the end zone for a touchdown. Miller's last sack also produced a Newton fumble, which the Broncos recovered. That set up C.J. Anderson's touchdown run to seal the victory.

It was, by far, the strangest of Denver's three Super Bowl–championship seasons. Yet, in the end, it produced the same result: a future Hall of Fame quarterback cradling the Lombardi Trophy.

"It's a special feeling," Manning said. "I certainly knew how hard it is to get here. It takes a lot of hard work and you got to have some good fortune and so we were very grateful to be here. It's very special.

"We had a great football team."

5 The Franchise

Floyd Little approached the 1967 AFL-NFL Draft with excitement.

A star running back at Syracuse University, Little was one of the top prospects in the country, and he knew he would be a first-round draft pick. The only question was who would take him, but even then he had a good idea of where he'd land. "I was expected to be drafted by the Jets," he said.

The Jets had the 12th pick and, according to Little, had told him he would be their pick if he made it that far without being taken. The Broncos, led by head coach Lou Saban, had the No. 6 pick and had made up their minds, too. "When the draft came up, the whole coaching staff had agreed to draft Gene Upshaw," Little said.

Just minutes before the draft, Little said, Saban turned his attention to Broncos director of public relations, Val Pinchbeck, who knew Little from Syracuse.

"My understanding is Lou Saban asked Val Pinchbeck, 'Tell me a little about Floyd Little,'" Little said. "From Val's conversation with me, he said to Lou, 'Floyd is a great guy, but we have all agreed to draft Gene Upshaw.' Saban said, 'Well, can we build our team around Floyd Little?'

"Val said, 'I don't know why that's relevant. We've all decided to draft Gene Upshaw. But we can. Floyd is a great guy, a great leader, captain of the team, but we're going to draft Gene Upshaw.'

"Saban said, 'I don't know. I'm going to draft Floyd Little.'"

Minutes later, the Broncos made the 5'10", 196-pound Little the No. 6 pick in the draft. "When I found out, I went, 'Holy shit! You've got to be shitting me! Denver? Where the hell is that?'" Little said.

To that point, the Broncos had never reeled in a top draft choice. From 1961 to 1966, three of their top picks were future Hall of Famers: Merlin Olsen in 1962, Bob Brown in 1964, and Dick Butkus in 1965; all of them signed with NFL teams instead. Little never got that option, because 1967 was the first year of the AFL-NFL common draft.

"My only choice was to go to Canada," Little joked. "I wasn't about to go to Canada. I didn't even know where Denver was, let alone Canada."

Before long, Little not only found out where Denver was, he put it on the map.

"I don't know that Denver would have a franchise if it wasn't for Floyd Little," said Tom Jackson, who joined the Broncos in 1973 and played with Little for three seasons. "That's what we called him for a long time…'the Franchise.'"

Prior to Little's arrival, the Broncos had been on shaky ground. Some found it a miracle that the franchise born in 1960 was still standing by 1967. At the time that Little arrived, the Broncos were on the verge of moving, yet wound up getting the financial support to keep the team in Denver.

Little played a significant role in drumming up that support, but his most visible contribution came on the field. He was every bit the star the Broncos hoped he'd be when they drafted him.

He rushed for just 381 yards as a rookie but finished the year with 1,604 all-purpose yards. That number increased to 1,825 in 1968, as he dazzled the fans by running the ball, catching it and returning punts and kickoffs.

Eventually, Little gave up the return duties and focused on running the ball. He proved to be one of the best running backs in the league, including an NFL-best 1,133 yards in 1971. From 1967 to 1975, only one player in pro football ran for more yards than Little: O.J. Simpson.

Little is the only player in Broncos history to lead the team in rushing for seven years in a row. Upon his retirement after the 1975 season, Little was the seventh-best rusher in pro football history, with 6,323 yards. Little still ranks second in team history in career rushing yards and career all-purpose yards (12,173). With Little, the Broncos never did get to the playoffs—and it wasn't until 1973 that they had a winning record. By then, however, Denver fans packed the stadium every time the Broncos played a home game. "I was like, *Why is it packed?* That really was my thought," Jackson said in recalling his rookie season in 1973. "It was about Floyd. It was all about Floyd. The reason people came to those games in droves is because Floyd Little was on display."

Billy Thompson, who came to the Broncos as a rookie in 1969, said he recognized Little's greatness immediately. "I didn't know that much about him before I got here, but once I got here and saw him and saw what he contributed, I started paying attention to who he was," Thompson said. "He was our guy. He was our leader. He was everything for this organization. As a friend, he was everything to me as a young player. He was my mentor, he was my friend—he was everything to me. One of the greatest players I've ever played with. No doubt in my mind."

Little was one of the greatest players in pro football history, but because he played in little ol' Denver, it took a while for people to realize that. It wasn't until 2010—35 years after his retirement—that Little was enshrined in the Pro Football Hall of Fame.

"Had he played back East, he would have been a Hall of Famer a long time ago," Thompson said.

Nevertheless, he got in and took his rightful place among football immortals. "The pain and anxiety dissipates over the years," he said. "It becomes a little more callous about why you're not in. It was a long ride, but we finally got in. I'm glad I'm standing straight up and not lying horizontal."

Little never did play for a chance to be in the Hall of Fame. He played for the thousands who paid to watch him do his job every Sunday in the fall. "The fans are what I really, really gave my best for because of their love for their team, their love for the city, their love for who the Broncos were and what they became," he said. "The Denver Broncos fans are why I love the Denver Broncos."

Little may not have known where Denver was on that day the Broncos drafted him, but he quickly fell in love, and it proved to be a mutual admiration. Little loved Denver, and Denver—its fans and its players—loved Little.

In his last game at Mile High Stadium, on December 14, 1975, Little had 150 yards in total offense and scored two touchdowns, including a 66-yard pass from quarterback Steve Ramsey, as the Broncos knocked off the Philadelphia Eagles 25–10.

"We won the game, and we carried Floyd off the field," Thompson said. "I'll never forget that. I had so much respect for him and what he had done for the organization."

6 The Mastermind

From the moment Mike Shanahan was hired as the head coach of the Broncos, on January 31, 1995, the organization took on a new attitude and a new level of expectations.

"Once he became our head coach, we had a chance to practice quite a bit differently than the way we had been practicing, and prepare differently," safety Steve Atwater said. "He just instilled a different mentality in us, in terms of 'we can play with anybody.' He'd been there. He won a Super Bowl with San Francisco, and we bought into it."

By his third year in Denver, Shanahan led the Broncos to their first Super Bowl championship. He led them to a second one in 1998. His tenure as Broncos head coach, from 1995 to 2008, is the most successful in team history, as he went 138–86 in the regular season and 8–5 in the postseason. Seven times the Broncos won at least 10 games in a season.

"Mike Shanahan was a great coach," said Sandy Clough, sports talk host on Denver's 104.3 FM The Fan. "He's at the top of the heap. There's no question about it."

Bowlen made it perfectly clear on that day he hired Shanahan that Shanahan would be in charge of every aspect of the Broncos. Shanahan ran the draft, made free-agent signings, controlled how the team practiced, and had his hand in just about every aspect of the team.

When things didn't go right the first time, he demanded it be done again.

"It was tough," Sharpe said of playing for Shanahan. "He was very demanding, very detail oriented. He expected perfection—not only in the games, but in practice—and he didn't deal with excuses."

Growing up in Illinois, one of six children in a typical Midwestern family in which his father was an electrician, Shanahan knew early in life that he wanted to be a coach. Always involved with sports, he was influenced by many of his youth and high school coaches.

As a player, Shanahan was a quarterback in a run-oriented wishbone attack—which is ironic, given his coaching history—and he wound up playing collegiately at Eastern Illinois, the only school to offer him a full scholarship.

While at Eastern Illinois, he nearly lost his life. During a spring scrimmage, he got hit hard on an option play. He finished the game, but afterward, back in his room, he urinated blood and filled the sink three times with vomit. Finally he went to the hospital.

At one point, his heart stopped, and during emergency surgery, doctors found that one of Shanahan's kidneys had been split open. A priest actually read last rites because the situation seemed so grim. "One doctor later told my father it was the closest he had ever come to losing a patient who actually survived," Shanahan wrote in his book, *Think Like a Champion.*

Shanahan survived, of course, but he wouldn't play football again. Instead, he began his long coaching career, helping out the staff at Eastern Illinois. Shanahan had several assistant coaching stints at the college level—at Oklahoma, Northern Arizona, back to Eastern Illinois, Minnesota, and then Florida. In those nine years, he helped his teams get to the postseason eight times, missing out only in 1979 at Minnesota.

In 1984, Shanahan got his first shot at the NFL. He interviewed with the Philadelphia Eagles and with the Broncos; both positions would have had him coaching wide receivers. He chose the Broncos because head coach Dan Reeves also promised a chance to work with the quarterbacks—a group that included a young John Elway. "He's a great football coach," Reeves said years later. "I hired him twice because he did a great job of coaching."

After his first year in Denver, Shanahan was promoted to offensive coordinator, a job he held through 1987, helping the Broncos get to two Super Bowls. In 1988, he was hired by Oakland owner Al Davis to coach the Raiders. It was Shanahan's first job as a head coach, and although the Raiders went 7–9, they did beat the Broncos twice. After a 1–3 start in 1989, Davis fired Shanahan, who still had another year and a half on his contract. Davis told him that if he went back to Denver, he wouldn't pay him. Later that season, he returned to the Broncos as quarterbacks coach. "I went to Denver, and he never did pay me," said Shanahan, who disputed with Davis for years over that money.

In 1991, Shanahan returned to his post as offensive coordinator and helped the Broncos to once again get to the AFC

Championship Game. It was his seventh year as a Broncos assistant and the fourth time he helped them reach the AFC title game. At that point, however, the tension between Elway and Reeves was thick. Shanahan got caught in the middle of it, and Reeves fired him at the end of the 1991 season. Years later, Reeves would not talk about his relationship with Shanahan but spoke of his respect for his former assistant. "Mike's record speaks for itself," Reeves said. "A lot of the things that we did through those years were because of ideas and the knowledge that Mike Shanahan had. There's no question he's a great football coach."

Shanahan spent the next three seasons in San Francisco, reaching the NFC Championship Game all three times and winning the Super Bowl in 1994. By the end of the 1994 season, the Broncos were in need of a change in direction—again. Reeves was let go after the 1992 season, replaced by Wade Phillips. But they were mediocre under Phillips, and he was fired. Shanahan—who was Bowlen's top choice to replace Reeves to begin with—returned to Denver.

"That was really a treat," Atwater said. "Everybody bought into the program, and we tried to execute the way he told us to execute. It all worked out well. I thought he was a very fair person in terms of, 'If you come out and practice hard, play hard, and give it your all, you're going to play for me.'"

He was fair, but he was also competitive. He did what it took to win, and he never forgot old grudges. It was never a secret how Shanahan felt about Al Davis, and he made sure to stick it to his old boss any chance he got. As Broncos head coach, Shanahan went 21–7 against the Raiders, including 11–1 in his first 12 games against them.

Shanahan also had a fractured relationship with Reeves after 1991. Against Reeves, who coached Atlanta from 1997 to 2003, Shanahan was 3–0, including a 34–19 win in Super Bowl XXXIII. That win came about 11 days after Reeves had opened old wounds during a press conference. "For Mike, this game was personal," Elway told *Sports Illustrated* after that win. "I've never seen him more ready for a football game. I knew it meant more to him than any game he has ever coached." In the same *SI* article, Shanahan said of Reeves, "We'll shake hands after the game—I'll shake anyone's hand in that context—but this will never be worked out."

To the media, Shanahan could be cold, but he never was one to blow up and lose his cool at the podium. When he didn't like a question, you could tell, but he'd often respond with a smile and a joke—often at the reporter's expense. Shanahan would warm to the media in some ways. He'd hold press conferences in relaxed settings, with him and the reporters sitting in chairs in a circle. He was honest about how his team was doing, yet he was very good at saying plenty without giving up too much. Whether it was the media, the players, or fans, everybody knew Shanahan was in charge, and with his success, he earned the nickname "the Mastermind." He was "very brilliant at organization," said Terry Frei of the *Denver Post*. "He knew what he wanted to do and did it."

Most of his players respected what Shanahan did during his 14 seasons as the Broncos' head coach.

"He definitely helped my career," Sharpe said. "I don't think I would have ended up being the player I became had I not had him as my coach for seven years."

Running back Michael Pittman, who joined the Broncos as a free agent in 2008 said, "That's one of the biggest reasons why I came here in the first place. I was always a fan of Shanahan."

One day after the 2008 season ended with a crushing loss in San Diego—a loss that ended the year at 8–8 and without a playoff berth for a third year in a row—Pittman talked about Shanahan's future. "I think he's a great coach, and I think if they ever try to release coach Shanahan or fire coach Shanahan, it would definitely be the wrong move," Pittman said.

The next day, Bowlen fired the head coach.

"I think it was time for the organization to move on and for Mike to move on," Bowlen said at the press conference.

Shanahan, who came to Denver with enormous expectations, guided the Broncos to two Super Bowl championships and made winning his main priority. The 2008 season was the 10th straight year the Broncos failed to win a championship. In those 10 years—all after Elway's retirement—the Broncos won just one playoff game. Shanahan raised the bar in Denver, and then failed to measure up. "It did catch me a bit by surprise," he said at the time of being fired, "but I can understand the reasoning behind it. It's always tough when you put your heart and soul into something and you're let go. I didn't get the job done. That's the bottom line. Your job is to win and win championships, and we have not won the championship for a while."

In the three years after Shanahan's departure, the Broncos went 20–28 and all the young talent Shanahan had began to develop—most notably quarterback Jay Cutler, receiver Brandon Marshall, tight end Tony Scheffler—had been traded.

"I just think after you've been a head coach in one place for a long time in today's NFL, you should probably consider moving on and try it again someplace else," former Bronco and current talk show host Alfred Williams said. "But in Denver, I do believe that what he was able to accomplish was fabulous, and if they would have left him alone with Jay Cutler, they would have had success again."

Shanahan wasn't out of work long. He sat out the 2009 season, but was the head coach of the Washington Redskins from 2010 to 2013. He led the Redskins to the NFC East division championship in 2012.

7 Denver's Best Owner?

Elway is the face of the Broncos. Shanahan was the mastermind behind the only two championships in team history.

Floyd Little, Shannon Sharpe, Terrell Davis, Dan Reeves, Tim Tebow, and even Josh McDaniels are all recognizable figures in Broncos lore.

While those men have taken the headlines, Pat Bowlen has steered the Broncos' ship for nearly three decades, with much of what he's done going unnoticed by the casual fan.

When Bowlen bought the Broncos in 1984, he already had a history of success, and he had no interest in changing that. "I remember when Pat first came here, his thing was, 'I want to win,'" Broncos Ring of Famer Billy Thompson said. "That's been his motto. He's always been that kind of a guy."

Bowlen was born in Wisconsin and obtained degrees in business and law from the University of Oklahoma. His father earned a fortune in the oil business in Canada, and Bowlen followed in those footsteps, earning millions in oil, natural gas, and real estate.

At 40 years old in 1984, he spent $78 million to purchase the Broncos from Edgar Kaiser. How'd that investment work out? In 2011, *Forbes* magazine tabbed the Broncos as the 12th-most-valuable franchise in the NFL, at an estimated worth of $1.05 billion.

Bowlen's tenure as owner has not been marked by the team's value, however. Rather, it has been defined by a rich tradition of success on the field, including seven Super Bowl appearances and three Super Bowl wins under his watch.

"There's no denying the record over more than a quarter century has been sensational," said Clough, who has covered the

Broncos since the late 1970s. "He's the best owner in the history of Denver sports."

Few that have played for Bowlen would disagree. In fact, few players in Broncos history—whether they played for Bowlen or not—would disagree.

Most Broncos players, past and present, have some sort of a relationship with Bowlen because of the priority he has placed upon the team's alumni.

It was Bowlen who established the Ring of Fame, which honors some of the greatest figures in team history. Bowlen has routinely invited past players to return to Denver for alumni events.

"I think one of the classiest things he does and has done for many years is invite all the players that ever played for the Broncos back and have a weekend for them," said Thompson, who now works for Bowlen as the team's director of community outreach. "This doesn't happen around the league, and he's done it for many, many years. He understands what a part of the history that is."

His loyalty was on display after cornerback Darrent Williams was killed on January 1, 2007. Bowlen paid for the funeral costs and even funded the costs of sending the entire team to Texas for the funeral.

Bowlen's loyalty isn't limited to the Broncos. He's loyal to the entire community, having donated millions of dollars to local charities over the years.

Of course, he isn't liked by everybody.

In his early years as team owner, he was viewed as arrogant because of his seemingly smug grin and the way he often stood on the sideline wearing a fur coat.

There are also some who didn't like Bowlen's role in getting taxpayers to help pay for the Broncos' new home, Sports Authority Field at Mile High. When it's all said and done, taxpayers will wind up paying 75 percent of the stadium's $401 million tab.

From the day he bought the team, however, Bowlen has been driven by just one thing: winning. He knows no other way than to strive to be the best. That's how he's run his businesses, and it's how he's conducted his personal life.

Although age has limited him in recent years, he has always been active, even competing in the Ironman Triathlon and other endurance events.

"You look at his pedigree, he understands what athletes go through," former Broncos linebacker Karl Mecklenburg said. "He understands the effort that goes into being a professional football player, which I think is pretty unusual for an owner."

Bowlen's pursuit of success has made him popular among just about anyone who has ever strapped on a helmet during his time as owner.

"His competitive drive—he wants to win more than anything," Mecklenburg said. "I love Pat. He'll do whatever he possibly can for you if you're doing whatever you can for him."

Love him or not, nobody can argue with Bowlen's results. From 1984 through 2015, the Broncos had a regular season record of 313–198–1. The Broncos went to the playoffs 18 times, won 13 AFC West titles, seven conference championships, and three Super Bowls. During that same time frame, Denver's three division rivals—the Kansas City Chiefs, Oakland Raiders, and San Diego Chargers—combined for 17 division titles, two conference championships, and no Super Bowl wins.

Bowlen has been one of the most influential owners in the NFL, playing key roles in labor and television negotiations for the league.

In 2015, the Broncos honored Bowlen by inducting him into the Ring of Fame during a game against the Green Bay Packers. It was a proud, and emotional day, for the Broncos. In 2014, Bowlen announced that he had Alzheimer's disease and was giving up control of the team. By 2015, his health had deteriorated to the point that he could no longer attend the games.

"[Alzheimer's] is a tough thing, and it's taken away from us and him the ability and this opportunity to be with a great team," Broncos president Joe Ellis told USA Today as the team prepared for Super Bowl 50. "I know it's a team that he is and would be very, very proud of. It's a shame that he can't be there like he was, because he would enjoy this. He would really appreciate how this team has conducted itself this year, with all these gritty wins and with this relentless effort each week."

After the Broncos' 24–10 win against Carolina in the Super Bowl, Elway held up the Lombardi Trophy and declared, "This one's for Pat!"

It was fitting, because throughout his time in Denver, Bowlen never lost sight of his goal.

"The focus has always been to win, to bring a championship to Denver," Thompson said. "He's never ceased in that. I've always admired him for that. He'll always be somebody special to me."

8 Sharpe Tongue

In Broncos history, there may not have been a better tight end than Sharpe. He may also hold claim to the most impressive physique and brightest smile in team history.

Loudest mouth? Well, that's no contest.

"That's my personality," Sharpe said.

A seventh-round pick from tiny Savannah State in 1990, Sharpe didn't figure to have much reason to talk when he got to the NFL. But he did anyway.

"He always had confidence in himself," said Reeves, who coached Sharpe from 1990 to 1992. "He was always fun to be around because he had that big smile and always was the guy that was talking. That became more and more [frequent]; as he became a bigger part of it and he became a better player, you can do more talking."

Sharpe didn't back it up as a rookie, catching just seven passes for 99 yards and one touchdown, but each season he became more integral to the offense. At the time of his retirement in 2003, he held NFL records for catches (815), receiving yards (10,060), and touchdowns (62) by a tight end. He was elected to the Pro Football Hall of Fame in 2011.

Drafted as a wide receiver, Reeves didn't take long to move the 6'2", 228-pounder to H-back, a hybrid of a fullback and tight end. "He was a mismatch for safeties and linebackers," Reeves said.

The more he grasped the offense, the more the Broncos used those mismatches to their favor.

"He was coming into his own as a player when I left there," said Reeves, who was replaced by Wade Phillips and then Shanahan. "They did a great job with him in making him the best player he could be."

Although he came from a small college, Sharpe wasn't a total unknown when the Broncos drafted him. His older brother, Sterling, led the NFL with 90 catches in 1989 and, at just 24 years old at the time, had established himself as one of the game's elite wide receivers.

Shannon always looked up to Sterling, who went to the University of South Carolina, was a first-round pick (chosen seventh overall in 1988 by Green Bay), and was a five-time Pro Bowler in seven seasons before being forced to retire, at the age of 29, because of a spinal injury.

During his Hall of Fame induction speech in 2011, Shannon said, "I'm the only pro football player that's in the Hall of Fame

Hall of Fame tight end Shannon Sharpe sizes up the competition during a 1997 game. Photo courtesy of Getty Images

[who is also] the second-best player in my own family. If fate had dealt [us] a different hand, there is no question, no question in my mind we would have been the first brothers to be elected to the Hall of Fame."

Shannon came in with good genes and a work ethic unmatched by most. It was a work ethic sparked by his draft position, Sterling said when he presented his brother at the Hall of Fame.

"Not getting drafted before the seventh round helped him more than anything or anyone, myself included, because it humbled him, broke him and made him a fierce competitor all at the same time," Sterling said.

Whatever the motivation, Shannon's work ethic was well known among his Broncos teammates. "He was a guy who was extremely disciplined, and he wanted to be the best," Atwater said. "He was the one always leading with the jokes and the pranks, but at the same time when we worked, he was one of the hardest workers out on the field, too."

Hard work played a pivotal role in Sharpe's rise, but so did his mouth. From the time he started playing football, trash-talking on the field was a part of his game. He loved facing the Broncos' biggest rivals, the Oakland Raiders and Kansas City Chiefs, because that brought some of his best trash-talking.

"I did that my whole life, so I didn't really see any need for me to stop once I got to the highest level, because that helped me get to that level," he said. "I just felt that I needed to continue to be Shannon.

"I felt that besides being a very good player and a hard worker, my job was to keep the guys loose. I didn't want the guys to get too caught up in the moment, the game, and all of a sudden get in awe of the moment. My job was to keep it loose. I kept it loose on the practice field, I kept it loose in games and in the locker room. When the game started, they knew I was going to be ready to play."

Some of his antics, such as wearing a giant Broncos horse head after big wins, endeared him to the fans. Perhaps no incident put Shannon's personality on display quite like what he did on November 17, 1996. That afternoon, the Broncos were in Foxborough, Massachusetts, to take on the New England Patriots, who went on to win the AFC championship. On that day, the Broncos owned the Pats, pounding them 34–8.

Late in the game, Shannon was on the sideline trash-talking with Patriots fans, with television cameras rolling.

"I'm calling the president," he said to them as he motioned to a sideline phone nearby.

Then he picked up the phone and, loud enough so the fans could hear, said, "Mr. President, we need the National Guard! We need as many men as you can spare because we are killing the Patriots!"

He hung up the phone and yelled up to the fans, "Help is on the way!"

Shannon's personality made him a favorite not only among the fans but among his teammates. However, as much as Shannon was known for his personality, it was his exemplary play that defined him. Prior to his emergence, the NFL hadn't seen many tight ends with the skill set he had.

"He had great hands [and] great speed—especially for a tight end," Atwater said. "He really had wide receiver speed."

Shannon combined his tremendous ability with his outgoing personality to become an emotional leader during the Broncos' Super Bowl championship seasons in 1997 and 1998. After the 1999 season, he left the Broncos and spent two years in Baltimore, helping the Ravens win their only Super Bowl, in 2000.

Shannon has no problem comparing his three Super Bowl wins. "The first one was the best," he said. "The rest of them, you're glad to be a part of them, you're glad you won, you would hate to think what the alternative is if you lost that game. Of the three Super Bowl parties we had, I only went to the first one. It was kind of expected the second time around, and in Baltimore, it was like, 'I'm tired, I just want to go back to the room and hang out with the kids and my family.'"

While he did win a Super Bowl during his two-year stay with the Ravens, Shannon never did want to leave the Broncos, but he felt the Broncos didn't want him anymore after the 1999 season.

"I wasn't bitter. I didn't quite comprehend it," he said. "I called my brother and I said, 'The Ravens have this offer on the table.' I just remember him telling me, 'If the Broncos want you, then they wouldn't have let you get in this situation.' That crystallized things for me. I just called my agent and told him, 'Let's do it.'

"Sometimes, maybe I took the Broncos for granted, maybe they took me for granted," he said. "But it was great for me to feel for once in my life like I was wanted [by the Ravens], that I was actually appreciated. Looking back at it and talking to Mike [Shanahan], I realize I was appreciated, but sometimes you want to hear it. I would have not wanted to leave Denver, but things happen, and it worked out for the best for everybody involved, and I got an opportunity to come back after two years and finish my career in Denver."

During his final two years, Shannon was the same stellar player he was during his first 10 years in Denver. Through 2015, he still ranked second in team history in catches (675), receiving yards (8,439), and touchdown receptions (55).

He gave the Denver fans one last thrill in 2009 when he was inducted into the Ring of Fame. Rather than walking onto the field, as other inductees have, Shannon jumped out of an airplane and parachuted to the field. Months before the ceremony, he was asked if he would do it and agreed.

"After the season, I was like, 'What did I just commit to?' That was never on my bucket list," he said. "When I went out there on

Saturday and practiced, I was like, 'What have I got myself into?' After doing it a couple times, I was like, 'Okay, this is the right thing, and the fans kind of expect me to do something crazy to match my personality.' I enjoyed it. It was crazy. It's not something that I really care to do again, but I'm glad the opportunity was presented to me and I took advantage of it."

Shannon is as well known in retirement as he was as a player. From 2004 to 2013, he worked as an analyst on *The NFL Today* on CBS and continued to express his opinions after that through various appearances and on social media.

"I definitely enjoy talking about football and keeping close to the game without actually being in the game," he said.

9 From Unknown to Superstar

Terrell Davis crossed the goal line, stood at attention, looked into the Mile High Stadium stands, and raised his right hand to salute the crowd.

For seven seasons—including four of the greatest by a running back in NFL history—Davis was a fan favorite whose "Mile High Salute" became a Broncos tradition.

An unheralded rookie in 1995, Davis became the greatest running back in Broncos history, at least statistically, and put himself in the Hall of Fame debate. His 7,607 career yards and 60 rushing touchdowns are both team records. Through 2015, he had three of the top four individual rushing seasons in team history.

"He gave us a really consistent, extremely good running game," said Atwater, who played with Davis from 1995 to 1998. "We had some backs in the past who played really well, but unfortunately we didn't have anyone that was as consistent as he was. He was a strong, fast, tough running back."

When Davis arrived in Denver in 1995, nobody could have imagined what would happen.

Davis had a difficult childhood in San Diego. His father, Joe Davis, was an ex-convict who wasn't always around, and when he was, good moments were mixed with abusive ones. Life got better for Joe, but he passed away when Terrell was 14. His mother, Kateree Davis, was married at 16 and had six children by age 23. Despite a number of challenges, including Joe's time spent in prison, she always worked hard for her kids.

Shootings, murders, drugs, and gangs were commonplace during his childhood. One of his brothers, Bobby, attempted to rob a woman and in the process shot her in the chest. She survived, but her unborn baby did not. Bobby was sentenced to prison.

During his first two years of high school, Terrell Davis often skipped school and therefore didn't have the grades to play football. At the end of his sophomore year, however, he realized he needed to change. He transferred high schools, went to summer school to boost his grades, and joined the football team at Lincoln High.

He played fullback, nose guard, and kicker for the Hornets as a junior, and then had a decent season as a senior, rushing for about 700 yards. He wound up getting a chance to play in college.

In 1990, he redshirted at Long Beach State, which was coached by Hall of Famer George Allen. Davis did well on the scout team, but at the end of the season, Allen passed away. Davis ran the ball a bit in 1991, but at the end of that season, Long Beach State dropped its football program.

Needing a new place to play, Davis landed at the University of Georgia, where he spent the 1992 season backing up star Garrison Hearst. In 1993, Davis was the starter and gained 824 yards, which didn't wow anybody, considering Georgia's tradition at running

Running back Terrell Davis, drafted late in 1995, was the linchpin of Denver's offense on the back-to-back Super Bowl–winning teams. Photo courtesy of Getty Images

back. In an injury-plagued senior season in 1994, he gained just 445 yards.

"They didn't get all the potential out of him in college," Atwater said. "When he came to Denver, he matured into one of the best backs that have ever played in the NFL."

In the 1995 NFL Draft, twenty running backs were drafted ahead of Davis, including five in the first round. It wasn't until midway through the sixth round that Davis got the call from the

Broncos. "I was thinking, *When you get drafted this late, all you are is camp meat,*" Davis told *Sports Illustrated* in 1996.

It was true that, as camp meat, very few gave Davis much of a shot to make the team, let alone become a starter. Davis, however, came to Denver at an opportune time. The Broncos had been through a host of mediocre running backs before 1995. They had the likes of Gaston Green, Rod Bernstine, and Leonard Russell pacing a rushing attack that didn't do much attacking. The Broncos ranked 23rd in the NFL in rushing in 1994, 18th in 1993, and 25th in 1992. During training camp, Davis' competition turned out to be not much competition, after all. Bernstine was getting long in the tooth, by running back standards; Aaron Craver was more of a fullback; and Glyn Milburn was too small to be an every-down back.

During the preseason, Davis made an impression by running the ball. He also made a lasting impression by delivering a vicious hit on a 49ers kick returner. One of 10 running backs to start camp, Davis quickly proved to be the best, and by the end of camp he had earned the starting job. "He worked extremely hard," said Sharpe, Davis' teammate from 1995 to 1999. "Every day you could see he was getting better. Here's a guy, kind of like my situation: late-round draft pick and all he wanted was an opportunity. When he got his opportunity, he never looked back. You can appreciate a guy that worked hard and his hard work is rewarded. That's what he did."

That season, Davis rushed for 1,117 yards, the most by any Bronco in five years. He also scored seven rushing touchdowns and caught 49 passes. All of a sudden, the Broncos had a star in the backfield, yet Davis was just getting started. He rushed for 1,538 yards and 13 touchdowns in 1996, then gained 1,750 yards and 15 touchdowns in 1997. In 1998, he became the fourth player in NFL history to rush for 2,000 yards, gaining 2,008, with 21 touchdowns. During that four-year stretch, Davis gained 6,413 yards and

56 touchdowns on the ground, while catching 152 passes for 1,181 yards and five touchdowns. In those years, he helped the Broncos win two Super Bowls, he was named MVP of Super Bowl XXXII, and he was the league MVP in 1998. "Nobody accomplished more than what he did in those four years," Sharpe said. "You're talking about a league MVP, a Super Bowl MVP, a 2,000-yard rusher. It doesn't get any better than that."

The Broncos had featured good running backs in the past, most notably Hall of Famer Floyd Little. During their three Super Bowl years in the 1980s, the Broncos had Sammy Winder and then Bobby Humphrey, both of them good backs. But, they weren't T.D.

"Having him run the ball and catch passes out of the backfield, pick up blitzing linebackers, it was invaluable," Atwater said. "We hadn't had that in the past. Really, that's one of the things that the teams who had gone to the Super Bowl in the past, one of the things that they missed was a running back that was as good as Terrell was."

That Davis went from a sixth-round pick to superstar was remarkable. Through 2015, seven players had compiled 2,000-yard rushing seasons, and Davis was the only one who wasn't a first-round draft pick. Of the 20 to produce a 1,750-yard season, only Davis and Atlanta's Jamal Anderson (seventh round) were drafted after the third round. Davis was one of just six running backs in history with two 1,750-yard seasons, joining Eric Dickerson, Barry Sanders, O.J. Simpson, Larry Johnson and Adrian Peterson.

Sharpe had just one complaint of playing with Davis: "He shortchanged me out of 150 catches," Sharpe joked.

In reality, what Davis did was make the Broncos' offense better and help turn them into champions.

"I love the guy," Shanahan told DenverBroncos.com at a team alumni dinner in 2007. "You knew right from the start this guy was going to be something special."

Those four years (1995–98) tell only half the story. During the fourth game of the 1999 season—Denver's first season in 17 years without Elway—Davis' career changed. Elway's replacement, Brian Griese, threw an interception during the first quarter. Trying to make the tackle on the defender-turned-ball-carrier, Davis tore up his right knee.

He was never the same. Trying to compensate for his right knee, his left knee became even worse.

From 1999 to 2001, he played just 17 games, gaining 1,194 yards and scoring four touchdowns. He played half the season in 2001, gaining 701 yards. He came back for the 2002 season, but the toll of his injuries was too much, and during the preseason he ended his comeback attempt and never played again.

"It's tough," he said in 2002. "I have mixed feelings. Obviously, I feel like I can still play, but I can't. The crowd's been great, Denver's been great, and I want to say thank you for all the support."

Davis went on to do some broadcasting, and he has helped to coach high school football. He's also got his own brand of barbeque sauce, called "Terrell Davis' Mile High Salute BBQ Sauce."

Because his career was so short, Davis will have a hard time getting into the Hall of Fame, but Sharpe believes Davis should be there.

"I'm a firm believer that greatness doesn't have a time limit on it," Sharpe said. "If you're great, you're great. I believe a guy should be rewarded if he's great for five years as opposed to being good for an extended period of time, and T.D. was great."

On September 23, 2007, Davis returned to Invesco Field at Mile High to be inducted into the Broncos' Ring of Fame. More than 75,000 fans cheered and chanted, "T.D.! T.D.! T.D.!" Wearing a suit and tie instead of a helmet and his familiar No. 30 jersey, Davis saluted the fans once more.

10 New Sheriff in Town

Throughout the 2011 NFL season, two quarterbacks gained more national attention than any others.

Peyton Manning, the out-of-this-world passer of the Indianapolis Colts, was a hot topic for what he *didn't* do. A neck injury sidelined him for the entire season—the first time in his 14-year career that he'd even missed a game.

Tim Tebow, the iconic, polarizing second-year quarterback of the Broncos, was the hottest topic in the NFL for what he *did* do. Throwing NFL convention out the window, Tebow rallied the Broncos from the dregs of the AFC West all the way to the playoffs.

As the 2011 season went along, few could have expected the two would become so inextricably linked in the spring of 2012.

Manning, after all, was *the* face of the Colts. The No. 1 overall pick in the 1998 draft, he played all 208 regular-season games for the Colts from 1998 to 2010. He played in 11 Pro Bowls, won four NFL MVP Awards, led the Colts to the playoffs 11 times, and won Super Bowl XLI on February 4, 2007.

Tebow wasn't exactly the face of the Broncos, and he hardly had the resume to match Manning—or even Kyle Orton. Despite struggling with basic fundamentals of NFL quarterback play, Tebow captured the hearts of Broncos fans and grabbed national headlines for the improbable comebacks he orchestrated during the 2011 season. It's not a stretch to say he had become the most popular Bronco since Elway retired in the spring of 1999.

Without Manning in 2011, the Colts started 0–13 and finished 2–14, earning the No. 1 pick in the 2012 draft. The prize of that draft was Stanford quarterback Andrew Luck, who many considered the best QB prospect since...Manning in 1998.

As March of 2012 rolled around, nobody was really sure if Manning would ever return to his Hall of Fame level, or if he could ever play again. The Colts had a major decision: pay a $28 million roster bonus to keep the 36-year-old Manning, or move on and draft Luck at No. 1. On March 8, Manning was cut by the Colts.

While Tebow led the Broncos to an 8–8 record, an AFC West title, and a first-round playoff victory, Elway never viewed him as the long-term answer at quarterback. So, when Manning became available, Elway pounced.

On March 20, 2012, Manning, nicknamed "The Sheriff," was introduced as the new quarterback of the Denver Broncos.

"I can tell this organization is committed to winning," Manning said that day in his press conference. "The Broncos, they do have incredible fans that love this team, and this truly is a special football environment, and I am glad to be a part of it. I am thrilled to be here, and I'm looking forward to meeting my new teammates and doing everything I can to help this franchise win another Super Bowl."

The next day, Tebow was traded to the New York Jets. Tebowmaniacs weren't happy about Elway's decision, but Bronco Nation would soon forget about the former Heisman Trophy winner.

During Manning's four seasons in Denver, the Broncos went 50–14, won the AFC West four times, won the AFC championship twice, and won a Super Bowl. Manning threw for 17,112 yards, 140 touchdowns, and only 53 interceptions.

And, Tebow? He played the 2012 season as a backup with the Jets, throwing just eight passes and accounting for no touchdowns. He was released after the 2012 season and never played another regular season game. The New England Patriots gave him a shot in 2013 and the Philadelphia Eagles signed him in 2015, but both teams cut him before the season.

Manning put any doubts about his health to rest early in the 2012 season. There were some early growing pains, as the Broncos began 2–3, but the Broncos won their last 11 games that season. Along the way, Manning set Broncos' single-season records for passing yards (4,659), completions (400), completion percentage (.686), touchdown passes (37), and passer rating (105.8).

The next season, Manning again led the Broncos to a 13–3 record, and he crushed the numbers he put up in 2012. He threw for a stunning 5,477 yards and 55 touchdowns, setting NFL single-season records in both categories. His 115.1 rating was the fifth-best in league history and he won his NFL-record fifth MVP award.

In 2014, Manning had stellar numbers once again, finishing with 4,727 yards, 39 touchdowns, and only 15 interceptions while taking the Broncos to a 12–4 record.

The 2014 season, however, signaled the beginning of the end for Manning. He was exceptional through the first nine games, with 29 touchdowns and seven interceptions. Everything changed in Week 10, though, when the Broncos were battered by the St. Louis Rams, 22–7. Starting with that game, Manning had just 10 touchdowns and eight interceptions the rest of the season, as he dealt with various injuries.

Although the Broncos went 5–1 after leaving St. Louis, there was a sense that they weren't the same team, and Manning wasn't the same quarterback. The Broncos won the AFC West division again, and then hosted the Colts in the divisional playoffs. Outplayed by the man who replaced him in Indy—Luck—Manning and the Broncos were beaten 24–13 in Denver.

There was some speculation that Manning would retire after the 2014 season, but he chose to return and work with new head coach Gary Kubiak. "I've been working real hard and I'm excited to be back with the Denver Broncos," Manning said to *The Denver Post*. "I'm excited to get to work and get to know the new coaches and looking forward to trying to make 2015 a special year."

For Manning, the 2015 season turned into an epic battle with Father Time. He was 39 years old and it showed. A maestro behind center who carried teams to victories for nearly two decades, Manning spent his final season in Denver struggling to get out of his own way. He kept throwing interceptions instead of touchdown passes. He couldn't stay healthy. His own fans booed him.

Had it not been for a historically sensational defense, the Broncos might have been buried by the halfway point of the 2015 season. While that defense managed to keep the Broncos on top, Manning was essentially buried—by fans, the general public, and the media—by Game 9.

Already the NFL's leader in interceptions that season, Manning spent the afternoon of November 15, 2015, making sure nobody would catch him in that category. A day that began with him getting the last three yards he needed to break the NFL's all-time record for passing yards ended with Manning standing on the sidelines after being benched for the first—and only—time in his career. Playing AFC West rival Kansas City, Manning threw 20 passes. Five were caught by the Broncos and four were caught by the Chiefs. Boos rained out of the Sports Authority Field stands after that fourth one, and Manning spent the rest of the afternoon watching his backup, Brock Osweiler, guide the offense.

During the next six weeks, Osweiler led the Broncos to a 4–2 record, while Manning nursed his ailing body and fought allegations that he had once used performance enhancing drugs—allegations he vehemently denied. For weeks, it appeared the final image of Manning would be that of him standing on the sidelines after that benching against the Chiefs.

Father Time always wins in the end, but the great ones find a way to go out in style. During the regular season finale, on January 3, 2016, against San Diego, Manning returned to uniform, this time as Osweiler's backup. It was, after all, Osweiler's team. Well… not quite.

Playing in front of the home crowd, the Osweiler-led Broncos sputtered on offense while the hapless Chargers built a 13–7 second half lead. Kubiak turned to Manning, in hopes of sparking the team. Statistically, Manning didn't do anything special, but he provided that spark. He led Denver to 20 points in the last 20 minutes, guiding them to a 27–20 victory that secured the No. 1 seed for the AFC playoffs. In doing so, Manning served notice that he was back in the saddle for one last ride. He wasn't going to let that sad image of him standing on the sidelines in mid-November be his last mark on the game.

Given two more weeks to heal his body before the start of the playoffs, Manning looked as healthy as he had all year when the Broncos hosted the Pittsburgh Steelers on January 17. Denver's defense was fantastic against the Steelers, and Manning avoided interceptions and was good enough in a 23–16 victory.

In the AFC Championship Game a week later, Denver's defense battered New England quarterback Tom Brady. Manning threw for just 176 yards, but he tossed a pair of touchdown passes—and, once again, avoided interceptions—in a 20–18 win.

Two weeks later, in Super Bowl 50, Denver's defense proved its dominance to the world. They pounded Carolina quarterback Cam Newton for a Super Bowl–record seven sacks, two of which led to touchdowns, and shut down the Panthers' high-powered offense in a 24–10 victory. Manning threw for just 141 yards and he did get intercepted once. Not that anyone will remember it.

The battle with age is always a losing one for athletes, but Father Time has a way of being cruel to them at the end of their careers. That's where Manning won. Manning didn't go out as an old, beaten and broken quarterback, limping off the field under a shower of boos. Manning went out as a cagey veteran with enough left in his tank to lift the Lombardi Trophy one last time and strut off the field under a shower of confetti.

On March 7, 2016, Manning announced his retirement, joining John Elway as the only quarterbacks to win a Super Bowl title in their last game. Manning will be best remembered for his time with the Colts, but Broncos fans will never forget Manning's exceptional four seasons in Denver.

"When someone thoroughly exhausts an experience they can't help but revere it," an emotional Manning said during his retirement press conference. "I revere football. I love the game. So, you don't have to wonder if I'll miss it. Absolutely. Absolutely I will. When I look back on my NFL career, I'll know without a doubt that I gave everything I had to help my teams walk away with a win.

"There's a scripture reading, 2 Timothy 4:7: 'I have fought the good fight and I have finished the race. I have kept the faith.' Well, I've fought a good fight. I've finished my football race and after 18 years, it's time."

11 Zim

Every quarterback needs a good tackle to protect his blind side.

John Elway was fortunate to have good left tackles throughout his career, including Dave Studdard during the QB's first five seasons.

No left tackle, however, protected Elway's blind side better than Gary Zimmerman did from 1993 to 1997. In fact, it's debatable whether any right-handed quarterback in NFL history could claim to have had a better left tackle than Elway did with Zimmerman.

"Gary was the best left tackle I ever saw play the game," Elway told the Associated Press in 2008. "His strength and athleticism were exceptional. He understood the game and was as tough as I have ever seen."

Elway's comments came on the day Zimmerman was elected to the Pro Football Hall of Fame, a fitting end to a brilliant 12-year NFL career.

"I'm shocked because I didn't think I had a chance," Zimmerman said to the *Denver Post*. "All the years they passed me over, I thought it was going to happen again. It's too good to be true."

Zimmerman may have been shocked, but nobody who played with or against him was the least bit surprised.

After spending two seasons in the United States Football League, he played seven seasons with the Minnesota Vikings. Then he had a falling out with Vikings ownership in 1993. The Broncos gave up a bundle to get him—sending a first-round draft pick, a second-round draft pick, and a sixth-round draft pick to the Vikings—but it proved to be well worth the investment. Zimmerman helped the Broncos win their first Super Bowl in 1997, and in 2008 he became just the second Bronco ever elected to the Pro Football Hall of Fame.

"He was a classic left tackle and very deserving of his election to the Hall of Fame," Elway told the Associated Press.

Zimmerman made the Pro Bowl three times in five seasons with Denver (and seven times overall in his career), and he started all 184 games in which he played during his NFL career, including 76 with Denver.

"Zim was a consummate pro," former Broncos teammate Alfred Williams said. "He was tough, he was smart, and he was actually brilliant. He knew where he could give up room to pass rushers, and he knew where he couldn't. It made his job great because he was a great athlete and he could just direct guys into corridors that wouldn't hurt the offense. He was just great at that."

It wasn't just his play that made Zimmerman great. He was also an exceptional leader on what proved to be a sensational offensive line for the Broncos. This section wouldn't be complete without his Denver linemates.

The group of Zimmerman, left guard Mark Schlereth, center Tom Nalen, right guard Brian Habib, and right tackle Tony Jones formed the best offensive line in Broncos history.

"I promise there aren't five linemen who play better together," tight end Shannon Sharpe told *Sports Illustrated* prior to Super Bowl XXXII. "They're very peculiar, and they have their own way of doing things, but they totally play for each other."

The group stuck together, played together, and kept each other in line. There was constant razzing between the five and way too many self-imposed fines to count. Tacitly agreeing not to speak to the press, they fined each other for talking to the media. Habib

"Stink" Made His Mark on the Broncos' Line

Many football fans today know Mark Schlereth as an outspoken NFL analyst on ESPN. Prior to his successful broadcasting career, though, Schlereth was a great offensive lineman who is one of the most interesting players in Broncos history.

Schlereth, affectionately known as "Stink," was unique in many ways. He's one of the few Alaskan-born players in NFL history, underwent 29 football-related surgeries, and was well-known for vomiting and urinating in his pants during games.

He also had unique talent, which he displayed during his 12-year career with Washington (1989–94) and the Broncos (1995–2000). He made the Pro Bowl twice and won three Super Bowl rings, two with Denver. "He couldn't move, he couldn't pull, he couldn't go left and right real fast, but if you stood up in front of him in a phone booth, he would absolutely destroy you," Alfred Williams said. "[He had the] strongest hands of any guy I ever played against."

Schlereth's drive to succeed passed on to his children, too. His daughter, Alexandria, went on to become a successful actress and his son, Daniel, was one of the Detroit Tigers' top relief pitchers in 2011.

was fined $3,000 for missing practice when his wife had their third child. Zimmerman wasn't immune to the fines, as the summer of 1997 would attest.

Zimmerman contemplated retirement and skipped training camp. Instead, he rode his Harley-Davidson to a motorcycle rally in Sturgis, South Dakota. After Zimmerman decided to return to the team, the kangaroo court slapped him with an $8,000 fine. Of that, $5,000 went for skipping camp, $2,000 was for the media coverage he got, and $1,000 because backup Scott Adams had to be cut to make room on the roster.

The quirks of the group were part of what made them special, because it certainly wasn't their girth. In fact, the Broncos had the smallest offensive line in football. While most of the league's quarterbacks were protected by 300-pounders, none of Denver's linemen hit that mark. Zimmerman was the biggest, at 6'6" and 295 pounds.

"They rank at the top of the league. I don't mean that individually but as a unit. Their strength lies in their ability to play together," San Diego general manager Bobby Beathard told *Sports Illustrated*.

The unquestioned leader of that group was Zimmerman, who was voted to the NFL's All-Decade Team not once, but twice—for the 1980s and 1990s.

"There are guys who try hard, like me, and I was relentless, but I wasn't a good athlete," Habib told the Associated Press. "And there are guys who rely on their talents but don't try hard to get better. Gary had more talent than anyone and also outworked everybody. That's what separates guys like Gary from the rest of us."

12 Broncos Are Born

Nowadays, the Broncos are known for Hall of Fame players, two Super Bowl championships, and the most polarizing figure in professional football.

The Broncos never would have gotten to this point, however, if not for a family of beekeepers with a desire to bring Major League Baseball to the Mile High City.

Bob Howsam was the founder of the Broncos, which is quite a story, considering his roots. Although born in Denver, Howsam grew up in the small southern Colorado town of La Jara, where his father, Lee, was a successful beekeeper.

"I figured honey producing would be my career," Howsam wrote in his book, *My Life in Sports*. "Dad was an outstanding honey producer and he had taught me well."

Howsam may very well have carried on the family business had he not married Janet "Janny" Johnson while attending the University of Colorado. Johnson's father, "Big Ed" Johnson, was a U.S. senator who also served three terms as governor of Colorado.

Through that relationship with Big Ed, Howsam went to work in Washington, D.C., and then was appointed by Big Ed to reorganize the Western League, a minor baseball league, in 1947. A stellar athlete in high school, Howsam eagerly accepted the appointment.

One of the teams in that league was the Denver Bears, and about 18 months into his job, Howsam learned the owners of the Bears wanted out. Howsam, his brother Earl, and their father pooled their money and bought the Bears for roughly $75,000 in 1948. That was the beginning of Rocky Mountain Empire Sports, which Bob operated.

Almost immediately, the Howsams built a stadium for the Bears, turning a city dump into a new facility for the baseball team. It was named Bears Stadium and later became Mile High Stadium. About a decade later, with the Bears a success, Bob and Big Ed formulated the idea for a new major league in baseball—the Continental League—with Denver as one of the franchises. With the idea of bringing Major League Baseball to Denver, Bob expanded Bears Stadium.

The Continental League never got off the ground, but it did have a significant impact on the MLB. Threatened by the new league, the two majors leagues—the National League and American League—got together and agreed to expand. They told Bob and other prospective Continental League owners that they would start by adding teams in Houston (the Colt .45s/Astros) and New York (the Mets), with the six other cities to come. Four other cities, Dallas–Fort Worth (the Rangers), Minneapolis– St. Paul (the Twins), Toronto (the Blue Jays), and Atlanta (the Braves) eventually got major league teams out of the deal—and Denver and Buffalo were left out in the cold.

So how do the Broncos fit into all of this?

Well, because of Howsam's success with the Bears, he developed a relationship with Lamar Hunt, a wealthy businessman with a desire to form a new professional football league. Hunt approached Howsam about having a team in Denver for Hunt's proposed football league.

Wanting to get more use out of Bears Stadium, Howsam bought in, and in 1959, the American Football League was formed. The Broncos played their first preseason game on August 5, 1960—just three days after the dream of the Continental League ended.

Howsam had a stadium, owned a radio station, and had professional sports experience. But, unlike Hunt, Howsam didn't have a lot of money—and it showed.

Austin "Goose" Gonsoulin, an original member of the Broncos and now a Ring of Famer, recalled his "locker" being a two-by-four with two nails in it. The penny-pinching didn't stop there. "Back then, I don't even know how we competed with the way that things were," Gonsoulin said.

The Howsams were counting on Denver citizens for support, which would translate into revenue, but that support was tough to come by. Local newspapers gave the team very little coverage. Only 18,372 fans showed up to the first game, despite it coming on a balmy 71-degree Sunday afternoon. By the end of the season, less then 8,000 fans were showing up to games.

Gonsoulin was only a rookie, but even he expected more out of professional football. When he first arrived in Denver, he attended a tryout for the Broncos at the Colorado School of Mines in Golden. "There [were] like 120 guys that were not drafted or anything," he said. "There were truck drivers, oil field workers, roughnecks, and all that. There was no organization. There [were] only three coaches. In my high school and junior high, I had more than three coaches. I'm thinking, *Oh, I made the wrong move.*"

Denver's first general manager was Dean Griffing, who had plenty of experience, but all of it in the Canadian Football League. The Broncos' first head coach was Frank Filchock, whose experience also came in the CFL. Their first quarterback was Frank Tripucka, who had played the previous seven seasons in—you guessed it—the CFL. The CFL would prove to be a big part of that first Broncos team.

"Every time they cut somebody in Canada, they would run them down here and everybody would sit on the sidelines in practice and watch the Canadian guys out there—trying to pick one out that's free probably," Gonsoulin said.

That first Broncos team was a far cry from the billion-dollar organization that it is today. In addition to the two-by-four lockers,

The First Game

The Broncos made history on September 9, 1960, when they squared off against the Boston Patriots in the first game in American Football League history. In front of 21,597 fans at Nickerson Field, home field of Boston University, the Broncos also became the first AFL team to win a game, edging out the Patriots 13–10. On the first play of the second quarter, Al Carmichael took a short pass from Frank Tripucka and went 59 yards for the first points and first touchdown in Broncos history. Gene Mingo booted the extra point for a 7–3 Denver lead. In the third quarter, Mingo returned a Boston punt 76 yards for a touchdown. Then, tired from that run, he missed the extra point, but Denver went on to win.

cheap players, and small coaching staff, Gonsoulin remembers the players using flimsy spiral notebooks to take notes, rather than having big, bulky playbooks. The team's first headquarters were located in a Quonset hut in Denver.

The most embarrassing part of that team, however, was the uniforms. Purchased used from the Copper Bowl, a defunct college bowl game, the home uniforms were brown and gold; the road uniforms were white and brown. The worst part about them was the socks, which featured vertical stripes. "I think the idea with the striped socks, one was that it was so unique," said Robert Howsam, Bob's son. "Number two, I think [Bob] went on some theory that because the striped socks went vertical that it made the guys looks taller. You're going for every little advantage you can come up with."

It was hardly an advantage, and to top it off, the Broncos wore cheap pads, or what Gonsoulin called "Mickey Mouse shoulder pads." From head to toe, the uniforms didn't bring any confidence to the players. In fact, they drew snickers and jokes from opponents around the league. "We were embarrassed about it," Gonsoulin said. "It was like we were putting on an exhibition as a bunch of clowns in funny-looking socks and uniforms."

Today, Gonsoulin looks back at those first years fondly. At the time, he knew the Broncos weren't a typical pro football team. "Everything was second-class," he said. "Nothing was first-class. I didn't think they'd make it at all. Even when I went back after my first year, I wondered if there was even going to be a team there. The way it was going, it was just terrible. The poor fans, they'd come out and there [were] maybe 6,000 or 8,000 people. In Texas, high school football was more advanced than that pro program back then."

Bob Howsam never pretended to have gobs of money. He did what he could to get a team in Denver and keep it in Denver. If that meant cutting corners, so be it, even if it meant putting his wife to work. "My mom used to wash the players' uniforms after the game," Robert said. "She'd take some of these things home, wash them up, and get them all ready to go."

While ownership worked on the cheap, the team struggled on the field. The Broncos actually started 2–0, and sat at 4–2 at one point, but finished 4–9–1. By season's end, Bob knew a change was in order. "I was convinced that someday professional football would be successful in Denver but I knew I didn't have the money to stick it out," he wrote in his book. "I didn't want to mortgage myself, my wife, and kids to a huge debt for the rest of our lives. I knew at the end of the football season that I would have to sell out."

In May 1961, Bob Howsam sold the Broncos, Bears, and Bears Stadium to a group of local businessmen headed by Calvin Kunz that included Gerald Phipps. Both were on the board of directors for Rocky Mountain Empire Sports. Bob Howsam was out of the sports business. "That evening, Janny and I went to the stadium, sat down, and looked over the whole complex," Bob wrote. "I cast my mind back over the past 14 years, thought about the twists that life takes, and I shed a few tears."

Bob may have lasted just one year with the Broncos, but his impact is still felt. Had it not been for Bob, the Broncos may never have come into existence. "He deserves the credit for taking the risk and putting it out there," Robert said. "I wish he could have kept it, of course. He believed in Denver, and he always did feel like we're one of the great sports cities. He gave it a shot and it worked getting here, and then other guys took it over. That's kind of the story with a lot of businesses."

Although money was tight, Bob always made moves with the team's best interests in mind. Even his last move as Broncos owner had the team and the city in mind. He had offers from businessmen in San Antonio and Chicago; had he taken those offers, the Broncos surely would have left town after one season. Instead, Bob took less money from the Kunz/Phipps group, which would keep the team in Denver.

"He could have made a small fortune and sold it to another city that wanted the club," Robert said. "But he's a Colorado guy, and he wanted to keep the club here. He felt like that would be part of his legacy. He started it. He's the founder. He certainly didn't have the finances of a Lamar Hunt and those people. But if he didn't get in on that initial round, Denver wouldn't have gotten a team for years."

Bob went on to a decades-long career in baseball, where he helped build championship teams with the St. Louis Cardinals and Cincinnati Reds. He also played a significant role in finally bringing Major League Baseball to Denver, with the Colorado Rockies' arrival in 1993.

Bob passed away in 2008. "All I can say is, 'Way to go, Dad,'" Robert said.

13 Riding out of Town?

There was a very real chance that the Broncos would leave Denver in the spring of 1961. As serious as that possibility was, however, it was nothing compared to the spring of 1965.

Truth is, the Broncos were an embarrassment at that point. Five seasons into their existence, they had a record of 18–49–3, by far the worst of the eight AFL franchises.

More troubling was the lack of support the Broncos got. In 1964, the team sold just 8,002 season tickets, and less than 17,000 fans, on average, attended home games.

To drum up support, players had to do their part.

"They would make us go to chamber of commerce meetings where these ladies would have a style show and we'd have to show up and try to convince people to come to the games," said Gonsoulin, who was a Bronco from 1960 to 1966. "It would be just about every week. You felt foolish. You felt like, 'This isn't pro football.'"

Save for those few fans who did show up, it seemed that nobody wanted the Broncos in Denver. Other AFL owners urged Broncos president Calvin Kunz to move the team elsewhere. If Denver didn't want the Broncos, plenty of others did. Chicago, Philadelphia, Atlanta, Cincinnati, New Orleans, and Seattle were all among the cities that were open to the idea of adopting the Broncos.

Denver natives Allan and Gerald "Gerry" Phipps, who helped save the team in 1961, wanted no part of losing the Broncos. They owned 42 percent of the stock in the team, and they expressed their love for the Broncos on, of all days, Valentine's Day, in 1965. The Phipps brothers refused to sell their stock when a group from

Atlanta offered roughly $6 million for the team. The team's board of directors met the next day. During a break in the meeting, Gerry Phipps went to the bank and took out a loan for $1 million. When he came back, he and his brother offered $1.25 million to purchase the 52 percent of the stock owned by Kunz and other members of the board.

Just like that, the Phipps brothers owned 96 percent of the Broncos, Denver Bears, and Bears Stadium. For the second time in four years, the Phippses saved the team.

"Why do we want to keep the Broncos in Denver?" Gerry Phipps said to *Sports Illustrated* in 1965. "I could sell out and make a pot full of money. We're not kidding ourselves that this will ever be a goldmine here. But we're trying to attract industry to this

Burn, Baby, Burn

Before the 1962 season began, the Broncos made a few significant changes. They released the team's original head coach, Frank Filchock, and original general manager, Dean Griffing. They replaced both of them with one man: Jack Faulkner. One of Faulkner's first moves was to ditch the ugly brown-and-yellow uniforms for orange-and-blue duds; the Broncos have worn orange and blue ever since. In July, Faulkner and the Broncos held a public ceremony in which they burned the old uniforms at an intrasquad game; thus, very few of the infamous uniforms and vertical stripes remain in existence today.

At 36, Faulkner was the youngest coach in pro football at the time, and he brought a no-nonsense approach to the Broncos. In 1962, the Broncos started 7–2 but ultimately finished 7–7. Faulkner was named AFL Coach of the Year. The burning of the old uniforms and the fast start aside, Faulkner had a rough tenure. After starting 7–2 in 1962, Faulkner went 2–20–1 during the rest of his time in Denver. He was fired after an 0–4 start in 1964. His replacement, Mac Speedie, didn't do much better, going 6–19–1 before being fired two games into 1966.

community. Nothing would hurt us more than headlines around the country saying Denver had lost its football team."

Phipps figured that in order to break even financially, the Broncos would have to sell 20,000 season tickets. That kicked off a remarkable ticket drive in the spring of 1965. Impressed by the show of support for the city of Denver, residents backed the Broncos like never before.

On February 16, a team-record 143 season tickets were sold. The surge continued, with 941 season tickets sold on March 5 alone. When it was all said and done, the Broncos sold 22,905 season tickets for the 1965 season. *Sports Illustrated* was so impressed by the ticket drive that the magazine wrote a story about it, with the headline reading, "A Love Affair With a Loser."

The team was saved and the fans finally threw in their support, but the Broncos continued to be losers, going 4–10 in each of the next two seasons. Just two years later, in 1967, the Broncos were in trouble again. As part of the AFL-NFL merger, which was announced in 1966 but set to take place in 1970, teams were required to have stadiums that could seat 50,000 fans. Bears Stadium had a capacity of more than 34,000 fans, and when Denver voters rejected a bond issue to build a new stadium, the Broncos once again had a foot out the door.

Rookie running back Floyd Little, the Broncos' first-round draft choice, had no idea where he'd actually be playing in 1967. "When I got there, I had heard that they were thinking of moving to either Chicago or to Alabama," Little said.

Before he ever stepped foot on the field in Denver, Little was asked to help save the Broncos. A nonprofit group stepped up with a fund-raising effort to purchase Bears Stadium from Rocky Mountain Empire Sports. Little was among the players who went door-to-door around the region looking for support in that effort, and in February 1968, the group purchased the stadium for $1.8 million. Shortly after that, an upper-deck section that seated

16,000 fans was constructed, pushing the stadium's capacity over the required 50,000 seats for the 1968 season. In December, Bears Stadium was renamed Mile High Stadium.

Once again, the Phipps brothers had a hand in keeping the Broncos in Denver. So did Little, who joined many others on a caravan through Colorado and such surrounding states as New Mexico, Wyoming, Idaho, and South Dakota in search of the funds needed to improve their stadium. It helped a great deal to have Little, the first first-round draft choice to ever sign in Denver, on board to pique the interest of fans. "We were trying to keep our team in Denver, and we did—and it became one of the best franchises in the National Football League," Little said.

Gonsoulin, who played through the ragtag, penny-pinching early days of Broncos history, was proud to see what the Broncos became and proud that they never left their birthplace. "I think it just hung on long enough that somebody came in with enough money to really make it a professional thing," he said.

14 Orange Crush

The 1970s featured some of the greatest defensive units in NFL history, and some of the great nicknames of all time. There was Dallas' "Doomsday Defense," the Los Angeles Rams' "Fearsome Foursome" defensive line, Miami's "No-Name Defense," Minnesota's "Purple People Eaters," and, of course, Pittsburgh's "Steel Curtain."

Denver's "Orange Crush" defense of the 1970s belongs not only on the list of great nicknames, but on the list of the great defensive units of all time.

"It started sometime in 1977, but I can't tell you where the moniker came from," linebacker Tom Jackson said. "I just remember at some point we started seeing it in the newspaper.

"Quite frankly, it's hard to be tough sometimes when you're wearing orange," Jackson continued.

This group managed to make orange look tough because of how they played.

"We really did take a lot of pride in that nickname," Jackson said. "We knew it was a compliment to what we did. I think it fit us perfectly. We really did pride ourselves on hitting and tackling and swarming to the ball. There was a time when I know that we felt that nobody could beat us."

The main cogs in the Orange Crush machine were acquired gradually. Safety Billy Thompson was the first, as a third-round draft choice in 1969, and defensive end Lyle Alzado came next as a fourth-round pick in 1971.

During the 1973 draft, the Broncos selected defensive end Barney Chavous and Jackson.

In 1974, the Broncos' first-round pick was linebacker Randy Gradishar. A less-heralded move that year brought linebacker Joe Rizzo into the fold as a free agent.

A year later was one of the most significant years in the construction of the Orange Crush. In the 1975 draft, the Broncos selected cornerback Louis Wright in the first round, nose tackle Rubin Carter in the fifth, and safety Steve Foley in the eighth. Also that year, linebacker Bob Swenson was acquired as a free agent.

The final piece arrived in 1977, when the Broncos acquired safety Bernard Jackson in a trade with Cincinnati.

Led by defensive coordinator Joe Collier, the Orange Crush defense showed signs of becoming a dominant unit in 1975. That year, the Broncos finished in the top 10 in the NFL in total defense and eight times held opponents to less than 20 points.

Late in 1975, the Broncos faced the AFC West–champion Oakland Raiders. The Broncos held the Ken Stabler–led Raiders to 178 yards. Late in the game, and the Raiders led 14–10, they had second-and-goal at the 1, but the Broncos stuffed them two plays in a row to force a field goal with 2:21 to play. Oakland won 17–10, but Denver made a statement.

"We lost the game, but during the course of the game, we really did battle them head to head," Tom Jackson said. "I thought at that moment we kind of all realized that we might be pretty good. From that moment on I think we had the kind of confidence that let us know we were all young and we were going to be together for a while."

For Thompson, the moment he realized the greatness of the Orange Crush came during the 1977 season. The Broncos were in Kansas City, holding a 14–7 lead in the waning moments when a fake punt gave the Chiefs first-and-goal at the Broncos 1 with just over a minute to play.

Chavous and Wright teamed up on a tackle on first down. Then Gradishar stuffed the Chiefs on the next play. On third down, Tom Jackson dropped a Chiefs running back for a six-yard loss, and on fourth down the Chiefs threw an incomplete pass. Denver won the game 14–7.

"When we were coming off the field, the offense was down like this," Thompson said, making a praying motion. "They were down on their knees. I thought then we had something that was more than special."

The Orange Crush made a habit out of special performances. From 1976 to 1978, the Broncos held 38 of 44 opponents to less than 20 points and 18 of those to less than 10 points.

"It's a dynamic defense that allows a lot of swarming, and it's about getting a lot of help to the ball, which we always prided ourselves in," Jackson said of Collier's system. "Then when you get to the ball, do some damage and make sure people feel it. That was

Rizzo and Swenson Aid the Crush

Two of the most underrated members of the Orange Crush defense were linebackers Joe Rizzo and Bob Swenson. They were the only two starters on that defense who weren't drafted by the Broncos or acquired in a trade.

Rizzo was a 15th-round selection of the Buffalo Bills in 1973 after playing at the U.S. Merchant Marine Academy. A knee injury, however, led him to fail a physical, and the Bills released him before he ever played a game for them. A year later, Rizzo benefited from a players' strike. Needing capable bodies in order to practice during the strike, the Broncos saw film of Rizzo, liked what they saw, and gave him a chance. Terry Frei of the *Denver Post* wrote in his book, *'77: Denver, the Broncos, and a Coming of Age* that Rizzo was about to ship off to the Persian Gulf as a Marine officer when the Broncos called. For a month, Rizzo practiced while the veterans were on strike. He made quite an impression, and even after the veterans returned in August, Rizzo made the team. He wound up starting next to Randy Gradishar in the middle of the Denver defense. From 1976 to 1979, Rizzo started nearly every game the Broncos played.

Perhaps his crowning moment came when he intercepted three passes in one game, a 30–7 win over the defending Super Bowl–champion Raiders in 1977. Through 2011, Rizzo is one of just three U.S. Merchant Marine Academy alums to play in the NFL, and the only one since 1967.

Bob Swenson never did get a lot of attention. He was a walk-on at the University of California–Berkeley and later proved himself enough to earn a scholarship as a defensive lineman. He switched to outside linebacker as a senior and then hoped to get a shot at the NFL. There were 17 rounds of the draft back then, but Swenson went undrafted. The Broncos offered him a chance to try out—he took it and made the most of it. Despite having just one year of experience as an outside linebacker, Swenson made the team in 1975 and played for eight seasons. He started 61 of 62 games from 1977 to 1981 and earned a spot in the Pro Bowl in 1981. Swenson, Frei said, became one of the NFL's best at covering tight ends. "I was always a big Bob Swenson fan," Clough said. "I thought he was colossally underrated."

our motto: a lot of hats on the ball and make sure that people feel it when you get there."

Denver's offense, which was a solid unit but not great, benefited from having the Orange Crush on its side.

"The great thing about our defense, they were like mobsters," quarterback Craig Morton said. "They just went toward the ball, and they caused fumbles and they caused interceptions. They weren't particularly giant guys, but they made things happen."

From 1976 to 1979, the Broncos gave up an average of 13.57 points per game and 280.83 yards per game. (Pittsburgh's Steel Curtain defense, which has the reputation for being the top defense in the NFL during that time, gave up 13.97 points and 257.55 yards per game during that same period.)

Despite their greatness, the Orange Crush has failed to garner the national recognition it deserves. Four members of the Steel Curtain defense have been enshrined in the Hall of Fame; the Orange Crush, meanwhile, has been left out.

"During the mid- to late '70s, their defense was just as good year in and year out as Pittsburgh's was," Clough said. "Their defense is very much, to me, underrepresented, in terms of Hall of Fame consideration. All those guys the Steelers have deserve to be in the Hall of Fame, but the Broncos should be represented by one or two of those guys off that Orange Crush defense. They were definitely Hall of Famers."

Jackson said the Broncos were victims of their location. "I don't want to say that the logistics of where you are affect the voting, but back then, when you didn't have every team getting the kind of national exposure, the Broncos quite frankly didn't," he said. "I don't think a lot of people knew who the Denver Broncos were. We weren't West Coast. We weren't East Coast. Had we won the Super Bowl in '77 and played a closer game, I think people maybe would have taken more notice of what we were doing."

That's the other thing that eluded the Orange Crush—a Super Bowl title. As good as the defense was, it didn't bring home the Lombardi Trophy, while Pittsburgh won four. Then again, the Steelers were helped by an offense that boasts five Hall of Famers, including quarterback Terry Bradshaw.

"Had we had Elway on our team, fuck! You're talking about five (Super Bowls)," Thompson said. "You're talking about one for the thumb if we had anything even similar to that. I'm not taking away from [future Broncos defenders] Steve Atwater, Dennis Smith, [and] Tyrone Braxton, but I'm saying give me that. Give me that 30 points a game and see what we would do.

"That team in '77 is, in my view, the greatest team to ever play for the Broncos defensively. There's no doubt in my mind. I'm not being overly boastful or anything. I'm just stating the fact. That's what it is. That team was just an exceptional team. It was a team that was unselfish, and it was a team that came to play every game."

The Orange Crush still holds most team records for defense. That group also produced five of the 17 shutout wins in team history.

15 Greatness Unnoticed

In 10 NFL seasons, Gradishar made 2,049 tackles—an astounding average of 14.1 per game. He played 145 games without ever missing one for injury. He intercepted 20 passes, taking three of them back for touchdowns.

Denver's first-round draft pick out of Ohio State in 1974, Gradishar started at linebacker for the Broncos from 1974 to 1983.

He made the Pro Bowl seven times, the All-Pro team twice, and was named the NFL's Defensive Player of the Year in 1978.

"Randy's probably one of the best tacklers that we had," said Thompson, who played with Gradishar from 1974 to 1981. "They set it up for him, and he didn't fail. Randy was a great player for us. There's no way you can not say that."

Every year, Gradishar's greatness is a discussion point in Denver. Those who played with him, watched him, and covered him in the media know he's great. And they all wonder why the Pro Football Hall of Fame won't acknowledge him as such.

"Randy Gradishar not being in the Hall of Fame is absurd," Morton said. "It just is a joke."

Gradishar is widely regarded as the best player on Denver's famed Orange Crush defense. "Had he been with the Pittsburgh Steelers, it wouldn't even be a question," Thompson said of Gradishar.

He came close. In 2003 and 2008, he was one of the Hall's 15 finalists. In 2005, 2006, and 2007 he was a semifinalist. Some thought it would finally happen in 2008—his final year of eligibility.

"It's been fun and exciting for me for the last two weeks to think about potentially making it to the Hall of Fame," he told the Associated Press just before the 2008 class was announced. "But if I don't get a call, I know the disappointment; I know it's not a good feeling."

He never got the call, and now his fate is out of the hands of voters. If he ever gets in, it'll come from the veteran's committee.

"My odds of winning the lotto would be better than my odds of going in as a senior candidate," he told the AP in 2008. "Of course, I joke that I can always go in posthumously, so I won't give up hope."

Gradishar's Hall of Fame chances took a hit because of where he played. Denver was fairly unknown during his career, and the

A seven-time Pro Bowler and Denver standout, Gradishar has been unfairly looked over by Hall of Fame voters.

Broncos didn't get much attention nationally. Some also say that playing linebacker in Denver's 3-4 defense works against him. The 4-3 defense was the typical alignment in those days, and former New York Giants great Harry Carson is the only inside linebacker from a 3-4 defense to be enshrined in the Hall. However, it should be noted that Gradishar led the Broncos in tackles and made the Pro Bowl in 1975, when they ran a 4-3 defense.

After defensive coordinator Joe Collier switched to the 3-4 defense in 1976, Gradishar's numbers flew off the charts. It was a defense that was designed to funnel plays to the middle of the field, giving Gradishar ample opportunities to make plays. And he made them. "It's easy to say we funneled it to him, but funneling it to him and having him make the plays are two different things," fellow linebacker Tom Jackson said.

Gradishar still holds the Broncos' all-time record for tackles, and his 286 stops in 1978 are a team record. From 1977 to 1983,

Gradishar made at least 219 tackles in all but one year: the strike-shortened 1982 season. He had 151 in nine games that year, which projects to 268 over a 16-game schedule.

Those numbers are even more remarkable when considering that since Gradishar's retirement, only two Broncos have come close to 200 tackles in a season—Al Wilson had 199 in 2002 and Steve Busick had 195 in 1984.

Ironically, Gradishar's tackle totals ultimately may be what have kept him out of the Hall of Fame.

"I've investigated, as well, as to why he is not in, and what I've heard is that there are people in that room when the conversation starts who don't believe the numbers, that it's impossible for a guy to step out of a game and have…17 unassisted tackles and three assists," Jackson said. "I can tell you for a fact that the numbers reflect exactly what he did on the field. The people who want to say the numbers don't add up really don't know what they're talking about. They really don't. They're trying to diminish what he did on the field. I was there for them, so I know the numbers are legit. It would be great if people would take the time to go look at a season's worth of film. But maybe even more of a compliment [to] go pick out any film. It wasn't just his greatness; it was his consistency of greatness. That, to me, really defines 'Hall of Fame.'

"No one could tell me that Randy is not a Hall of Fame linebacker. It's ridiculous."

Gradishar's greatness has been recognized by the Colorado Sports Hall of Fame, the Broncos' Ring of Fame, and the College Football Hall of Fame. It's the only hall he's not in, however, that defines him today, but it certainly hasn't tarnished his legacy in Denver.

Said Clough: "Randy Gradishar is a Hall of Famer, whether he's officially acknowledged as such or not."

16 Always a Bronco

Like several players drafted in the 1960s and early 1970s, Thompson wasn't exactly thrilled when the Denver Broncos called his name during the 1969 draft.

"I had no clue at the time where Denver was," said Thompson, a third-round pick from Maryland State (now known as Maryland–Eastern Shore). "Back East, when you got the weather reports [for Colorado], it was always from Fraser or somewhere frozen—and I was going, 'I don't want to go there.'"

Like several players who wound up coming to Denver, Thompson fell in love, and he's never left.

"Denver is a wonderful place to be and live and raise a family," he said. "A lot of guys from other teams who haven't played for the Broncos live here."

Thompson came to the Broncos before they had ever posted a winning season. Playing cornerback and then safety, he had a significant role in the team learning to win in the early 1970s and then was a key cog in the Orange Crush defense that led the team to the playoffs three years in a row from 1977 to 1979.

For a team that has had a history of exceptional defensive backs, Thompson may be the best of them all.

"The guy that was consistent his whole career was Billy Thompson," said Little, who considers Thompson the best player with whom he suited up in Denver.

Thompson was the first player to reach 13 years of service with the Broncos and he's still the only player in team history who was a part of three different decades, as he wrapped up his career in 1981.

"Billy Thompson was great in so many different ways," Tom Jackson said. "I think as a cover guy, as a tackler, as a skilled safety,

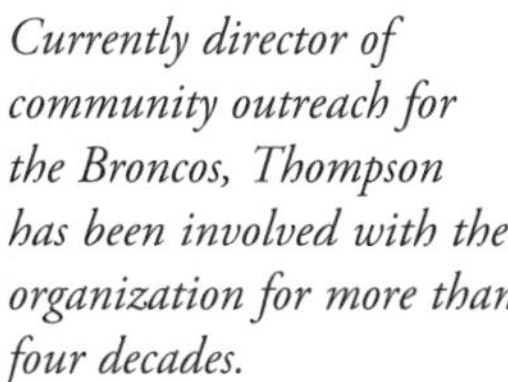
Currently director of community outreach for the Broncos, Thompson has been involved with the organization for more than four decades.

I don't think that anybody has played the position better than Billy. He was also a great return man—not only punt return but kickoff return as well, earlier in his career.

"For Billy, who spent time on teams that weren't very good, to maintain his level of play for as long as he did, that speaks to how good of a player he was."

Thompson began his career as cornerback and returner. Although he spent just five years as the Broncos' primary punt returner, he still ranks second in team history in career punt-return yards (1,814). He also ranks third in team history with a career average of 25.13 yards per kickoff return.

It was on defense that he made his biggest impact. He started out at cornerback and was one of the game's best at that position. Had it been up to Thompson, he probably would have stayed at corner, but defensive coordinator Joe Collier had another plan for the 6'1" 200-pounder. Collier moved Thompson to safety in 1972, and he started there in every game through 1981. In all, Thompson was in the starting lineup for 156 games from 1971 to 1981—still the longest streak in team history.

"He said, 'You'll be more valuable to us [at safety],'" Thompson said. "He always put me where he thought the action was going to be."

Collier asked a lot of Thompson. As a safety, he was asked to be an integral part of stopping the run, but Collier also wanted Thompson to cover receivers.

"I loved it," he said. "I enjoyed that role immensely because it made me pay attention to the teams that were coming into play, and it taught me more about football. I knew every week I was involved—big time involved. It made me a better player and it gave me a better understanding of the defense."

Few players understood the defense like Thompson did, and his presence made those around him better. Charley Johnson, who quarterbacked the Broncos from 1972 to 1975, said he and Thompson "always were trying to pick on each other" in practice.

"He was just a talented athlete to start with, and then he learned about playing safety and what he could do to wreck offenses and upset their timing," Johnson said. "He was very, very smart in what he did."

Combining his talent and intelligence, Thompson finished his career with 40 interceptions (third in team history), 21 fumble recoveries, and a team-record seven defensive touchdowns. Going into 2016, his four career fumble returns for touchdowns ranked fourth in NFL history.

Thompson takes great pride in the role he played in helping the Broncos become winners. He also takes pride in being a Bronco. Following his playing career, he joined the Broncos' front office and still works as the team's director of community outreach.

"I don't take it lightly," he said of being a Bronco. "It's something that I'm honored to do, to be a part of something that

I think is great. In the capacity I'm serving now, it gives me an opportunity to help other people that have been supportive of the Broncos forever and supported the team when the team wasn't successful."

17 Broncomania

Denver did not embrace the Broncos right away; but when it did, it became an unconditional love. Broncos fans have a passion for their team that few NFL teams can boast.

"I had never seen anything like it," former linebacker Karl Mecklenburg said. "Coming from Minnesota, people there are pretty stoic. Coming out here and experiencing the excitement and just the commitment of the fans to the Denver Broncos was something I had never seen anything like."

A strong relationship between the fans and the team began to form in the 1960s, when Little and others personally went out to meet fans in an effort to drum up support for the team. "It's always been there," said Little, who joined the team in 1967. "Broncomania was always there."

The Broncos didn't win much when Little arrived, and that's when he discovered the fans' love for their Broncos. "Even after we lost, we'd see the whole [airport] corridor decorated with Bronco stuff after we got our butts beat. Fans in Denver supported us whether we won or lost, our whole time there."

Since 1970, the Broncos have sold out every home game (with the exception of two games during the 1987 strike when replacement players were used). With all those sellouts, it's little wonder that the stadium can get a little rowdy at times. Charley Johnson quarterbacked the Broncos from 1972 to 1975, when the capacity at Mile High Stadium was just above 50,000. "That was a noisy place," he said.

The fans in the south stands at old Mile High Stadium became legendary for their rambunctious ways, and they were like that during Johnson's day, too. "They were loud and vociferous and they attacked all the teams that came to town," Johnson said.

As the Broncos got better on the field, the fans got louder and more passionate about their team. "They came out rain, sleet, or snow—like the postman," Little said. "They never wavered. They supported and they rooted for us."

Broncos fans don't simply express their love by showing up to the stadium on game day. Their passion comes alive during pregame tailgate parties. It comes alive with the thousands who paint their faces, hair, or personal property.

While Broncomania had been alive for several years, the 1977 season is often associated with the peak of Broncomania. That season, a stadium expansion added nearly 25,000 seats. Also, for the first time in franchise history, the 1977 squad went to the playoffs and reached the Super Bowl. Fans could sense how good the team was all season. Thousands of fans greeted the team at the airport after road games. The city had Broncos fever like never before.

"It was Denver's first time in the national sporting spotlight," said Terry Frei of the *Denver Post*. "It was the Broncos' first time as a legitimate championship threat, even as a legitimate franchise in some ways. There was a naïveté and freshness to it in an almost collegiate zeal that just could never be repeated."

Quarterback Craig Morton still remembers the 1977 season as one of the most magical of his career—and it was because of the fans and the burst of Broncomania.

"People painting their cars orange, their houses orange," Morton said. "They'd come to practice lined up. Guys identified with the fans. We took all the time necessary [with the fans]. We signed their cars, would go to their houses and sign their house. We'd go to restaurants, and people would stand up and cheer. Nothing was weird there. It was something real special because the city and the people had a chance to really live the dream that they had been wanting to happen. There was none of this real distance between player and fan. It was all just one happy huge Denver family that really, really had great times."

The passion for the Broncos has not diminished since 1977, but it has changed. "We became a more mature and jaded market as time went on, and that team in '77 was really a part of the change," Frei said.

Unlike fans in 1977, fans today have experienced a lot of winning and they expect a lot of winning. From 1977 to 2011, the Broncos won two Super Bowls, appeared in four others, played in eight AFC Championship Games, and won 11 AFC West division titles.

Anything under That Barrel?

Perhaps no fan has ever embodied the spirit of Broncomania like Tim McKernan, also known to the Broncos faithful as "the Barrel Man." In more than 40 years, starting in 1967, McKernan missed just four games. For one game, he painted a barrel to look like a can of Orange Crush soda. Shirtless, he wore the barrel, held up by suspenders, along with cowboy boots and a cowboy hat. The reason? McKernan had made a bet with his brother that if he wore it, he could get on TV. The barrel stuck, and McKernan wore it to games for years—regardless of the weather. A United Airlines mechanic, McKernan gained fame for wearing the barrel and leading cheers in the Mile High Stadium stands. McKernan stopped wearing the barrel in 2007 and in December 2009, the 69-year-old passed away from lung failure. The biggest question people always had was, "What's he got on under the barrel?" He never answered that question.

Broncomania may never be like it was in 1977, but even today, you can spot orange and blue cars around town every now and then. And on game days, the city of Denver gets caught in a wave of Broncomania.

18 1977 Playoffs

With Broncomania at its peak, the team entered the 1977 playoffs with excitement and great hope.

At 12–2, they had the best record in the AFC and were tied with Dallas of the NFC for the best mark in the league. One of their biggest wins was against perennial power Pittsburgh, 21–7 at Mile High Stadium in Week 8.

But the Broncos had to face the Steelers again, this time in the first round of the playoffs on Christmas Eve. Denver had never been to the playoffs. Pittsburgh, on the other hand, was in the postseason for the sixth straight year, including Super Bowl championships in 1974 and 1975. Although the Steelers were just 9–5 that season, this was still the *Steelers*—Terry Bradshaw, Franco Harris, Rocky Bleier, Lynn Swann, John Stallworth, "Mean" Joe Greene, Jack Ham, Jack Lambert, Donnie Shell…and on and on.

Although the Broncos had never been to the playoffs, there was a measure of confidence. It helped that they had defeated the Steelers earlier in the season. It also helped that they were at home. In two years, the only team that had come into Mile High Stadium and defeated the Broncos on their home turf was the Oakland Raiders.

"We had home-field advantage, so that was the best thing in the world, because people didn't like playing in Mile High,"

Morton said. "First of all, we had the best fans and the loudest fans. Then we had the stigma of the mile-high air. Everything was played up. The [local newspapers] did a good job.

"Everything was new to everybody, but nobody panicked. Nobody thought anything different. We just had a lot of confidence we could beat these guys."

With two of the great defenses of the era on the field, neither team did much on offense. Although the final score—Denver 34, Pittsburgh 21—suggests a lot of offense, Denver finished with only 258 yards, Pittsburgh with 304.

Denver's defense, and Tom Jackson in particular, had a fantastic day. The Broncos scored on six possessions in the game, and on five of those the defense set up the offense in Steelers territory. John Schultz blocked a punt, and Jackson recovered a Steelers fumble to set up first-half touchdowns. In the third quarter, a defensive stand pinned Pittsburgh deep, and that set up another Broncos touchdown.

The Broncos led 24–21 when Pittsburgh took over with 7:05 to play in the game. That's when Jackson stepped up. He picked off Bradshaw and returned the ball 32 yards to set up a Jim Turner field goal.

Now down by six, Pittsburgh had five minutes to go, but Jackson did it again, intercepting another Bradshaw pass. With less than two minutes to play, the Broncos were at the Pittsburgh 34 when Morton made a gutsy call.

During a timeout, the Broncos discussed their strategy. Morton wanted to throw a deep pass to Jack Dolbin, who hadn't caught a pass all game but had 26 that year. It was a bit of good fortune for the Broncos, however, because Pittsburgh's future Hall of Fame cornerback Mel Blount had an injury and didn't play in the game. That put backup Jimmy Allen in the lineup covering Dolbin.

Denver head coach Red Miller didn't like the idea of the pass, but when Morton got in the huddle, he called it anyway. "I just said, 'To hell with it. I'm calling this play because I know what they're doing,'" Morton said. "'We're going to call this play and we're going to make a touchdown and that'll be it.' That's exactly what happened."

Dolbin reached out and caught the ball over a diving Allen. The touchdown put Denver ahead 34–21 with 1:44 to play. When Morton got back to the sideline, he passed by Miller.

"He kind of smiled at me," Morton said. "He's not going to say anything. It worked."

Morton injured his hip late in the season, and it kept getting worse, but he fought through it to beat the Steelers and send the Broncos to the AFC Championship Game against the hated Oakland Raiders on January 1, 1978.

Morton's chances of playing in the title game looked bleak, at best. He spent the entire week in the hospital, nursing his painful hip. He didn't practice a single play with the team all week.

"From my hip down, it was just solidly covered with every color you could imagine," he said. "It was all broken blood vessels. It was horrible. It just was very painful. I didn't think there was any way I could play when I woke up Sunday morning in the hospital. I had even gotten out of bed and I couldn't do anything. They would come in and try to get the blood out. They put needles in my leg and started trying to withdraw it."

"Make Those Miracles Happen"

For seven seasons, from 1974 to 1980, Jon Keyworth was an exceptional fullback for the Broncos. The 6'3" 230-pounder could block, he could run (2,653 yards and 22 touchdowns), and he could catch (141 receptions for 1,057 yards). Keyworth's most memorable contribution to the Broncos came in a recording studio, however. During the 1977 season, Keyworth wrote a song about the team, "Make Those Miracles Happen." The record flew off the shelves as the Broncos made a run to the Super Bowl. "We thought it was wonderful," quarterback Craig Morton said.

Morton's good friend, Loren Hawley, came to pick him up from the hospital that morning.

"What do you think?" Hawley asked.

"Loren, I don't know if I can play," Morton responded.

"Bullshit! You've worked all your life to get another chance to do this. You're going to play," Hawley barked back.

"You're right," Morton said.

Years later, Morton said, "A little kick in the ass is what I needed because I was feeling sorry for myself."

Morton went to the stadium to get ready, and while he was on the training table, several teammates walked in to check him out.

"I could see in their faces, saying, 'Holy shit, he's not playing,'" Morton said.

Nevertheless, he went out to the locker room and put on his uniform. Then he slipped his feet into his shoes but couldn't bend down to tie them.

"Red came over to me and said, 'What do you think?' I said, 'Coach, you tie my shoes, I'll play, and we'll win the game,'" Morton said. "He got down in front of everybody, everybody came around, and he tied my shoes, and I said, 'Let's go.'"

The next three hours were three of the most magical hours in Broncos history. Morton had his best playoff performance in a Broncos uniform, throwing for 224 yards and two touchdowns, the defense was sensational once again, and the Broncos got a couple fortunate breaks to knock off the defending Super Bowl–champion Raiders 20–17.

In the first half, Oakland's future Hall of Fame receiver Fred Biletnikoff injured his shoulder when he was hit by Denver's Joe Rizzo and Steve Foley. That took one of the Raiders' top weapons off the field for the rest of the day.

Another break came in the third quarter. Leading 7–3, the Broncos were at the Raiders 1 when running back Rob Lytle fumbled. The Raiders recovered, but officials had blown the whistle and the Broncos kept the ball. On the next play, Jon Keyworth scored to up the lead to 14–3.

Along with those breaks, the Broncos made several big plays. Both of Morton's touchdown passes went to Haven Moses, the second one putting the Broncos ahead 20–10 midway through the fourth quarter. That clinching score was set up by Bob Swenson's interception of a Ken Stabler pass.

"The excitement of the whole thing, I don't remember if it was [painful] or not," Morton said of his hip. "Once you get going, you just tend to forget about it."

Stabler responded by throwing his second touchdown pass of the day to Dave Casper with 3:16 to play to cut the Broncos' lead to 20–17, but the Broncos offense ran out the clock with a pair of first downs.

The win was monumental not only because it propelled the Broncos into the Super Bowl, but it came against the Raiders. Oakland had gone 13–0–2 in its previous 15 trips to Denver, including a 24–14 win earlier in the 1977 season. Beating the Raiders was a remarkable addition to perhaps the most thrilling season in Broncos history.

"It was real magic," Morton said. "Nothing could be like that again. I was lucky, very fortunate to be with great guys, a great team, and great coaches and great owners, and we just had a great time. Everybody had the best time doing it. We just knew we were part of something extremely special, and the fans were part of it. We knew that. The fans were like a teammate."

Frei said the Broncos, in many ways, did what they were supposed to do as the AFC's best team, but it didn't diminish the magic.

"I don't think it bowled everybody over in terms of being shocked, but there still was kind of that 'pinch me' quality to it," he said.

Especially for Thompson. He arrived in Denver as a rookie in 1969 and had played eight seasons without going to the playoffs before 1977. "The night of the championship game against the Raiders is embedded in my memory," he said. "It was a pivotal moment for me, because quite frankly I was the only one left from 1969, that rookie group, that was still on the team in '77. It was an incredible moment for me. All the guys I had played with, Floyd [Little] included…all these guys I had played with didn't get to experience what I was experiencing with this thing now."

The win had another significant meaning to Thompson. He was one of the players who had nudged management to fire coach John Ralston after the 1976 season and bring in Miller.

"After that, they came to me and said, 'Hey, we gave you what you asked for. Now let's see what you're going to do,'" Thompson said.

For Thompson and many of the Broncos, it was Super Bowl or bust that season, and beating the Raiders got them to where they wanted to be.

"I knew if we hadn't, I was in trouble," Thompson said.

19 Super Bowl XII

After the thrill ride of the AFC playoffs, the team headed to New Orleans to take on the powerful Dallas Cowboys in Super Bowl XII on January 15, 1978. These were the Cowboys of Roger Staubach, Tony Dorsett, Ed "Too Tall" Jones, Randy White, and Thomas "Hollywood" Henderson. The Cowboys led the NFL in total offense and total defense that season. Only one team—the Raiders—scored more points throughout the year.

Denver, of course, countered with the Orange Crush defense and had Morton's veteran presence to lead the offense. The Denver defense was exceptional all night, but the offense broke down, setting a Super Bowl record with eight turnovers in the 27–10 loss. Morton threw four interceptions and nearly threw a fifth before he was relieved by backup Norris Weese.

"Normally, that many turnovers in that kind of a game, it's a blowout," Thompson said years later. "If we got a couple of breaks, I think we could have won the ballgame, but it's really hard to overcome eight turnovers. Eight! Think about it: eight turnovers in a championship game."

Both teams traded punts to start the game, and on the TV broadcast Pat Summerall said, "If anybody looks tight, it's Dallas." Seconds later, Rubin Carter sacked Staubach and forced another punt.

Then the turnovers began. Morton threw his first interception to set up Dallas at the Denver 25. Five plays later, future Hall of Fame running back Tony Dorsett powered into the end zone from three yards out.

Two plays later, Morton's pass was tipped and intercepted, giving the Cowboys the ball at the Broncos 35. The Cowboys wound up with a field goal for a 10–0 lead.

The second quarter may have been one of the ugliest 15 minutes in Super Bowl history. The Broncos had a stunning five turnovers in that quarter alone, and Dallas managed just three points, as the Denver defense kept the Broncos in the game.

"The defense played really well, and we had a few opportunities there to get into the game," Morton said in recalling that game. "If we ever would have gone ahead, we probably would have done a lot differently."

They never did get the lead, but kept themselves in the game.

In the third quarter, Weese relieved Morton and finished off Denver's only touchdown drive. The Broncos actually scored 10 third-quarter points to pull within 20–10 and, remarkably, had a chance with 20 minutes to play.

The Broncos' offense never could get comfortable, though. They generated 121 yards on the ground, but Morton and Weese combined for just 61 yards through the air, completing just eight of 25 passes.

"We just did not match up well against them, our offensive line against their defensive line," Morton said. "We could not hold them out. I tried to make plays, which my very essence for being there was not to try to do some of the things I tried to do. Of course everything just kind of backfired and it was a horrible experience."

The Cowboys had just four sacks, but their relentless pressure forced many of Denver's mistakes. Cowboys defensive linemen Harvey Martin and Randy White shared the MVP Award after they absolutely destroyed Denver's offensive line. It was the only time the Super Bowl has had co-MVPs and, through Super Bowl XLVI, was one of just two in which defensive linemen were honored.

"They blitzed a lot up the middle, and we just never had the blocking arrangements," Morton said. "There was always somebody free and they were always kicking my ass."

The turnovers were crippling, but the Orange Crush defense never backed down.

"During the game you don't even think about that," Thompson said. "You're just saying, 'We don't give a shit where [the ball] is, we're stopping them. We've got to go play.'"

All things considered, the Broncos did a great job against the Dallas offense. The Cowboys did have 325 yards but needed 71 plays and more than 38 minutes of possession time to get those yards.

Dallas had 16 offensive possessions. A stunning seven of them began within 40 yards of the end zone, but those possessions netted just 17 points for the Cowboys. Denver's defense held Dallas to no more than one first down on 11 of the 16 possessions, and only one Dallas drive went for more than 41 yards.

"After it was over, it felt like we had played two games," Thompson said. "We played so many snaps in that game that it wasn't even funny."

After the game, Cowboys coach Tom Landry told Thompson, "You've got the best defense we played."

Unfortunately for Morton, nobody remembers what the Broncos defense did that day. But they sure do remember how he played. The hero so many times during that magical season, he completed 4 of 15 passes for 39 yards and four interceptions. His 0.0 quarterback rating is the lowest in Super Bowl history.

"That's one of the things I don't like about Super Bowl time because they start showing these movies again," he said. "That's rated the worst performance of any quarterback in the history of the Super Bowl, and I doubt anybody will ever do worse than I did."

20 Von & the Orange Rush

Carolina quarterback Cam Newton never saw Von Miller coming. Late in the first quarter of Super Bowl 50, Newton and the Panthers trailed the Broncos 3–0, and Newton dropped back to pass.

Bouncing around his own 5-yard line, Newton surveyed the defense, hoping to find an open receiver. To Newton's right, Miller raced past Panthers tackle Mike Remmers as if Remmers wasn't even there. Just as Newton appeared to find a possible target, Miller slammed into him. As Newton fell to the ground, Miller ripped the ball from his hands, and then watched it bounce into the end zone, where Broncos' defensive lineman Malik Jackson fell on it for a touchdown.

If the football world had any questions about the dominance of Miller and the Denver defense, those questions were all answered on February 7, 2016, as the Broncos destroyed the Panthers for a 24–10 win in the Super Bowl. Miller cemented his status as one of the game's premier defensive players by registering 2.5 sacks, five tackles, and two forced fumbles, both of which led to Denver touchdowns. Miller was named the games' Most Valuable Player (MVP), just the 10th defensive player to win the award.

"It just shows what type of defense that we've been playing. It's honestly not about me. If I could cut this award, I would give it to DeMarcus [Ware] and [Derek] Wolfe and all the other guys. That's what I would do. This is all great and stuff, but for me, I want to be with my guys. I would take the ring, the MVP is great, but I'll take the ring. I want to go in there with my teammates," Miller said after the game.

It wasn't just about Miller, but he had quickly become the brightest star on the Denver defense. Selected No. 2 overall in the 2011 NFL Draft out of Texas A&M, Miller was the highest draft pick in Broncos history. In fact, it was the first time in 20 years that the Broncos had a top-10 pick and only the fourth time since the common draft began in 1967 that they had a top-five pick.

Miller immediately lived up to the hype, tying the team rookie record with 11.5 sacks in 2011. The next season, he established a new single-season team record with 18.5 sacks. He added five more in a suspension/injury-shortened 2013 and 14 more in 2014, before registering 11 in 2015. Hall of Famers Reggie White and Derrick Thomas were the only players in NFL history to reach the 50-sack mark quicker than Miller.

Ware, a veteran who was also a gifted pass rusher, noticed a special quality in Miller and developed a great camaraderie with his younger teammate. "I say, 'It's Miller time.' I tell him that all the time. When he feels that and I can see it in his eyes, I know that he turns it on," Ware said.

In addition to his sacks, Miller forced a whopping 17 fumbles during his first five years and he may have led the league in sack-dance variety and creativity. Charismatic and entertaining on and off the field, Miller enjoyed a remarkable celebrity tour after the Super Bowl, including appearances on *The Ellen DeGeneres Show* and *Today*, and guest spots on *Saturday Night Live* and at the Grammy Awards. He was also a contestant on *Celebrity Family Feud*, and topped it off by competing on *Dancing with the Stars*.

"He's even more fun [in person]," Broncos cornerback Chris Harris said. "You're not getting all of Von Miller when all you see is on TV. He's even more fun without the TV, behind the closed doors. It's great, playing with Von. Me and him came in the same class [in 2011]. It's been an amazing ride, and we just want to continue to win games."

With Miller leading the way, the Broncos did win a lot of games, but in 2015, he was hardly alone in lifting the defense to the top of the NFL. In the 1970s, the Broncos had the Orange Crush defense. In 2015, it was the Orange Rush, because nobody in the league could rush the quarterback like the Broncos. They led the NFL with 52 sacks during the regular season before adding 14 more in the playoffs. If it wasn't Miller getting to the quarterback, it was Ware, or Wolfe, or Shaquil Barrett, or Jackson, or rookie Shane Ray.

Ware, who played his first nine seasons with the Dallas Cowboys, revitalized his career by signing with Denver in 2014. Among the all-time leaders in sacks, Ware got to the 100-sack mark in only 113 games (White was the only player in history to get there quicker). Ware teamed with Miller to give the Broncos a devastating starting duo.

Denver's defense also featured Pro Bowl cornerbacks Aqib Talib and Harris, Pro Bowl safety T.J. Ward, two of the best young defensive linemen in the game (Wolfe and Jackson) and two of the best young linebackers (Brandon Marshall and Danny Trevathan).

The Orange Rush finished first in the NFL in yards allowed, first against the pass, third against the run, and fourth in points allowed. What truly made the group special, though, was its uncanny ability to rescue a poor offense time and time again.

In four different wins, the Broncos returned interceptions for touchdowns, two by Talib. A fumble return for a touchdown by Bradley Roby was the difference in a win at Kansas City. In two other games, the Broncos forced fumbles in the closing seconds or overtime to secure wins. Seven times during the regular season, they held the opposition to 15 points or less.

During the playoffs, the Broncos smothered the high-powered Pittsburgh Steelers, frustrated the defending-champion New England Patriots, and put together a masterful performance in the Super Bowl. The Panthers' No. 1 offense never stood a chance, as Denver forced four turnovers and racked up a Super Bowl–record seven sacks.

At the forefront of the defense was coordinator Wade Phillips. Long considered a defensive mastermind, Phillips re-joined the Broncos in 2015.

"He just brought personality, man, and he trusts us," Harris said. "He kept everything so simple. The defensive game plans weren't difficult. He made it to where guys didn't have to think and they could just play. That was a huge key to us getting better."

Phillips, who had coached in Denver previously from 1989 to 1994 (including 93–94 as head coach), finally won a Super Bowl in his 38th NFL season as a coach, and he could not have been more thrilled.

"Tremendous performance all through the playoffs. We almost led the league in every category, so we've got to say this is a special, all-time defense. I've been lucky to be around a lot of great defenses and a lot of great games, but this one topped it off," Phillips said.

21 Fan Favorite

The ink had barely dried on Tom Jackson's first pro contract when he flew back to Kentucky and, with friends by his side, walked into a Chevrolet dealership in the spring of 1973. The 22-year-old Cleveland native had just finished his college career at Louisville, had a signing bonus of $15,500, and knew exactly what he wanted to buy first.

"It was one of the proudest moments of my life," he said. "I bought a colonial gold Monte Carlo with a sunroof and an eight-track tape deck. The gentleman who sold me the car, he's got a bunch of college kids in his showroom, and he goes, 'So how are you going to pay for it?' I said, 'Cash.'

"I was just so glad to be able to get a car and glad to be able to pay cash for it."

That was the first of what proved to be a career full of great moments for Jackson. The younger generation of football fans knows Jackson as the energetic and outspoken analyst for ESPN. But from 1973 to 1986, he was a standout linebacker, a team leader, and one of the most popular players in Broncos history.

"He's the same guy you see on TV—outspoken, loving life, [and] had great fun playing football," Karl Mecklenburg said. "He's kind of the Shannon Sharpe before Shannon Sharpe—the real character in the locker room. Great, great guy."

At 5'11" and 220 pounds when he was coming out of college, Jackson was considered too small by some to play a significant role in the NFL. He had dreams of playing for his hometown Browns but was picked up by the Broncos in the fourth round. "My mom had passed away when I was very young, when I was 13," he said. "She never really got a chance to see me play. But my sister and my dad, they were happy for me to be in the NFL. I don't know that I was jumping [for] joy that I got drafted by the Denver Broncos, but I was very, very pleased to be in the NFL."

When he got to town to sign his contract, Jackson said, "I thought it was one of the most beautiful places I had seen in my life."

Riding into town in his brand-new Monte Carlo, Jackson made an immediate impact on a Broncos defense that was growing up and learning to dominate.

Inducted into the Broncos' Ring of Fame in 1992, he's one of just five Broncos to play 14 years for the team and ranks among the top five in team history in games played (191) and games started (177).

Jackson recorded 44 sacks, 20 interceptions, and scored three touchdowns during his remarkable career.

"Tommy Jackson is as good of a linebacker that's ever played football," Morton said.

As a rookie in 1973, Jackson got into the starting lineup when veteran Chip Myrtle suffered a bad knee injury during a preseason game. Defensive coordinator Joe Collier turned to Jackson and told him to get into the game.

"I remember the only thing Joe told me when I went in was, 'Watch the sweep,'" Jackson said. "The first play they ran my way went for about 60 yards. I let them get the corner. I felt horrible. After that I kind of settled into a pretty good game. From that point on, I felt pretty confident about my skills.

"The game never overwhelmed me. I knew between Paul Smith and Lyle Alzado and Billy Thompson, [and] Leroy Mitchell, I knew we had some pretty good players. Tommy Graham was playing the middle at that point. As bad as the team had performed in the past, I knew we had some pretty good players, and I was just glad to get my opportunity and wanted to take advantage of it."

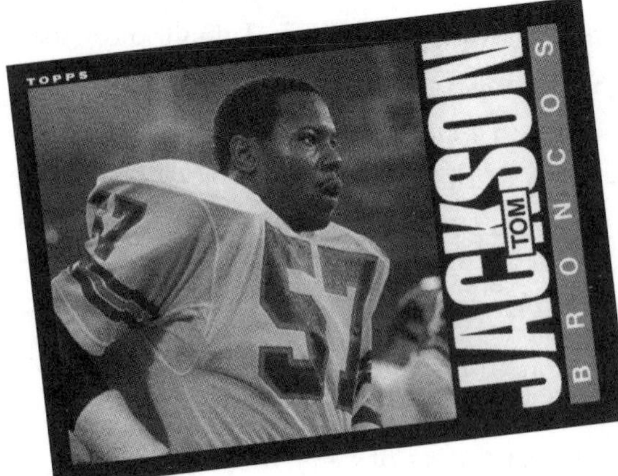

A familiar face to football fans around the nation as a television commentator, Jackson has long been beloved in Denver.

A middle linebacker through high school and college, Jackson had an injury-plagued rookie season. When the season was over, Collier made a decision that changed Jackson's career by moving him to weak-side linebacker in order to take advantage of Jackson's speed and overall skill.

"I always told Joe that was probably the best move and the best decision on the field that anybody ever made for me," Jackson said. "When he moved me outside, it got me out in space. It just worked out much better for me."

Jackson was a regular in the starting lineup through the end of his career in 1986. During his career, Jackson played with Broncos greats Floyd Little and John Elway, and he was one of the few players to play in both Super Bowl XII and Super Bowl XXI.

"He doesn't get as much credit, but he was a great, great player," Thompson said.

He was a great leader, too.

"Tom Jackson was as inspirational as any player was," talk radio host Sandy Clough said.

Jim Saccomano, who has spent several years in the Broncos' media-relations department, said Jackson was the only player who ever got a standing ovation from the media at his retirement press conference.

"I always had a great relationship with our media," Jackson said. "I was always open with them. I always did things, hopefully, the right way."

He has continued to do things the right way as a member of the media himself. He joined ESPN in 1987 and has been a part of its NFL coverage team ever since.

"I work for a great company, but I'm also very fortunate to work with people that I like," he said. "We're just having fun. If you have real fun, people at home will feel it, and it will be as if they're joining you in a conversation that's real. If you get that, you've got it."

Jackson has it as a broadcaster, and he had it as a player. Fans were always drawn to how he played the game. In retirement, he's had knee-replacement surgery, hip-replacement surgery, and a pin put in his shoulder. Even so, to Jackson, the pain and injuries were "all part of the fun that was had."

"I wouldn't trade the time in which I played for anything," he said. "I know we didn't win the Super Bowl, and I always wish we would have; I wish we would have been able to win that first one for them, but we didn't. I would not trade a single thing, other than winning those two games, about anything about my career."

22 Shutdown Corner

Every once in a while, a cornerback comes along that changes a defense. In the first round of the 1975 draft, the Broncos found one of them. With the 17th pick in that draft, the Broncos selected Louis Wright, from San Jose State.

Wright wasn't thrilled to leave his native California for Denver. But for 12 seasons he was one of the best corners in the NFL and perhaps even the best corner in the 50-plus-year history of the Broncos. Wright was selected to the Pro Bowl five times, a franchise record for corners until Champ Bailey came along. Yet to those who played with or against Wright, or watched him play, he was still underrated when measured against his peers.

"The best player who has not gotten the credit he deserves, by far, is Louis Wright," the *Denver Post* sportswriter Terry Frei said. "He's so low-key and I would say unflashy in the sense of not calling attention to himself. As many have said, he was a shutdown corner before anybody called it that."

Guys like Mel Blount, Darrell Green, Mike Haynes, and Deion Sanders earned their way to the Hall of Fame for their ability to completely take their side of the field away from the opposition's passing attack. Herb Adderley and Mel Renfro, who both played in the 1960s and '70s, are Hall of Fame corners who flashed the same type of ability.

"Louis Wright—there's not a better cornerback," Morton said. "I played with Herb Adderley and Mel Renfro and against all the great players. He's as good as any of them."

At 6'2" and 200 pounds, Wright was as dominant as anyone in his era. Opposing receivers rarely caught passes against him, and his shutdown ability created opportunities for the rest of the Broncos defense. Tom Jackson, who played with Wright throughout Wright's career, described how everybody on the defense would play off the guy next to them. Well, almost everybody. "What we would do, that was true of 10 of us," Jackson said. "And then coach Collier would take Louis and put him on the best receiver on the field and go, 'Take that guy away.'"

What made Wright stand out in Jackson's mind was not just his cover skills, but that he could do everything else well, too. "Louis also would come up and tackle, and Louis would also do all the dirty work that you expect from a corner," Jackson said.

Wright was blessed with physical ability like few players in team history. "Louis is one of the greatest corners I ever played with," Thompson said. "He could just flat-out run. I've never seen anything like it."

He also had great football instincts and was often in position to make big plays. He finished his career with 26 interceptions, 11 fumble recoveries, and four defensive touchdowns. His interception total might be a bit low for an elite corner, but that was in part because teams didn't throw his way and in part because Wright did have one fault, Thompson said. "Louis was a great corner, but he had bricks for hands," Thompson joked.

Nobody ever questioned what Wright brought to the Broncos, though. He played 166 games in a Broncos uniform and ranks among the franchise leaders with 163 starts. In every game he played, he was one of the best athletes on the field. "Louis Wright was the best pure football player I think they ever had here," Clough said.

Prior to Wright's arrival, the Broncos had never been to the playoffs. During his 12-year career, they got to the playoffs six times and reached the Super Bowl twice. He played in each of the franchise's first 10 postseason games.

Wright retired after the 1986 season, citing a desire to go out while still playing at a high level. A strained relationship with head coach Dan Reeves likely played a role, too.

By the time his career was over, Wright decided Denver was a fine place to live, and he's been there ever since. Wright has spent several years coaching high school football and teaching at the high school and middle school levels. "Deep down, I have the personality to teach, even if it's not football," he said to the *Aurora Sentinel*. "With friends, with family, with children, I catch myself teaching all the time."

Wright was inducted into the Colorado Sports Hall of Fame in 1992 and the Broncos' Ring of Fame in 1993.

23 Koobs

Who was the best quarterback the Broncos drafted during the 1980s?

Ask the casual fan that question and they're sure to laugh and say, "John Elway, of course." But, they'd be wrong, likely forgetting that Elway was acquired in a trade, not through the draft in 1983.

During the 1980s, Denver drafted just three quarterbacks—Mark Hermann (1981, fourth round), Gary Kubiak (1983, eighth round), and Buddy Funck (1985, 10th round). Hermann played just two games in Denver before being a part of the deal that brought Elway to town. Funck never made it onto the roster. Kubiak, meanwhile, became one of the more impactful people ever brought into the organization.

Kubiak spent his entire nine-year playing career as Elway's backup, retiring after the 1991 season. From 1995 to 2005, he spent 11 seasons as the Broncos' offensive coordinator. And, in 2015, he returned to Denver again, this time as head coach. The 2015 season was Kubiak's 21st in the organization. In those 21 years, the Broncos played in six Super Bowls—winning three of them—won nine AFC West division championships, reached the playoffs 14 times, and had a winning record 16 times.

During the course of his nine-year playing career, Kubiak mostly served as Dan Reeves' right-hand man on the sideline. "Gary was great for me, being on the sideline," Reeves said. "He used to keep all of the statistics—what defense they played, what the coverage was. I can't tell you how many times Gary Kubiak would make a suggestion to me and he would see something that normal players don't see. He was just awesome, and I knew he was going to be a great coach."

When Kubiak did get a chance to play, he often came through. He finished his career completing 58.1 percent of his passes (173-for-298) for 1,920 yards, 14 touchdowns, and 16 interceptions. "Gary never ever played poorly when he was called upon," Reeves said.

Kubiak started just five games during his career, but beat Seattle as a rookie in 1983 and subbed for an injured Elway to beat the Los Angeles Raiders in 1984. In 1989, a year in which the Broncos won the AFC, Kubiak started in place of Elway, who was ill, and beat the Redskins in Washington. In perhaps his most valiant effort, Kubiak came into the 1991 AFC Championship Game in Buffalo in relief of Elway, who injured his thigh in the fourth quarter. The Broncos trailed the Bills 10–0. Kubiak completed 11-of-12 passes for 136 yards, and his three-yard touchdown run with 1:43 to play brought the Broncos within three at 10–7. A late Broncos fumble ended their hopes of winning, but Kubiak had given them a chance in what turned out to be his final game as a player. He retired at the end of the season.

"He's one of the more unselfish people I think I've ever been around," Reeves said. "The thing that's difficult is not [being] the starter, not that John had an easy job. But it's a lot easier to prepare yourself week in and week out knowing you're going to start. How difficult is it for you as a backup guy to be the one that you've got to sit there and be ready in case that guy goes out?"

Immediately upon his retirement, Kubiak signed on as an assistant coach at his alma mater, Texas A&M University, spending two years on the Aggies staff. In 1994, he served as the quarterbacks coach for the San Francisco 49ers, where he worked with Mike Shanahan. When Shanahan got the Broncos' head coaching job in 1995, he hired Kubiak as the offensive coordinator. With that, Kubiak was back working with Elway—this time as his boss.

Kubiak guided the Broncos offense for 11 seasons, helping them reach the playoffs seven times, including two Super Bowl

A tale of two coaches: backup quarterback and future head coach Gary Kubiak takes cues from Denver head coach Dan Reeves. Photo courtesy of Getty Images

"I walked in, and the first question he asked me was, 'What is it going to take for you to be my head coach?'" Reeves said in his signature thick Southern accent. "He never asked me what my philosophy was or anything. I had gone through probably about six or eight interviews [with other teams] and did the interview process and when I finally [got] a job nobody asked me one single question about what my philosophy was or anything."

A recommendation from good friend Fran Tarkenton, a Hall of Fame quarterback, was all Kaiser needed. Two weeks after buying the team, Kaiser fired Red Miller and named Reeves as his head coach, on March 10, 1981.

"[Kaiser] was great to work with and got me the contract I needed to get the job done and gave me a great opportunity," Reeves said.

During the next 12 years, Reeves led the Broncos to great success. He won 110 regular-season games, second in team history to Mike Shanahan. He took the Broncos to the playoffs six times, won five AFC West titles, got them to four AFC Championship Games, and directed them to three Super Bowls.

"Dan was as driven to win as any coach I've ever met," said Karl Mecklenburg, who played for Reeves from 1983 to 1992. "It doesn't matter if you're flipping a coin or watching a horse race, Dan has to win. That's his nature, and we won a lot of games because of that drive. There was no question about what was the most important thing to the Denver Broncos at that point. It was to win games."

Reeves implemented much of what he learned from Landry, who was the only head coach he had worked for.

A running back from South Carolina, Reeves played for Landry's Cowboys from 1965 to 1972, helping them to their first Super Bowl in 1970 and their first Super Bowl win in 1971. Reeves then worked as an assistant coach in Dallas from 1974 to 1980, going to three more Super Bowls, including a win over the Broncos in Super Bowl XII.

In Denver, Reeves took over a team quarterbacked by his good friend and fellow 1965 Dallas rookie Craig Morton.

"I was at the supermarket, and they announced it over the intercom," Morton said of how he found out about Reeves' hiring. "I went to the pay phone, called him, and told him, 'Congratulations. Be yourself. Don't try to be Landry.'"

Reeves relied on the strong arm of Morton that first season, going 10–6 and falling just short of the playoffs.

"Usually when you go into your first head coaching job, you're going in because you've got a bad football team," Reeves said. "That wasn't the case. I came in to a good situation, to a team that had been in the playoffs [in 1979]. They had just come off of an off-year, and I was able to really benefit from having a great football team my first year coaching there."

It wasn't long before Reeves put his stamp on the franchise. He had his way, and that wasn't going to change.

"Dan was old school," said Thompson, whose final season as a player was Reeves' first year in Denver. "His whole mentality was 'You make a mistake, you run. You pay a price for your mistake.' I think he overdid it a little bit at times, where the team was tired. He was kind of relentless, but that was kind of his iron way doing it. He was hard, but he was at least fair. You did your job, you didn't hear from him. You didn't do your job, you heard from him big time. He hated mistakes."

Reeves' iron will and run-oriented offense proved to be his trademarks with the Broncos. Under Reeves, the Broncos typically played good defense and a conservative brand of offense.

Reeves won a lot of games with the Broncos but is often accused of holding Elway back and not turning his Hall of Fame quarterback loose.

"There's criticism of his coaching style," former Broncos play-by-play radio announcer Larry Zimmer said. "I think the only reason that criticism came was because he had a great quarterback in Elway, and I think a lot of people didn't think he used Elway to his advantage. The truth of the matter is, Dan won football games—and without ever having a great running back."

Whether you liked his style or not, nobody could argue with the results. He had just two losing seasons with the Broncos and four times came within one win of making the playoffs.

Wade Phillips

Throughout the Broncos' Super Bowl championship season of 2015, Wade Phillips was a bit of a star. The defensive coordinator was the mastermind behind the defense that led the NFL and dominated the New England Patriots and Carolina Panthers in the playoffs.

For Phillips, it was a triumphant return to Denver, where a previous tenure didn't end well. Phillips was the Broncos defensive coordinator from 1989 to 1992, with mixed results that included a Super Bowl appearance in 1989. After the Broncos went 8–8 in 1992, the Broncos fired head coach Dan Reeves and handed the reins to Phillips. In his first-ever job as a head coach, Phillips went 16–16 in two seasons before being fired after the 1994 season.

"It was a big change [from Reeves]. I think it was too much of a change, and that may be why we didn't have the success," linebacker Karl Mecklenburg said. "I played under Wade as a defensive coordinator for years, and he's a very gifted football guy. But that drastic change I think was too much."

From 1995 to 2014, Phillips had success in several jobs, mostly as a defensive coordinator. He also had successful runs as a head coach with the Buffalo Bills (1998–2000) and Dallas Cowboys (2007–2010). He took Buffalo to the playoffs in 1998 and 1999, before being fired after the 2000 season. Through 2015, the Bills hadn't been to the playoffs since. In two of his three full seasons in Dallas, he took the Cowboys to the playoffs. In the five seasons after he was fired, the Cowboys got to the postseason just once.

"No doubt he was a good coach," Thompson said. "You come from the Landry system of football and, like it or not, they were successful. That's what he brought. He was successful with it. We were always in the running. We were always in the game.

"His drawback was that he wouldn't change."

Humbling defeats on football's biggest stage didn't help, either.

Reeves had taken the Broncos to three Super Bowls, but they were crushed in all of them. And, over time, key relationships—with Elway, owner Pat Bowlen, and defensive coordinator Joe Collier, to name a few—went sour.

"Probably his downfall was that both the height of his reign here and his downfall were linked to going to three Super Bowls in four years," Clough said. "They did a lot of winning on the one hand, but the Super Bowl losses almost obscured the winning because they were by such huge margins and almost ended up doing more damage. You have relationships that were once pretty solid—for example, between Dan and Pat Bowlen—that showed some signs of deterioration through the losing of the Super Bowls."

After an 8–8 season in 1992—which included four straight losses late in the year with an injured Elway on the sideline—Bowlen chose not to renew Reeves' contract.

Although Reeves' tenure in Denver ended in disappointment, his success will be forever remembered.

He went on to prove himself further with head coaching stints with the New York Giants (1993–96) and Atlanta Falcons (1997–2003). He took the Falcons to their only Super Bowl in 1998, losing to Denver and Elway. It was the fifth time he was on the sideline for a Super Bowl involving the Broncos.

"That's probably the best record I've got. I was 1-for-2 against them and 0-for-3 when I was coaching with them," he joked.

Reeves finished his coaching career in 2003. He is among the all-time leaders in victories (190), games coaches (357), and playoff victories (11). As a player, assistant coach, or head coach, he got to nine Super Bowls—the first man in league history to get there that many times.

"He's another guy who should be in the Hall of Fame," Morton argued.

25 Meck

Reeves and Collier always had admiration for a versatile defensive end from the Miami Dolphins named Kim Bokamper. An original member of Miami's "Killer B" defense, Bokamper was a quick and powerful defender who was exceptional at getting to the quarterback as well as stopping the run. During the 1983 NFL Draft, Reeves saw University of Minnesota prospect Karl Mecklenburg as having that same type of potential. "We looked at him and said he could be just like [Bokamper]," Reeves said. "He turned out to be that and more."

Taken in the 12th round, 310th overall, in the draft, Mecklenburg hardly projected to be the star that he became. At 6'3" and 240 pounds, he was too small to play defensive line, which he played at Minnesota, and he didn't really have the prototypical look of a linebacker. There was something undeniable about Mecklenburg, though: he could play.

"Dan drafted me. I owe a lot to Dan," Mecklenburg said. "Dan seemingly every year would keep somebody who was kind of the underdog, the guy that nobody expected to make it, a guy that reminded Dan of himself. I was that guy that year. Dan saw that I could play the game and gave me a shot, and a lot of coaches wouldn't have done that."

The man, the myth, the Meck. Photo courtesy of Getty Images

During his 12-year career, Mecklenburg proved to be one of the greatest finds in the Broncos' draft history. He finished with 1,145 tackles, recorded 79 sacks (second in team history), and intercepted five passes.

"If we had known he was that good, we would have drafted him a lot higher than we did," Reeves said. "He was quicker and faster than we thought, and he got bigger than what we thought he could be."

Mecklenburg made his mark not as a linebacker, not as a defensive end, and not as a defensive tackle. He made his mark by playing all of those positions. Mecklenburg frustrated the opposition, which never knew where he'd line up.

"It was great fun," he said. "It's hard to imagine this, but football can get boring. If you're sitting in the meeting room five days a week, and we were…after a while it becomes repetitive and difficult. Instead, we had 110 different defenses with options off of each of them at the high point of Joe Collier's defensive coordinating. We did all kinds of stuff. Every week it was difficult. It was mentally stimulating, as well as effective."

Collier and linebackers coach Myrel Moore always found unique ways to use their players' skills, but particularly with Mecklenburg. "Joe and Myrel said, 'We can take advantage of him from a tactical standpoint and put him in positions where he's used to playing against offensive tackles. Now all of a sudden he's pass rushing on a running back or tight end,'" Mecklenburg said. "It was an amazing thing."

Of course, it wouldn't have worked if Mecklenburg didn't have the talent and mental ability that he did. "He was so competitive, very smart, and he worked hard," Reeves said.

Running back Sammy Winder, who played with Mecklenburg from 1983 to 1990, considered Mecklenburg to be the best player—outside of Elway—with whom he played in the NFL.

Rulon Jones

From 1980 to 1988, Rulon Jones was one of the top pass rushers in the NFL, reaching the Pro Bowl in 1985 and 1986. A second-round draft choice from Utah State in 1980, Jones was a 6'6", 280-pound defensive end who wreaked havoc. He recorded 73½ quarterback sacks, which ranked second in team history at the time of his retirement. Jones had 11½ sacks as a rookie, a mark that still stands as the team's rookie record (Von Miller tied the mark in 2011). Jones' 13½ sacks in 1986 was a single-season team record at the time. Jones also recorded a Broncos-record three safeties—the only player in team history with more than one—and he returned a fumble for a touchdown in a 1984 game.

"That was a guy that wasn't very fast, he had decent size, decent strength, but somehow he just knew how to get to the ball," Winder said. "I tell stories of him all the time.

"When we'd have linebacker drills, where the back would block the linebacker, I would always call him out. He would always win, of course, but the next day I'd still call him out. I said, 'I want Meck' every day."

Mecklenburg was a fan favorite throughout his career, and he shared that admiration for the fans.

"I loved every minute of it," he said.

Since retirement, Mecklenburg has stayed involved with football as a coach on the high school level. He also has embarked on a successful career as a motivational speaker and authored a book, *Heart of a Student Athlete*, which gives advice to athletes and their families.

26 Hard Work Pays Off

When Rod Smith was a star at Missouri Southern, he worked hard. After he tore up his knee as a collegian, he worked hard. When all 28 NFL teams passed him up during the 1994 draft, he worked hard. When the Broncos put him on their practice squad, he worked hard. Throughout his Pro Bowl career, he worked hard.

"When you watch his work ethic, just think about this: 600 practices, 13 years, and he never missed one," Mike Shanahan said on the day Smith retired in 2008. "I always say, to win championships you have to have a work ethic, but you've got overachievers and you've got overachievers with ability, and you got overachievers with great ability. If you don't have those guys, you don't win. If you've got overachievers with great ability, then you have a chance to get in the Hall of Fame. That's what we have in Rod Smith."

Smith is the best receiver in the history of the Broncos. He caught 849 passes for 11,389 yards and 68 touchdowns from 1995 to 2007. All three of those numbers rank, by far, No. 1 in team annals. "Honestly, I don't know how to measure who goes in the Hall of Fame," Smith said during his retirement press conference. "I did everything I could, and I would love to have a speech there one day." It's a testament to Smith's will that the Hall of Fame is even a possibility for him. In fact, it's a remarkable feat that he even got to have a retirement press conference.

Smith was a star at a small college but left the field in his last game there with a severe knee injury. He went undrafted in 1994 but earned a spot on the Broncos' practice squad that year. "Every day at practice, on scout team, he wanted to be the Tim Brown, he wanted to be the Jerry Rice, he wanted to be the Cris Carter," tight end Shannon Sharpe said. "He always got the opposing team's best guy's jersey. You could see him working every single day for the scout team, and when he would get his one or two reps for the offense, he'd go all out and try to make it happen."

Safety Steve Atwater remembers Smith as a young player with a relentless desire to excel. "The great thing about Rod is that Rod bought in early to, 'I've got to work hard,'" Atwater said. "He just continued to do better. He would do anything the coaches asked of him. He would be full speed on special teams. Everybody on the team loved him. He had a great personality."

Gifted Receivers

Rod Smith was, without question, the best receiver in Broncos history, and he was greatly missed after finishing his career in 2006. Over the course of the next decade, however, the Broncos did a nice job of finding other stellar receivers to lead the passing game:

Brandon Marshall (2006–09): After learning under Smith in 2006, Marshall exploded. He posted at least 101 catches in three consecutive seasons, becoming the first Bronco with three 100-catch seasons. Maybe the most gifted receiver in team history, he was also one of the most complex on and off the field. He was traded to Miami after the 2009 season.

Eric Decker (2010–13): A third-round pick out of Minnesota, Decker has two of the best seasons in team history in 2012 and 2013, averaging 86 catches, 1,176 yards, and 12 touchdowns in those seasons. Seeking a bigger contract, Decker signed with the New York Jets after the 2013 season.

Demaryius Thomas (2010–15): Still with Denver going into 2016, Thomas set a team record with 1,619 receiving yards in 2014 and tied the team record with 14 touchdowns in 2013. Prior to his arrival, there were only five times in team history when a receiver had at least 1,300 yards in a season. Thomas did it four years in a row from 2012 to '15.

Emmanuel Sanders (2014–15): Signed as a free agent in 2014, Sanders' career exploded in Denver. During his first two seasons as a Broncos, he racked up 177 catches, 2,539 yards, and 15 touchdowns.

Smith's hard work and determination impressed Shanahan so much in 1995, Shanahan's first year as head coach, that he put Smith on the active roster. "What you do when you first come in as a head coach is try to look at film all the time," Shanahan said. "And you're watching the wide receivers going against our defense and you have the scout-team offense going against your first-team defense. And you keep on looking at a guy and saying, 'Why can't they cover this guy?' Our starters should be able to cover our scout-team wide receivers. Then you watch him on special teams and as a scout-team special team player. Then you say, 'Holy cow. I've got myself a football player.'"

In Week 3 of the 1995 season, Smith finally caught his first NFL pass. The Broncos and Redskins were tied at 31, and on the final play of the game, Smith caught a leaping 43-yard touchdown pass from John Elway to win the game 38–31.

"When they called his number, he stepped up and he never looked back," Sharpe said.

That play kick-started a career in which Smith made the Pro Bowl three times, caught at least 100 passes in a season twice, and had eight 1,000-yard seasons, including six in a row from 1997 to 2002. In 2012, he was named to the Broncos' Ring of Fame.

Smith played in an era where brash wide receivers, such as Terrell Owens, Randy Moss, and Chad Johnson, grabbed the headlines. Statistically, Smith was as good or better than just about everyone in his era, but he didn't get a lot of national attention because he was far from brash. He never once did a dance in the end zone after a touchdown, called out his quarterback in the media, or stood in front of a microphone and demanded he get the ball more often. He simply showed up to work every day of his career.

"Not a lot of people realize how good he was," Atwater said. "I don't know that Rod got the publicity that he deserved. I'm not surprised that he ended up being as productive as he was, because he was a great young guy and he just took on a leadership role. He just became all that he can be, and I'm really happy for him."

Smith didn't get the attention that many of his counterparts got, but he left the game with something Owens, Moss, and Johnson never got: a Super Bowl ring. Two of them, in fact.

"That's the only thing we do is chase those two rings day in and day out," Smith said upon his retirement, while wearing both rings.

Few people in team history ever worked harder for those rings than Smith.

27 The Elway Trade

May 2, 1983, was a big day for the Denver Nuggets.

Trailing three games to none to the San Antonio Spurs in the National Basketball Association's Western Conference semifinals, the Nuggets needed a win to stay alive. The Denver media gathered at McNichols Arena for Game 4 of the series.

Broncos head coach Dan Reeves was among those in attendance. Then, midway through the game, the media started scrambling. Reeves left the building.

While the Nuggets fought for their playoff lives, the Broncos were working on the biggest transaction in the history of the franchise: acquiring prized rookie quarterback John Elway. Elway had recently finished a record-setting career at Stanford University and he was, without question, the best player going into the 1983 NFL Draft. By virtue of their league-worst 0–8–1 record in 1982, the Baltimore Colts had the No. 1 pick.

Elway and his father, Jack, had been adamant that Elway would not play for the Colts. It was nothing against the city of Baltimore or Colts owner Bob Irsay. The Elways just simply didn't respect Colts head coach Frank Kush. In Elway's back pocket was the threat that he would play baseball instead of playing for the Colts. Exceptional on the diamond, Elway had played for the New York Yankees' Class A affiliate in Oneonta, New York, in 1982 and did fairly well, hitting .318 with four homers, 25 RBIs, 13 stolen bases, and a .432 on-base percentage in 42 games. He also played flawlessly in the field.

Although most believed Elway was a better prospect in football, baseball at least gave Elway some leverage. "I'll just let them all do the wheeling and dealing and then I'll decide," Elway said before the 1983 draft. "I know I can be happy either way. I won't look back."

The whole sporting world knew Elway had no desire to play for the Colts. The Raiders tried to trade for the No. 1 pick to get him. So did other teams. The Broncos were in on talks for the pick before the draft, too. Reeves had talked with Kush before the draft, and the two discussed possibilities. "He said, 'If we get the pick behind you, would you be interested in trading?'" Reeves said. "That pick behind us was San Diego. I knew when he said that, he wanted Chris Hinton." Hinton was a guard from Northwestern and arguably the top offensive lineman in the draft. The Broncos, of course, were interested in acquiring the top pick to get Elway, but after discussions with Kush, Reeves gave up on that thought. "We had tried to work out a trade with them prior to the draft, but they were asking so much for him we couldn't possibly do what they wanted to do," Reeves said.

On the day of the draft, the Colts took Elway No. 1. The Broncos selected Hinton at No. 4. A pair of Pro Bowl running backs, Hall of Famer Eric Dickerson and Curt Warner, went between those picks. The next day after the draft, Reeves got a call from Broncos owner Edgar Kaiser.

"Would you be interested in getting Elway?" Kaiser asked.

"Yeah, we'd be interested, but I don't see how we can make a deal with what they're asking for," Reeves said.

"Well, I almost bought the Colts with Irsay, and I have a pretty good relationship with him," Kaiser replied. "Let me check it and see."

Reeves hung up the phone and went about his business. The next day, Kaiser called Reeves again. Kaiser listed Hinton, Broncos backup quarterback Mark Herrmann, and a 1984 first-round draft choice.

"I'm waiting and waiting, and I said, 'Is that it?'" Reeves said.

"Yeah," Kaiser replied.

"Oh God, I'd do that in a heartbeat," Reeves told his boss.

Not long after that, the Broncos flew Elway in to see if the two sides could come to an agreement on a contract. They did. "First time I had met John Elway, it was on an airplane in one of the private airports in Denver," Reeves said. "He was there, and they worked out the contract right there on the airplane. That's basically how the thing came around. I hated to give up Chris Hinton, but we needed a quarterback, with Craig [Morton] reaching the end of his career."

Hinton was a key to the deal, and he proved worthy of the No. 4 pick, playing in six Pro Bowls in seven years with the Colts. In all, he had a 13-year career and made the Pro Bowl seven times—just two fewer than Elway. Ron Solt, whom the Colts drafted in 1984 with the pick obtained in the deal, also made a Pro Bowl and played nine solid years in the NFL. Herrmann had an 11-year career, mostly as a backup.

The roots of the Elway trade went back to the NFL players' strike of 1982. The Broncos had finished .500 or better every year from 1976 to 1981, and they were 1–1 in 1982 when the strike hit. The strike wiped out seven games, and it was more than two months before play resumed. "We were a pretty good football team at the time the strike hit," Reeves said. "We were so out of shape when we came back."

The tired, out-of-shape Broncos went 1–6 after the strike to finish 2–7. That put them in position to get Hinton and, ultimately, Elway. "All of that was brought about because we had such a bad year the year before with the strike," Reeves said. "If we wouldn't have had that high of a pick, we would have never been able to work that deal out."

Back at McNichols Arena on May 2, the Nuggets continued to battle the Spurs and the media continued to scramble. Word of the Elway deal had leaked out.

"When everybody started scrambling around, everybody knew what was going on," said Terry Frei, who covered the Nuggets for the *Denver Post*.

Once the Broncos and Elway came to a contract agreement, they didn't wait long to announce it. They called a press conference for 10:30 PM that night.

The Nuggets finished off a 124–114 win over the Spurs, staying alive in the playoffs. It was a big win for the Nuggets, but it certainly wasn't the biggest win of the day for Denver. Like Reeves, most of the media left before the game was over, and headed to the Elway press conference.

"Everybody pretty much bailed," Frei said. "It was pretty much [just] me talking to [Nuggets coach] Doug Moe after the game."

Two days later, the Nuggets were eliminated from the playoffs.

28 The Drive

Cleveland was a magical place to be during the 1986 NFL season. Their Browns, who hadn't won an NFL championship in 22 years, had the best team in the AFC, with a 12–4 record. Since their 1964 championship, the Browns had been through more heartache than most teams. They lost NFL Championship Games in 1965, 1968, and 1969—the last two of which would have sent them to the Super Bowl.

Going into 1986, the Browns hadn't even won a playoff game since 1969, so when they defeated the New York Jets in overtime on January 3, 1987, in the divisional playoffs, Cleveland became a crazy place.

"The Dawg Pound," a name given to a section of fans at Cleveland Stadium, was ferocious and became the identity of the Browns, who were just one win away from going to their first Super Bowl. All they had to do was beat the AFC West–champion Broncos in Cleveland.

The night before the game, KOA radio announcers Bob Martin and Larry Zimmer, along with *Rocky Mountain News* columnist Dick Connor, went to see the Cleveland Orchestra at Severance Hall.

"At the end of the concert," Zimmer said, "the orchestra stood up and started to bark."

The next day, the Broncos, who were 0–4 all-time in road postseason games, encountered 79,915 barking fans at Cleveland Stadium. It was an overcast, dreary, and snowy afternoon with the wind chill at 5 degrees below zero. The rabid fans in the Dawg Pound not only spent the day barking at the Broncos, but throwing dog bones at them. Elway and other players literally spent time during pregame warm-ups kicking dog bones out of their way and trying to avoid being hit by biscuits.

"That game, under those circumstances, with as hostile of a crowd as I've ever seen, it was us against the world right there," linebacker Karl Mecklenburg said.

However hostile the crowd was at the start of the game, it was intensified with 5:43 to go. Browns quarterback Bernie Kosar had just thrown a 48-yard touchdown pass to Brian Brennan, giving Cleveland a 20–13 lead and putting the Super Bowl within grasp.

On the ensuing kickoff, the Broncos failed to field the ball and it hit at the 15-yard line and took an awkward bounce. The Broncos' Ken Bell picked up the ball near the 1-yard line, but he was immediately tackled between the 1- and 2-yard lines. "You may have just seen the straw the broke the Broncos' back," Martin said on the radio broadcast.

With 5:34 to play, the Broncos were 98½ yards away from the end zone. In the huddle, left guard Keith Bishop eased some tension with a quote that has gone down in Broncos lore. He told the rest of the offense, "We got 'em right where we want 'em."

The next five minutes were a roller coaster of emotions for the fans of both teams. Every play that went in favor of Denver gave Broncos fans hope of a comeback. Every play that went in favor of Cleveland gave the Browns fans in attendance a belief that the Super Bowl was a reality.

The 15-play possession went down in NFL history as "the Drive." The entire 15-play sequence:

1. First-and-10, own 2: Elway five-yard pass to Sammy Winder
2. Second-and-5, own 7: Winder runs to right for three yards
3. Third-and-2, own 10: Winder runs up the middle for two yards
4. First-and-10, own 12: Winder runs to left for three yards

5. Second-and-7, own 15: Elway scrambles to left for 11 yards
6. First-and-10, own 26: Elway completes pass down the middle to Steve Sewell for 22 yards
7. First-and-10, own 48: Elway completes pass to the right to Steve Watson for 12 yards
8. First-and-10, Browns 40: Elway incomplete to Vance Johnson
9. Second-and-10, Browns 40: Elway sacked by Dave Puzzuoli for 8-yard loss
10. Third-and-18, Browns 48: Elway completes pass to left to Mark Jackson for 20 yards
11. First-and-10, Browns 28: Elway incomplete to Watson
12. Second-and-10, Browns 28: Elway completes screen pass to the left to Sewell for 14 yards
13. First-and-10, Browns 14: Elway incomplete to Watson
14. Second-and-10, Browns 14: Elway scrambles to right for nine yards
15. Third-and-1, Browns 5: Elway completes pass down the middle to Jackson for a five-yard touchdown

Jackson came from the left and slid low to catch the ball in his stomach and then rolled once, popped up, and raised his hands to signal the touchdown. "It was a low-heater, too, because if Mark didn't get it, nobody was going to get it," Elway said of the touchdown pass on NFL Films. "I remember seeing Mark Jackson wide open and saying to myself, 'Get this ball to him as fast as you can get it to him.' I don't remember throwing a ball as hard as I threw that ball." The touchdown came with 37 seconds left on the clock, and when Rich Karlis kicked the extra point, it tied the game at 20–20.

Elway's final throw sealed the drive, but there were some incredible moments along the way, including both long passes to Sewell. On the 10th play, the Broncos had a bit of good fortune.

The moment every Denver fan will forever remember and every Cleveland fan wishes they could forget: Mark Jackson (80) notches six during "the Drive."
Photo courtesy of Getty Images

Elway was in the shotgun and the snap hit Watson, who was running in motion, glancing off his hip. Elway made a good play to snag the ball, set his feet, and made an accurate throw to Jackson for a first down.

Cleveland ran out the clock to go to overtime and then got the ball to start the overtime period. The Broncos forced the Browns to punt and got the ball at their own 25. Elway had two key passes, a 22-yarder to Orson Mobley and a 28-yarder to Watson, to get the offense into field-goal range. On fourth-and-3 from the Browns 15, Karlis and his bare right foot lined up for a game-winning field goal. Karlis put his foot into the ball and sent it sailing into the air. It curved to the left, and the officials under the goal posts raised their hands. The Broncos won 23–20. Although replays of that kick suggest it might not have been good.

"We still might be playing that thing if they had instant replay and they looked at Karlis' field goal there at the end," Mecklenburg said. "I don't know if it was good or not. It didn't look very good. I'm pretty sure it wasn't. It didn't matter at the time. The refs' arms went up, and we were going."

Reeves, to this day, doesn't dispute the kick.

"There's no question," he said. "I saw the official throw his hands up, and I knew he made a good call. I really don't know. You couldn't tell. From the angle that we were [at], it looked good, and I was watching the official. When he threw his hands up underneath the goal post, I never even questioned it. I didn't even know it was close."

Karlis and holder Gary Kubiak made it onto the cover of *Sports Illustrated* the next week with the headline, "Victory!"

"To win a game in that situation was awesome," Reeves said. "It was an unbelievable accomplishment in as tough of an environment as you could get. They had just taken the lead, and all of a sudden you have to go 98 yards with less than five minutes to go in the game, that's pretty amazing."

It was Elway's drive that was the signature of that game. He had more than 10 fourth-quarter comeback drives to his credit before that day, but the Drive put Elway on a different level.

"John had some good moments, John had some comebacks," Tom Jackson said. "But when John put together the Drive, that was his moment. The moment where he took the step was in Cleveland. After that we knew he would never be the same."

Said Clough: "The game in Cleveland changed everything for John. It changed his reputation, it changed the arc of his career."

Elway would win 14 postseason games in his career, in 21 starts, but it was the Drive that let football fans around the country know that he could deliver in the clutch.

29 The Fumble

The Broncos were a defeated team. The scoreboard didn't show it, but they were on the verge of losing the AFC Championship Game to the Cleveland Browns on January 17, 1988. "Oh yeah, I knew it," Mecklenburg said.

With the final minutes of the fourth quarter melting away, the Broncos were clinging to a 38–31 lead. Cleveland had already torched the Broncos defense for 28 second-half points, and the Browns wanted more. Taking over at their own 25-yard line with three minutes, 53 seconds to play, the Browns marched down the field. Quarterback Bernie Kosar completed two big passes to Brian Brennan. Running back Earnest Byner had three big runs. With 72 seconds left to play, the Browns were at the Denver 8.

"They had all the momentum," Mecklenburg said. "It was over."

Not quite.

Byner, a 215-pound bundle of muscle, took the handoff up the middle and bounced out to the left. He had almost a clear path to the end zone for his third touchdown of the day. At worst, he would have been tackled just short of the goal line, giving Cleveland a first down. A last-second decision by Broncos reserve cornerback Jeremiah Castille changed all of that.

Before the ball was snapped, Castille, listed at 5'10" and 175 pounds, was lined up outside on a Browns receiver, and he was in position to play bump-and-run coverage. Recalling that play, Castille told NFL Films, "Right at the last minute, I decide, 'Hey, I got beat last time bumping this guy.' I said to myself, 'Why don't I back off so I can get a real good picture of everything as it's happening?'"

Castille slowly backpedaled about four yards, keeping his eyes on Kosar. When the ball was snapped, Cleveland's receiver failed to sell his route, and Castille looked inside to see that Byner was getting the handoff. "By backing off and getting about six, seven yards off of him, when the draw play happened, I could see the play developing," Castille said. Castille immediately made a run at Byner. "Earnest Byner never saw him coming," then–Browns head coach Marty Schottenheimer told NFL Films.

Much smaller than Byner, Castille didn't tackle him.

"Jeremiah [was] probably the smallest guy on the field, and there's no way he was going to take on Earnest Byner on the goal line and not get knocked back into the end zone, so he just went for the ball and picked him clean," Mecklenburg said. "It was unbelievable." Castille stripped the ball out of Byner's hands and then fell on top of it. In the final minute, the Broncos gave the Browns a safety to provide the final points, but it was Castille's play that secured the 38–33 win and sent the Broncos to their second straight Super Bowl. "You talk about Mile High Magic," Mecklenburg said.

Up to that point, the game had already been an epic battle between the two best teams in the AFC.

Elway threw for 281 yards and three touchdowns, while Winder and Gene Lang paced a ground attack that totaled 156 yards.

The Broncos led 21–3 at halftime and then took a 28–10 lead after Elway threw an 80-yard touchdown pass to Mark Jackson.

During the second half, though, Cleveland dominated. Kosar finished with 356 passing yards and three touchdowns. Byner had a sensational day as well, rushing for 67 yards and a touchdown and catching seven passes for 120 yards and another touchdown.

"That game was strange in that we dominated the first half, and then all of a sudden Cleveland just came on and dominated us defensively," Mecklenburg said. "They were able to move the ball at will, seemingly, against us in the second half."

Kosar and the Browns had tied the game at 31–31 early in the fourth quarter. Elway and the Broncos responded with another score, a 20-yard touchdown pass from Elway to Winder. That set up Cleveland's final drive.

"We were definitely on our heels," Mecklenburg said of the Broncos defense. "They had something figured out, and whatever we tried, they were one step ahead of us during that second half. I'm not sure what was going on. It was getting scary."

Then Castille stepped in to save the game.

"We were just hanging on, and to have Jeremiah make that heady play that he made was pretty tremendous," Mecklenburg said.

Castille played two years for the Broncos; that was the only fumble he forced and the only fumble he recovered.

30 The Broncos' Savior

For all the great things Pat Bowlen has done as Broncos owner, Gerald Phipps might have had the most impact of any owner in the team's history.

After all, if it wasn't for Phipps, there would have been no Broncos for Bowlen to buy in 1984.

A Denver native, Phipps began his relationship with sports in 1947, when he was on the board of directors for Rocky Mountain Empire Sports—the group that owned the Denver Bears baseball team and, later, the Broncos.

In 1961, Phipps stepped up as part of the ownership group, headed by Calvin Kunz, which kept the Broncos from being sold to out-of-town investors. When the threat of the Broncos moving came up again in 1965, Phipps and his brother Allan purchased Kunz's stock and, once again, kept the team in Denver. Then, in 1967, a drive to increase Mile High Stadium's attendance to 50,000—thus allowing them to join the NFL in 1970 rather than moving or folding—saved the team again.

The Phipps brothers did more than just keep the Broncos in Denver. They were with the organization from 1961 to 1981, and during that time, they helped pave the way for the team to grow on and off the field. Perennial losers in the AFL, the Broncos became winners during the Phippses years as owners. During their last eight years, 1973 to 1980, the Broncos went 69–46–3 and made the playoffs three times, including one Super Bowl trip.

Along the way, they earned tremendous respect from their players. In particular, Gerald, who was more involved with the

Edgar Kaiser

Edgar Kaiser's tenure as Broncos owner didn't last long. He bought the team from Gerald Phipps on February 25, 1981, and sold it to Pat Bowlen on March 23, 1984. Kaiser did, however, orchestrate two of the most significant moves in team history. Shortly after becoming owner, he fired Red Miller and hired Dan Reeves as head coach. Then, in 1983, he engineered the trade that brought John Elway to Denver. Together, Reeves and Elway took the Broncos to three Super Bowls. Years after selling the team, Kaiser lost a court battle with Bowlen over a right to buy back his stake in the team. A businessman and philanthropist, Kaiser passed away on January 11, 2012.

day-to-day operations of the team, was visible to the players. Allan preferred to stay out of the spotlight.

"Gerry and Allan Phipps are two super, super guys," Floyd Little said. "[Gerry] wasn't what you would call hands-on like a Jerry Jones [in Dallas], but he would be in the locker room. He would come and support you and he would be at practice from time to time and he was [well] liked by all the players."

Charley Johnson, who quarterbacked the team from 1972 to 1975, called both Phipps brothers "very, very nice gentlemen."

"I think they appreciated the players that worked for them," Johnson said.

While the Phippses weren't as hands-on as some owners are today, including Bowlen, they did have a noticeable impact. "Whenever he came on board, you could tell a difference in the attitude, just the way he would handle things," said Ring of Fame safety Goose Gonsoulin.

Gerald and Allan were also known for their intense involvement in the community and their many philanthropic efforts.

In 1981, the brothers sold the Broncos to Edgar Kaiser for $40 million. Gerald passed away in 1993 after battling liver cancer. Allan passed away in 1997.

Gerald Phipps' tremendous contributions to the Broncos were recognized by Bowlen when Phipps was inducted into the team's Ring of Fame in 1985. He remains the only non-player to be honored. He was also inducted into the Colorado Sports Hall of Fame in 1982.

Prior to owning the Broncos, Gerald Phipps became known for the construction company he founded—Gerald H. Phipps Construction, which still thrives today. Among GH Phipps' most well-known projects are Sports Authority Field at Mile High, the new $410 million Children's Hospital Colorado campus at Fitzsimmons, and renovations to the Denver Museum of Nature & Science—which includes the Phipps IMAX theater.

31 Mile High Stadium

For a baseball field, Mile High Stadium turned out to be quite a home for football.

The facility opened in 1948 as Bears Stadium, home to the Denver Bears baseball team. The Howsam family had purchased the Bears for about $75,000 early that year and then nearly got the land for the stadium for next to nothing. The Howsams had a deal in place with Denver mayor Ben Stapleton to purchase the land, about 15 acres that were used for a city dump, for $1. At the time, Stapleton was running for reelection, but he ultimately lost. New mayor Quigg Newton sold the land to the Howsams for $32,000. For another $275,000, Bears Stadium was built. The Bears played their first game there on August 14, 1948. The stadium had about 10,000 seats.

Over the years, the stadium went through several changes. When the Broncos became a charter member of the AFL in 1959, the south stands were built, as well as the movable east stands, pushing capacity to more than 34,000. The east stands were unique in that they moved to accommodate for football and baseball. The structure of the east stands was 535 feet long, 135 feet tall, and weighed almost 9 million pounds. To set up for baseball, the stands were moved back 145 feet. They moved along a thin layer of water, with hydraulic rams pushing the stands, according to the Broncos media guide. The process, at a rate of three feet per minute, took about two hours.

One of the most significant changes came in 1968. In order for the Broncos to join the NFL in 1970, they needed a stadium with 50,000 seats, so a 16,000-seat upper deck was built on the west side. That was also the year the name was changed to Mile

High Stadium. An expansion project in 1977 increased capacity to 75,100, and the final addition, with 60 suites, in 1986, brought capacity to 76,098.

But numbers don't tell the whole story. The stadium provided years of memories for sports fans in Colorado. In the 1950s, it was future baseball legends such as Don Larsen, Whitey Herzog, and Tommy Lasorda that starred at Bears Stadium. In later years, Andre Dawson, Gary Sheffield, and Greg Vaughn were among the top baseball stars to play their minor league ball in Denver.

In 1993 and 1994, Mile High Stadium finally hosted Major League Baseball, as the Colorado Rockies played their first two seasons there before moving to brand-new Coors Field in 1995. The Rockies set a major league attendance record in 1993, with 4,483,350 fans.

It was football that made Mile High Stadium nationally known. It gained a reputation for being a nightmare stop for opposing teams and one of the loudest stadiums in pro football.

"It was loud, and it was like the fans were right up on you, right up on the sidelines," Steve Atwater said.

During their 41 seasons at the stadium, from 1960 to 2000, the Broncos won 63.8 percent of their home games (190–108–7). During John Elway's 16 seasons, from 1983 to 1998, the Broncos went 102–26 during the regular season at Mile High Stadium, including 24–0 in his last three seasons. In postseason play, the Broncos were 11–2 all-time at Mile High Stadium.

"The attachment of Denver's fans with their football team and stadium stands out as unusual even in a city that has as strong an affinity for all its teams as does Denver," Jim Saccomano, the team's vice president of media relations, wrote on the team website. "Mile High Stadium was the birthplace of Broncomania. The stadium nurtured both the fans and the team, and watched Broncomania become a national phenomenon."

Mile High Stadium was replaced by a new stadium in 2001 and was later torn down and turned into a parking lot. While the building itself is no longer there, it never will be forgotten by millions of fans who had the pleasure of watching a game there, and it won't be forgotten by the hundreds of players who had the privilege of playing there.

"There was just something electric about the old Mile High," Shannon Sharpe said. "I was very fortunate...to play a lot of years in that stadium and have a lot of great memories in that old stadium."

32 Mile High Magic

For 41 years, Mile High Stadium was the home of the Denver Broncos, and in that time, the stadium was the stage for some of the most amazing games in team history—and NFL history. Because of that, Broncos fans have come to believe in "Mile High Magic."

Although Mile High Stadium has been replaced by a new venue, the magic has continued. Whenever the Broncos come through with a thrilling or improbable win, fans often credit the Mile High Magic.

Some of the most amazing home games in the Broncos history:

- **Broncos 26, Oilers 24—January 4, 1992**: In the AFC divisional playoffs, the Broncos quickly fell behind Warren Moon and the Houston Oilers 14–0 and still trailed 24–16 early in the fourth quarter. An 80-yard touchdown drive by the Broncos cut the Houston lead to 24–23 midway through the fourth quarter. Moon, a future Hall of Fame quarterback, had a brilliant game, but Denver held the Oilers offense on the next possession. That gave Denver one last chance, but it wasn't a good one. The Broncos took over at their 2-yard line, with 2:07 to play and no timeouts. Enter John Elway. The Broncos quarterback led the team 87 yards down the field in 12 plays, converting two amazing fourth downs along the way, including a floating pass to receiver Vance Johnson on a fourth-and-10 with under a minute to go. With 16 ticks on the clock, David Treadwell booted a 28-yard field goal, sending the Broncos to the AFC Championship Game. Some still refer to this game as "the Drive II."

- **Broncos 38, Browns 33—January 17, 1988**: For the second straight year, the Broncos played the Browns in the AFC Championship Game. And for the second straight year, it came down to last-minute heroics. The Broncos were clinging to a 38–31 lead with the Browns marching down the field. Cleveland running back Earnest Byner took a handoff and was headed for the end zone with more than a minute to play when small defensive back Jeremiah Castille reached in and stripped the ball. The Broncos recovered and, after giving the Browns a safety, finished off another great win.
- **Broncos 29, Steelers 23 (OT)—January 8, 2012**: Big-time underdogs at home to the defending AFC champion Steelers, the Broncos' Tim Tebow had the game of his life. He led the Broncos to 20 second-quarter points and a 23–13 lead going into the fourth quarter. The Broncos gave up the lead in the final 10 minutes but ended the game quickly in overtime. On the first play of overtime (and under new overtime rules eliminating sudden death unless the first team in overtime possession scores a touchdown on their first drive), Tebow threw an 80-yard touchdown pass to Demaryius Thomas. They scored 11 seconds into overtime—the quickest overtime score in NFL history.

- **Broncos 30, Chargers 24 (OT)—November 17, 1985**: After Denver's Rich Karlis kicked a game-tying field goal with five seconds to play in regulation, San Diego started overtime with a march down the field into field-goal range. Chargers kicker Bob Thomas set up for a 40-yard attempt, but Broncos safety Dennis Smith blocked it. Unfortunately for the Broncos, someone on the team had called a timeout, so the play was nullified. Thomas got another chance, and again Smith blocked the kick. It bounced directly to Louis Wright, who scooped it up and ran 60 yards for the game-winning touchdown.
- **Broncos 17, Packers 14—October 15, 1984:** With *Monday Night Football* in town, Denver was in the midst of a snowstorm. At the start of the game, the field was covered in snow, and heavy flakes continued to fall. Green Bay got the ball to start the game, but on the first play, the Packers fumbled. Broncos safety Steve Foley picked it up and ran 22 yards for a touchdown. Green Bay received the kickoff again, and again on the first play the Packers fumbled. This one was picked up by Wright, who ran 27 yards for a Denver touchdown. Rich Karlis gave the Broncos a 17–0 lead in the second quarter, and then the Broncos held on. Despite just 193 yards of offense (compared to 423 for Green Bay), the Broncos pulled off the win.
- **Broncos 23, Raiders 23—October 22, 1973**: In the Broncos' first-ever prime-time appearance, they faced the hated Raiders on *Monday Night Football*. The Raiders had won 15 of the previous 16 meetings with the Broncos and had a team that wound up in the AFC Championship Game that year. The Raiders' George Blanda put his team ahead with a 49-yard field goal with 44 seconds to play. Denver responded, though, with a march down the field that set up Jim Turner's game-tying 35-yard field goal in the closing seconds. There was no overtime in the NFL at that point, so the game ended in a tie.

The enthusiasm of Broncos fans is the primary reason why Denver is considered an inhospitable place for teams to play on the road. Photo courtesy of Getty Images

- **Broncos 31, Patriots 24—October 23, 1960**: During their inaugural season, the Broncos found themselves in a 24–0 hole early in the third quarter. That's when quarterback Frank Tripucka went to work. He threw four second-half touchdown passes, including two to Al Carmichael. Gene Mingo added a nine-yard field goal. The 24-point deficit is the largest ever overcome by the Broncos (and was matched 19 years later against Seattle).

- **Broncos 21, Colts 19—December 11, 1983**: The first fourth-quarter comeback win in John Elway's career came against the team for which he refused to play. Just months after trading the disgruntled No. 1 overall draft pick to Denver, Baltimore seemed to have the last laugh, protecting a 19–0 lead going into the fourth quarter. Instead, Elway poured salt on the Colts' wounds, throwing three touchdown passes in the fourth quarter, including a 26-yard strike to Gerald Willhite with 44 seconds to play.
- **Broncos 37, Seahawks 34—September 23, 1979**: Down 34–10 with 9:28 to play in the third quarter, few figured the Broncos would win this one. But quarterback Craig Morton threw three touchdown passes in a span of 79 seconds in the third quarter to pull Denver within 34–31. In the fourth quarter, Morton led the winning touchdown drive, capped by Rob Lytle's one-yard run.
- **Broncos 23, Steelers 16—January 17, 2016**: In the divisional playoffs, offense had been a struggle all day. Early in the fourth quarter, the Broncos trailed 13–12, and Pittsburgh was knocking on the door to add more points. Steelers running back Fitzgerald Toussaint took a handoff and ran to the left, but Broncos cornerback Bradley Roby reached out and punched the ball away from Toussaint. The Broncos' DeMarcus Ware recovered the fumble with 9:52 to play. Denver's offense came alive, with a 13-play drive that took 6:52 off the clock. C.J. Anderson powered his way into the end zone from one yard out, with three minutes to play. Another defensive stand was followed by a Brandon McManus field goal that helped to seal the win.
- **Broncos 20, Chiefs 19—October 4, 1992**: Down 19–6 with two minutes to play, the Broncos seemed headed for a sure defeat. Fans were already on their way out of the stadium. Yet Elway managed to find a way again. Just after the two-minute

warning, Elway connected with Mark Jackson on a 25-yard touchdown pass. The Broncos defense forced the Chiefs to punt, and a 28-yard return by Arthur Marshall put the Broncos in business at the Chiefs 27. Moments later, Elway threw a 12-yard touchdown pass to Vance Johnson with 38 seconds to play. Treadwell's extra point put the cap on the remarkable comeback.

- **Broncos 38, Redskins 31—September 17, 1995**: The teams were tied at 31 with 1:07 to play and Denver on its own 20-yard line. Seven plays later, the Broncos were on the Redskins 43 with just six seconds left. Elway threw the ball downfield and Rod Smith, who had never caught a pass in an NFL game, snagged it out of the air and scored the 43-yard touchdown on the final play.
- **Broncos 39, Chargers 38—September 14, 2008**: It will forever be known as the "Ed Hochuli Game" in Denver. The Broncos trailed 38–31 in the final minute but were driving for the tying score. Quarterback Jay Cutler dropped back to pass and lost his handle on the ball. The Chargers picked it up, but Hochuli, the head official, ruled it an incomplete pass. Ultimately, it was ruled a fumble, but Denver kept possession because the whistle had blown. Seconds later, Cutler threw a four-yard touchdown pass to Eddie Royal, and then the two hooked up for the game-winning two-point conversion. Hochuli later admitted he got the call wrong and that San Diego should have taken over possession.
- **Broncos 30, Patriots 24 (OT)—November 29, 2015**: Facing the 10–0 Patriots, the Broncos were down 21–7 in the fourth quarter on a snowy Sunday night. Backup quarterback Brock Osweiler and the offense sputtered all game, but Mile High Magic struck again. The Broncos were forced to punt early in the fourth, but the Patriots muffed the return and the Broncos recovered. Four plays later, C.J. Anderson scored on a 15-yard

touchdown run. That sparked a 17–0 run to give Denver a 24–21 lead. The Patriots tied the game at the end of regulation, but in overtime Denver prevailed. Anderson busted through the Patriots defense and glided through the snow for a 48-yard touchdown run.

33 The Right QB at the Right Time

Morton never was a star quarterback in the National Football League. He had some very good years throughout his 18 seasons, however, and forever will be remembered as one of the top signal-callers the Broncos have ever had.

The need for a leader at quarterback played a role in head coach John Ralston being fired in January 1977 and Miller being hired as his replacement. Miller immediately addressed the quarterback position, sending quarterback Steve Ramsey and a fifth-round draft pick to the New York Giants for Morton.

"When I was traded, I was back in Dallas," Morton said. "I got a call from John McVay, who was the coach of the Giants at the time. He said, 'Craig, sorry to have to tell you this, but we've traded your rights to the Denver Broncos.' I said to him, 'Thank you very much. You can't give me a better present.' The Giants were going no place in those days.... So it was a pleasure going."

In a bit of irony, one of Morton's last games as a Giant came against the Broncos at Mile High Stadium. "I always thought, *Boy this is a heck of a defense, and if they had a quarterback that wouldn't make any mistakes and was wise enough and smart enough to play the defense, you could probably do pretty well,*" Morton said.

Turns out, he was that guy. Morton was already 34 years old and 13 years into his career when he arrived in Denver, but he was exactly what the Broncos needed. He had started 81 games in the NFL, led the Dallas Cowboys to their first Super Bowl in 1970, and was a part of the Cowboys' 1971 Super Bowl championship team. In 1977 he had little trouble beating out the rest of the competition, which included former Heisman Trophy winner and future college coaching legend Steve Spurrier. "There [were] a lot of quarterbacks, but that didn't make a difference," Morton said. "I knew that nobody was going to beat me out. So it was great. I was very, very ecstatic about having the opportunity to play there."

To the rest of the team, especially the veterans who pushed Ralston out, Morton gave them instant credibility. "The first time I ever walked in the locker room, Lyle Alzado was sitting in the locker room," Morton said. "His locker was right across from mine, and he looked up at me and said, 'Now we'll win a championship.' That gave me a lot of confidence. Lyle was a phenomenally great player and he just kind of gave me a little *oomph.*"

Not quite like the *oomph* Morton gave the team. His numbers from 1977 didn't turn any heads. In starting all 14 games, he threw for a modest 1,929 yards and 14 touchdowns, hitting 51.6 percent of his passes. However, he did exactly what the Broncos needed him to do, in terms of giving the team a presence on the field and by taking care of the ball. He threw just eight interceptions.

"I thought Craig Morton brought stability to that position," said Thompson, who was one of the players pushing for a quarterback change. "Craig got beat up a lot that year, but he didn't give the ball up. He took a lot of sacks.

When Elway stepped in to Denver in 1983, it was Morton's shoes he was trying to fill.

"He understood that by not turning the ball over and being productive with the ball, we could do a lot. There was no doubt we had the top defense, in our minds."

With Morton leading the way, the Broncos went 12–2, won their first AFC West title, and got to the playoffs for the first time ever. Once in the playoffs, Morton's leadership really blossomed. He had two of his better games in leading the Broncos past the Pittsburgh Steelers and Oakland Raiders to get to Super Bowl XII.

"He was the right guy at the right time when Red Miller brought him in here," said Zimmer. "He did a great job in that '77 season and it continued into '78. He was a good quarterback through that particular era."

Morton led the Broncos to a 10–6 record and another playoff appearance in 1978—the first year the NFL went to a 16-game schedule. In 1979, he guided them to another 10–6 record and another playoff appearance.

Morton continued his solid play in 1980, but the Broncos slipped to 8–8 and Miller was fired. The coach was replaced by Dan Reeves, one of Morton's good friends and former teammates. Morton had the best statistical year of his career in 1981 with Reeves in charge, throwing for a career-high 3,195 yards, tying his career high with 21 touchdowns and completing 59.8 percent of his passes. Reeves and Morton were rookies with the Cowboys in 1965, and Reeves said there's no telling how good Morton could have been had he not hurt his shoulder early in his career. "Extremely talented, very bright," Reeves said. "He knew everybody's assignments. He could read defenses. He had the strongest arm you'd ever seen. Not to take anything away from Roger [Staubach], because Roger was a great quarterback, too, but it would have been interesting if Craig was completely healthy, what he could have done."

Reeves was happy to take advantage of having Morton in the twilight of his career, though. "He still had a lot left as far as playing in the National Football League," Reeves said. "You really were at the point you could reap all the benefits of all the things he had learned over the years."

Morton returned for the 1982 season but was replaced early in the season by Steve DeBerg. Morton retired at the end of the season. "My legs, they were gone," he said.

Shortly after retirement, Morton coached the Denver Gold of the USFL, and he dabbled in business and media. In 2000, the University of California, where he had starred as a collegian, hired him to help with fund-raising efforts. He still lives in the San Francisco Bay Area.

34 Lighting the Fire

Just as Morton was the perfect quarterback at the perfect time, Robert "Red" Miller was the perfect coach at the perfect time.

A longtime NFL assistant coach, Miller was tabbed as the Broncos' new head coach on February 1, 1977, and he got the job because general manager Fred Gehrke and owner Gerald Phipps believed he could get the team to the next level. Miller took over a team that had never been to the playoffs but went 9–5 in 1976 and was on the verge of something special. "He was the guy who lit the fire underneath them and convinced them they could win and challenged them to do well," the *Denver Post* sportswriter Terry Frei said.

It was a long journey for Miller to get into the head job with the Broncos. Raised in Macomb, Illinois, Miller was born in 1927 and grew up during the Great Depression. For the Millers, as with so many other families at that time, money was hard to come by. Miller's father, John, was a coal miner and worked other jobs, as well, to put on the table. From a young age, Miller learned the value of hard work and earning an honest wage. He also learned to love sports and lettered 12 times in high school, playing four different sports: football, basketball, baseball, and track. After a stellar high school career, he starred at Western Illinois, where he also became a Golden Gloves boxing champion. Shortly after college, he began his coaching career in high school and then became an assistant to Lou Saban, who later coached the Broncos, at Western Illinois.

When Saban was hired as the head coach of the AFL's Boston Patriots in 1960, Miller went with him (coincidentally, Miller coached against the Broncos in the first AFL game in history, in

1960). Miller then had several assistant coaching jobs, including with the Broncos, from 1963 to 1965, coaching the offensive line. He spent four seasons with the Patriots, from 1973 to 1976, before getting the head job with Denver.

Miller was a welcomed addition to a team that needed a spark from its head coach, and as soon as he traded for Morton, the veteran Broncos were ready to roll with their new leader.

"What Red did was, he understood what we needed [at quarterback] and he went about at least attempting to change that position and say, 'Okay, I'm going to do this, but I'm going to need you guys,'" safety Billy Thompson said. "I think Red was really pivotal in doing that and understanding his team. We loved him."

Even without Morton, the Broncos were loaded with talent, thanks to John Ralston, so there's no telling how they would have done without the coaching change. But Miller proved to be the right man to lead that talent.

"I loved Red," said Morton, who is a friend and fellow Cal alum of Ralston. "I have to give a lot of credit to John Ralston because he put together that team. The foundation was set because of John's uncanny ability to look at talent. Then Red was the coach that everybody responded to because he was so much fun. He was just so exuberant all the time.

"I think it was exactly what [the Broncos] needed. Red was just at the right time for his personality to get guys enthused. Everybody had a great time."

From the start, Miller's energy was infectious on the veteran club. He combined that with the strong work ethic he learned as a boy.

"I didn't know Red from a man in the moon," nose tackle Rubin Carter said in Frei's book, *'77: Denver, the Broncos, and a Coming of Age*. "But I know this: He came in with energy and enthusiasm that were unbelievable. There's an old saying that the speed of the leader is the speed of the pack. Well, you better keep up with Red Miller because when he got to the field, he hit it running."

In 1977, the Broncos started 6–0, including a stunning 30–7 win in Oakland against the defending Super Bowl–champion Raiders. The Raiders snapped the Broncos' win streak in Week 7, but Miller's squad followed that with another six-game win streak. The Cowboys beat the Broncos and backup quarterback Norris Weese in the regular-season finale.

At 12–2, the Broncos had their best record ever, won their first AFC West title, and reached the playoffs for the first time.

At one point during the 1977 season, radio broadcaster Larry Zimmer bumped into Ralston at a local health club. Ralston told him, "Red Miller did something I never was able to do—he got them to play together."

Miller kept the Broncos hungry in 1978 and 1979, reaching the playoffs both seasons. With the players from the 1977 squad getting older, the 1980 season ended in disappointing fashion. After a 7–5 start, they lost three in a row, two of them to Oakland and one to Kansas City. They finished 8–8 and missed the playoffs. Two months after the season ended, Phipps sold the team to Edgar Kaiser. Less than two weeks later, Kaiser made a change at head coach, firing Miller and bringing in Dan Reeves. "I was surprised," Morton said. "But Edgar told me that he just wanted his own coach."

With a 40–22 regular-season record and three playoff appearances, Miller at least left the team in good standing. "It was unusual, in that Red had been fairly successful over four years," Sandy Clough said. "They were coming off an 8–8 year and they were kind of an older team. It was kind of an interesting time with an older team that seemed to be in decline. Making the playoffs three years in a row for a team that had never made the playoffs [before], over time if you look back with some degree of distance and objectivity, Red did a hell of a job."

Miller returned to coaching for a brief time in 1983 with the Denver Gold of the United States Football League (USFL), but he clashed with owner Ron Blanding and was fired 11 games into the season. Morton was named as his successor. That was Miller's last coaching job. He had a successful career as a broker before retiring in 1999. He still lives in Denver and follows the Broncos.

35 The Magician

Marlin Briscoe walked into the Broncos locker room and saw an unfamiliar jersey in his locker. Healthy again after a hamstring injury, he knew the Broncos had a choice: activate him or release him.

"So I go to my locker and open up my locker and there was a No. 15 [jersey]," he said. "My first thought was that I knew we needed a quarterback and that I was cut. My number was 45. I thought the No. 15 in my locker was for the new quarterback that they needed."

It was.

"I turned around and there was [head coach] Lou Saban," Briscoe said. "He said, 'That's yours, and you're now a quarterback.' I had to be cool, but my heart was pumping."

A quarterback through high school, Briscoe became a record-setting passer at the University of Omaha. Yet, when he was drafted by the Broncos it was as a defensive back—and he wasn't taken until the 14th round. This was 1968, and the civil rights movement was at a boiling point. Civil rights leaders Martin Luther King Jr. and Robert Kennedy were both assassinated that year. U.S. President Lyndon B. Johnson signed the Civil Rights Act of 1968 in April. During the Summer Olympics, Tommie Smith and John Carlos gave their Black Power salute on the medals stand. James Brown's song, "Say It Loud—I'm Black and I'm Proud," hit the top of the R&B charts. It was a time in which African Americans were discriminated against in every walk of life, including sports.

Pro football executives and coaches thought black athletes could be exceptional assets on their teams. Just not at quarterback. That was a problem for Briscoe, who is black. "First of all, [the black quarterback] wasn't intelligent enough and then he didn't have throwing mechanics," Briscoe said of the common perception at the time. Briscoe, nicknamed "the Magician," knew it was absurd. "I could throw and I could think," he said.

He wanted a chance to prove it, so Briscoe negotiated for a three-day tryout at quarterback during camp that summer. Competing against seven other quarterbacks, Briscoe didn't get an equal opportunity, but he made the most of it. Fans and media in attendance at the tryout could tell that Briscoe was the best of the bunch.

Nevertheless, Briscoe made the team as a defensive back. He would have started at cornerback, he said, had he not injured his hamstring. The injury kept him out of the first two games of the season. The starting quarterback, Steve Tensi, missed those games himself, with a shoulder injury. His backups, Jim LeClair and John McCormick, struggled. After starting 0–2 at the beginning of the 1968 season, Saban gave Briscoe his No. 15 jersey. It never would have happened without Briscoe's performance at the three-day tryout that summer, Briscoe said. That week, his dream came true. LeClair and the Broncos were playing poorly at home against the Boston Patriots on September 29, 1968. It was the fourth quarter, and Denver needed a spark. Quarterbacks coach Hunter Enis yelled for Briscoe to get in the game.

"It was kind of cold that day, and we had the hooded coats on," Briscoe said. "I took it off and ran onto the field."

Receiver Eric Crabtree greeted Briscoe in the huddle. "Don't be nervous, now," Crabtree told him.

First play, Briscoe completed a 22-yard pass to Crabtree. Later, Briscoe scored a touchdown. The Broncos lost the game, but Briscoe nearly led the comeback.

A week later, on October 6, 1968, Briscoe made history, becoming the first black quarterback to start a game in modern professional football. Briscoe didn't play well and Tensi, healthy by that point, actually came in and led the Broncos to the victory that day, but Briscoe had made his mark. His landmark achievement was celebrated by African Americans around the country. "I was anointed by God or somebody else to be the first, to prove the naysayers wrong," Briscoe said.

Briscoe started four more games that season, after Tensi was injured again. In all, he played in 11 games, finished sixth in the AFL in passing yards (1,589), and still holds the Broncos' rookie record for touchdown passes, with 14. Briscoe also ran for 308 yards and three touchdowns on just 41 attempts—a remarkable 7.5 yards per rush. To this day, the 5'11", 178-pound Briscoe is the smallest quarterback in Broncos history. But he was a thrill to watch.

"Of course, a guy 5'10", 5'11" in the National Football League doesn't have too much of a chance today, but it certainly was a good opportunity for us at the time," said former Broncos running back Floyd Little, who led the team in rushing in 1968. "He did a great job for us at the time. He was the best quarterback we had."

By season's end, it appeared Denver had found its quarterback of the future. But Saban had other ideas. Tensi was back for the 1969 season, and Saban signed Canadian Football League star Pete Liske. With Briscoe finishing his degree in Omaha, Saban held meetings with his other quarterbacks. Briscoe found out and showed up to meet with Saban. "I stood outside the office while they were holding their meetings, and they came out and Lou

Saban couldn't look me in the eye," Briscoe said. "Hunter Enis and Saban came out of there, and it was like they saw a ghost, but they kept going. At that point, I knew I was not going to get an opportunity to compete for the job. I went to camp, and sure enough, [in] those first few days, it was obvious. It was like I wasn't even there."

Briscoe could have remained in Denver had he agreed to change positions, but he felt he deserved a chance to play quarterback. So he asked Saban for his release. Saban agreed but made Briscoe wait four days. "Within those four days, he released me and nobody would touch me, so I know that during those four days, my name was sullied," Briscoe said.

Briscoe never played quarterback again. After being released by the Broncos, he was signed by Buffalo to play wide receiver. He played three years in Buffalo before Saban was hired to coach the Bills. Saban immediately traded Briscoe to Miami.

In all, Briscoe played eight more seasons after leaving Denver, all as a receiver. He played in a Pro Bowl while with Buffalo and won two Super Bowls as a key member of the 1972 and 1973 Miami Dolphins.

After football, Briscoe's life took a downward turn. He got heavily involved with drugs, became homeless, and wound up in jail. "I moved out to California," he said. "I wasn't a big-city kid, and I didn't really realize the pitfalls of making bad choices. I was always conscientious as a player of getting in shape, staying in shape. When I got to L.A., I kind of let my guard down. At first, I was having fun, but that fun turned into something else. It turned into a bitter addiction that I never thought would take me out like that."

Briscoe later became a counselor for youth and an influential figure in the Long Beach, California, area. An independent film company has tried for years to make a full-length feature about Briscoe's life. It is a life that has been filled with ups and downs, even during his short time in Denver. Briscoe, however, harbors nothing but good thoughts about Denver and the Broncos. "I feel very grateful that they gave me an opportunity, because they really didn't have to," he said. "They could have completely not addressed it and chose not to play me, but they knew I could play."

In fact, Briscoe believes Denver was the right place for him in the racially charged year of 1968. "It couldn't have happened in 1968 in any other city but Denver, I feel," he said. "The fans gave me that much love and support. I can't see it happening, really, in any other city."

Briscoe is proud to have been the first black starting quarterback and routinely gets a thank-you from those that followed him, including Hall of Famer Warren Moon and current star Michael Vick.

The only regret, from Briscoe and his 1968 teammates, is that he didn't get to play quarterback longer.

"If he had stayed and played, our won-and-lost record would have been a lot better than it was, and we would have been more competitive with Marlin there," Little said. "We won games with Marlin Briscoe."

36 The Champ

As good as Louis Wright was during his 12 seasons in Denver, Champ Bailey is right there with him, if not better.

Billy Thompson sat in his office one winter's day and was asked which one he'd pick as the best corner in team history. He couldn't decide.

"Louis Wright or Champ Bailey? If I had my choice? I couldn't lose on that one," he said. "Both of them will hit. Louis Wright will knock you in the ground, and Champ will do the same thing."

During his career, from 1999 to 2013, Bailey was one of the elite cornerbacks in the league. Some might argue others were better, but for more than a dozen years, the discussion of the NFL's best shutdown corners always included Bailey.

Roland "Champ" Bailey was the seventh overall pick in the 1999 draft by Washington. In high school and at the University of Georgia, he was not only a star on defense, but on offense, too. In five seasons with the Redskins, he started all 80 games at cornerback, made the Pro Bowl four times, and even got to play on offense a little bit.

The trade that brought him to Denver could arguably be considered the second-biggest trade in franchise history—superseded only by the John Elway deal. Prior to the 2004 season, the Broncos traded Pro Bowl running back Clinton Portis to Washington for Bailey. There was a heavy debate at the time, and in the years following, about which was more crucial to a team: a shutdown corner or an elite running back. At the time of the trade, Bailey expressed his confidence that he would be worth the investment, which included a new $63 million contract. "I won't be a disappointment," he said at the time. "I can guarantee that."

He was right. By 2011, Bailey's eighth season in Denver, the debate over who got the better end of the deal had long since faded away. In those eight seasons, Bailey made it to the Pro Bowl seven times, missing out only in 2008 when injuries limited him to nine games. "He's still playing at a very, very high level," Shannon Sharpe said after the 2011 season. "He doesn't have the foot speed that he once had, but he's still a top-three or -four corner in the National Football League. I believe Revis is slightly better, but Champ will take more risks than Revis will. He still believes to the utmost in his ability."

Bailey became the first cornerback in NFL history to get to the Pro Bowl 12 times. He had 34 interceptions as a Bronco, tied for the fourth-best total in team history at the time of his retirement.

His 10 interceptions in 2006 are the second-highest single-season total for the Broncos. "He's a true pro," former Broncos defensive lineman Elvis Dumervil said. "He's a big mentor to me, and I've learned a lot from him. Just having a guy like that on the team, a shutdown corner, is just tremendous."

Early in his career, Bailey relished the personal honors he received, but as he got older he started looking more at team success. Through his first 13 seasons, he went to the playoffs just four times, winning only three playoff games. "I want to be the best I can be. I want to be the best in the game," he said prior to the 2009 season. "But I want to be [part of] the best team, too. That's what is more important to me right now. The older you get and you don't have a ring...that's all you start thinking about is trying to get that ring. I would definitely feel unfulfilled if I don't win a Super Bowl. Forget just getting to it. I want to win it. Whether I'm a Hall of Famer or not, that's one thing that will always stick out, that I didn't get that ring."

Injuries limited Bailey to just five regular season games in 2013, but he was healthy enough for the playoffs and helped the Broncos reach the Super Bowl, finally giving him a chance to play on the NFL's biggest stage. In what turned out to be Bailey's final game, the Broncos lost 43–8 to Seattle in Super Bowl XLVIII.

After the season, Bailey was released by the Broncos. He signed with the New Orleans Saints, but was released just before the season and two months later announced his retirement.

Bailey never did get the ring he coveted, but he was one of the game's true greats and one of the best to ever play in Denver.

37 All-Around DB

Dennis Smith's greatness is often overlooked because of whom he played with during his football career.

He was an All-American at Southern California but was not nearly as touted as his teammate and fellow safety Ronnie Lott. During his professional career, he was a six-time Pro Bowler but often overlooked because fellow safeties Steve Foley and Steve Atwater were not only great players, but popular, too. Lott was elected to the Pro Football Hall of Fame. Atwater is mentioned as a Hall of Fame candidate. Foley holds the Broncos' record for career interceptions.

And Smith?

Well, he was one of the all-time greats in Broncos history—an incredible talent with a nose for the football and the ability to hit with the force of a truck.

"I've seen some great safeties through the years, but Dennis combined the speed and the size and his hitting ability," said Dan Reeves, who made Smith his first draft pick after taking over in Denver in 1981. "That turned out to be an awesome pick for us."

The 15th overall pick in 1981, the 6'3", 200-pound Smith played 14 seasons for the Broncos, from 1981 to 1994. In that time, he amassed 1,171 tackles, 15 sacks, 30 interceptions, and 17 fumble recoveries.

Smith, who lettered three times in track at USC, played his NFL rookie season at cornerback but moved to safety in 1982 and stayed there for nearly every game through 1994.

"A guy that was as tough of an individual as you'd ever see," Karl Mecklenburg said. "There were players across the league who were just scared to death of Dennis. He would knock somebody out every third or fourth game—out cold. He knocked me out cold one time by accident. I remember seeing the ball, and the next thing I saw was the trainer."

Even Atwater, who built a reputation for destructive hits, admires Smith's ferociousness, comparing Smith's hits to a train wreck. "He was an old throwback guy and one of the hardest hitters I've ever witnessed in my life," Atwater said. "I tried to mimic him, but I still couldn't do it as good as Dennis did it. He was full-speed. He had no fear. He was a great athlete and he had great speed. He could hit with the best of them."

Atwater recalls several of Smith's greatest hits, but one stands out above the rest. "We were playing against the Indianapolis Colts in Denver," Atwater said. "Roosevelt Potts was playing fullback. I'm thinking I'm running to the ball fast and Dennis, he comes flying by me and slams into him—*bam!*—and knocks him out cold. Dennis, he was getting up, wobbling around. We didn't want him out of the game because we didn't want anybody to know he was dinged, too. We just pulled him up to the huddle and Roosevelt Potts, he was out." Potts, at 250 pounds, outweighed Smith by a good 50 pounds.

Smith and Atwater are often mentioned together because for six seasons they formed one of the best safety tandems in pro football. Three times in those six seasons they both made the Pro Bowl. Because they are often linked together, there is a natural debate about which one was better.

"Atwater was an unbelievable player, but Dennis was the all-around thing," Mecklenburg said. "He could be a head football coach with his knowledge of the game and his passion."

Atwater agrees. "Dennis, he took me under his wing and tried to teach me everything he knew," Atwater said. "Some of the stuff he did, I couldn't do."

Smith was inducted into the Broncos' Ring of Fame in 2001. Today, he and his wife, Andre, live in Hollywood, California, and Smith owns a real-estate investment company.

38 The Smiling Assassin

Christian Okoye was a 6'1", 255-pound bulldozer of a man. A native of Enugu, Nigeria, the Kansas City Chiefs running back earned the nickname "the Nigerian Nightmare," and he certainly lived up to it. Okoye led the NFL in rushing in 1989 with 1,480 yards on 370 carries that punished the opposition more than it did himself. Another big game by Okoye in the 1990 season opener helped the Chiefs to a win.

Week 2 brought the Chiefs to Denver for a *Monday Night Football* contest. Denver's two starting safeties, Smith and Atwater, were ready. "I remember leading up to the game, Dennis and I were talking, 'Man, we've got to hit him. Whoever has the opportunity, we've got to just come up and bring it,'" Atwater recalled years later. "I guess my number was called."

Atwater's number was called in the fourth quarter. Okoye took the handoff and ran up the middle. Atwater, a power-packed 6'3" and 217 pounds, sprinted ahead, squared up, and delivered a crushing hit to the big back. Okoye had a full head of steam but was stopped dead in his tracks and knocked backward.

"It's the first time that I've probably ever seen a 260-pound back run into a free safety and go flat on his back," Elway said during an NFL Films piece about the hit. "It was exciting."

That hit, while maybe not the best or most important of Atwater's career, earned him an instant reputation for being one of the hardest-hitting safeties in the NFL. "I don't know if I have one in my mind that's the best hit, but I definitely remember that one," Atwater said.

Nicknamed "the Smiling Assassin," Atwater had an infectious smile and a killer instinct on the field.

"He was the enforcer," Sharpe said. "He was the intimidator we had that would make sure that receivers and tight ends...he would throw them off line when they came through the middle to make sure he let them know it was unacceptable for them to run through his house."

Denver's first-round draft choice in 1989, Atwater came to the Broncos after becoming a two-time All-American at the University of Arkansas. He still held the Arkansas record for career interceptions, with 14, as of 2012 and is a member of the school's Hall of Honor. Dan Reeves sensed Atwater's greatness during a pre-draft workout. "When we brought him in, we needed somebody to direct the secondary.... There was no question he was that guy," Reeves said. "He had all the things you needed and looked for in being a leader. That's what he did the whole time he was there. He was a great leader for that secondary."

Atwater immediately earned a starting job next to Smith. They spent six seasons terrorizing the opposition together. "Steve learned from Dennis and was able to do many of the things Dennis was able to do," Mecklenburg said. "Steve was just a great athlete and an unbelievable player. The interesting thing with Steve, he was an unbelievable player from day one. He made a couple plays his rookie year that I'd never seen anybody make. It was unbelievable. He did a couple things that year that were athletically unparalleled."

During his 10 years with the Broncos, Atwater missed just five games. He was in the starting lineup for all 155 games that he played for the Broncos. He was exceptional not only in pass coverage, but against the run, as his hit on Okoye proved. Atwater made 1,301 tackles and intercepted 24 passes as a Bronco.

DBs under the Radar

The Broncos have seemingly always had Pro Bowl–caliber defensive backs, but they've also had several who were fan favorites which didn't necessarily get national recognition.

Tyrone Braxton, nicknamed "Chicken," was a 12th-round pick in 1987 out of North Dakota State. During his first stint with the Broncos (1987–93), he was a starting cornerback. After one year in Miami, he returned to Denver (1995–99) and started at safety. In 1996, he led the NFL with nine interceptions and made his only Pro Bowl. Through the first 50 seasons of Broncos football, only three players had more interceptions than Braxton's 34.

Ray Crockett started nearly every game at corner from 1994 to 2000. He didn't intercept many passes (17) but was a top-flight cover corner and a leader on a defense that helped the Broncos win two straight Super Bowls.

Mike Harden was one of the toughest hitters the Broncos have had. From 1980 to 1988, he played in 128 games and started 98 of them. A corner and then safety, heading into 2012 he ranked fifth in team history with 33 career interceptions. He was released before the 1989 season to make room for rookie Steve Atwater and played his last two seasons with the Los Angeles Raiders.

He played one of his best games in Super Bowl XXXII. Helping the Broncos beat the Packers 31–24, Atwater had six tackles, a quarterback sack, a forced fumble, and two passes defended. In his last game as a Bronco, Atwater had seven tackles in the team's 34–19 win over Atlanta in Super Bowl XXXIII.

By the end of the 1998 season, the Broncos decided to part ways with the aging Atwater. He had lost a step in his speed, and surgeries on his shoulder, bicep, and knee contributed to him no longer being the same player. The Broncos waived him, and Atwater signed with the New York Jets. In his third game as a Jet, Atwater had seven tackles to help his team to a 21–13 win over the Broncos at Mile High Stadium. He retired at the end of the 1999 season. "Sometimes I regret making that decision to go and play for the Jets for a year, but that was a decision I had to make back then," he said. "It was cool. We had a good experience up there, as well."

Atwater's greatest experiences, though, came in Denver, and he proved more than worthy of the No. 1 pick the Broncos invested in him.

"I pretty much expected to do well, and I think I had a pretty decent career," he said. "If anything, in the end, I wish I could have done a little bit more.

"Those were some of the best times of my life."

In 2005, Atwater was inducted into the Broncos' Ring of Fame. He lives in Atlanta where, after years of owning a property-management company, he teams with his wife, Letha, in raising their four children.

39 The Goose

Even before Austin "Goose" Gonsoulin played his first professional football game, the Denver Broncos had a hunch he would be pretty good.

The team's 1960 media guide, published before the team's inaugural season, include these words about Gonsoulin: "The first day in camp Gonsoulin was tried at defensive half and he's been there ever since. Speed, size and good hands make him a potential great as a defensive back. Can do everything well and for a rookie has amazing reactions in pass coverage." One of the original Broncos, he was as good as they thought he'd be, if not better.

From 1960 to 1966, Gonsoulin was one of the Broncos' best players and was arguably the best safety in the AFL. He played in five AFL All-Star games, and it would have been six, except the game in 1960 was canceled. In the Broncos' first game of 1960, Gonsoulin intercepted two Boston Patriots passes. The next week, he picked off four Buffalo Bills passes, and the week after that, he got an interception against the New York Titans, giving him seven in the first three games. "I ended up thinking, *Man, this isn't too bad*," Gonsoulin said years later.

The Texas native had been a star at Baylor University and was selected by the Dallas Texans in the 1960 AFL Draft. Shortly after the draft, the Broncos swung a deal, sending fullback Jack Spikes to Dallas in return for Gonsoulin. It was the first trade in Broncos history, and there haven't been many others better than that one.

Gonsoulin's four interceptions against Buffalo are still a single-game franchise record. His 11 interceptions in 1960 are still a single-season record for the team. In addition, his 43 career picks were a team record (and the most in the AFL's 10-year history) until Steve Foley broke the mark in 1986. Foley finished with 44.

It was a remarkable ride for the Port Arthur, Texas, native.

"My family was real poor growing up," he said. "Didn't have a telephone or television, didn't have a car. We were dirt poor back then, but I loved every minute of it."

In the 1960s, players didn't become wealthy like they do now, but Gonsoulin was intent on giving back to his parents. "I finally got enough that I bought my mom and dad a house," he said. "That was more pride than anything I've ever done, to finally get them out. I bought them a duplex so they could rent the other half out. That way they could pay for some of their groceries and stuff."

In another glimpse into what life was like for pro football stars in the 1960s, Gonsoulin spent his first two off-seasons in the army reserves. "Back in those old days you had to join the service or get drafted, and you'd stay in there two years," he said. Gonsoulin never did have to go overseas for the military, and that proved to be convenient during his second off-season. He reported for duty, but, "About a week later, I get a letter saying I made the Pro Bowl. I had to go to the head guy and ask if I could get a week or two off to play in the Pro Bowl. It was like pulling teeth, but they let me off."

Getting into the Pro Bowl was a big deal for Gonsoulin, who took great pride in being an elite player and making sure he was ready to excel on the field. "I took it serious," he said. "I worked out hard in the off-season and ran a lot and tried to stay in good shape, and it paid off."

Other than never being a part of a winning team, Gonsoulin's only regret about his time in Denver was how it ended. Training camp for the 1967 season was about to start and Gonsoulin, who was a team captain, was still not under contract. The Broncos hired a new coach, Lou Saban, and Gonsoulin had yet to hear from Saban. He drove up to Denver and was staying in a hotel when he got a call from the Broncos, telling him he'd been put on waivers. "I couldn't believe it," Gonsoulin said. "[Saban] never talked to me. Never called me. Never said anything. It was disheartening, because I felt like me and Denver had given each other a lot. It was rude in the way that he handled it. It really upset me."

He signed on with the NFL's San Francisco 49ers and played an injury-plagued 1967 season before retiring because of a neck injury. "I loved playing football," he said. "I just loved it."

Gonsoulin was an original Ring of Fame inductee in 1984 and is often honored by fans as one of the best defensive backs ever to play in Denver. "After all these years to still be remembered is wonderful," he said. "[Being traded to Denver] was a real disappointment back then. I'm glad it happened now."

Gonsoulin ran a construction company in Texas for several years before retiring. A proud Bronco throughout his adult life, Gonsoulin spent his final years battling prostate cancer. He passed away on September 8, 2014, in Beaumont, Texas, at the age of 76.

40 Denver's First QB

In putting together the first Broncos squad in 1960, head coach Frank Filchock looked north in search of an assistant coach. Filchock, a veteran coach in the Canadian Football League, asked Frank Tripucka to help him on the Broncos. Tripucka had finished a stellar CFL career the year before and had expressed interest in coaching.

With 11 years of professional football experience, Tripucka figured to be a great asset to Denver's quarterbacks. A former All-American quarterback at Notre Dame, Tripucka played four seasons in the NFL before joining Canada's Saskatchewan Roughriders in 1953. In six seasons with the Roughriders, Tripucka led the league in passing four times. He then played for the Ottawa Rough Riders in 1959 before wrapping up his playing career—or so he thought. Tripucka arrived in Denver with hopes of helping the Broncos develop a quality starting quarterback and to get his feet wet in the coaching ranks.

The Broncos had at least eight QBs in camp, including George Herring—yet another Canadian product—veteran NFL backup Tom Dublinski, and three local players: Dick Hyson from the University of Colorado, Bob Miller from the University of Denver, and John Wolf from Colorado State University. Early on, Filchock could tell the talent level at quarterback was low. His best quarterback wasn't in uniform. So he approached Tripucka about trading in his coach's whistle for a jersey and helmet. That's how Tripucka, at age 32, became the first starting quarterback of the Broncos, a job he held for the better part of three seasons.

"He made a big difference," Gonsoulin said. "Had we not had him, we would have been in trouble. That was the best move they made was getting him to come play and quarterback for us. Frank had a good feel for the game. He was older. He was almost like our dad out there. When he said something, everybody paid attention and listened to him. He was like a player/coach."

The Broncos didn't win much in those years. In fact, they won just 13 of the 39 games Tripucka started, but, Gonsoulin said, "He had this authority about him and he tried real hard. He just had that character of a winning-type quarterback."

Tripucka threw for an AFL-leading 3,038 yards in 1960. He also tossed 24 touchdown passes, which stood as the Broncos single-season record until Elway threw 25 in 1993. (Unfortunately, he also threw 34 interceptions, which is still a team record.)

After a rough 1961 season, Tripucka led the AFL in passing again in 1962, throwing for 2,917 yards and 17 touchdowns. He helped the Broncos get off to a 7–2 start that season, but they lost their last five games to finish 7–7. He returned for the 1963 season, but at the age of 35 didn't have much left in the tank. He threw just 15 passes that season, as he gave way to youngster Mickey Slaughter.

As the passing game has developed over time, Tripucka's statistics have been buried in the Broncos' record books, but his

Picked Off

Broncos quarterbacks threw interceptions at a historic rate in the team's early years. Frank Tripucka's 34 interceptions in 1960 are still the third-highest single-season total for an individual in pro football history. As a team, the Broncos threw 45 interceptions in 1961—including 22 by George Herring and 21 by Tripucka—which still ranks as the second-highest total in pro football history (the Houston Oilers threw 48 in 1962). Overall, the Broncos threw 120 interceptions from 1960 to 1962 and finished with at least 29 in each of their first seven seasons. Since 1967, the Broncos have had as many as 29 interceptions just twice.

Quarterback Frank Tripucka brought veteran leadership to the nascent Broncos franchise. Photo courtesy of Getty Images

contributions to those early Broncos teams, both as a passer and, more important, as a leader, were significant. Throughout the rest of the 1960s, the Broncos went through a lot of quarterbacks and never found anyone that gave them the stability who Tripucka gave them in those early years.

In 1986, Tripucka's role in team history was recognized when the team named him to the Ring of Fame. He is one of four quarterbacks—along with John Elway, Charley Johnson, and Craig Morton—to receive the honor.

Following his playing career, Tripucka returned to his native New Jersey and began a long business career. One of his seven children, Kelly, made his own sports legacy, leading Notre Dame's basketball team to four NCAA Tournament appearances and playing 10 seasons in the National Basketball Association.

41 Becoming Winners

The Broncos didn't reach the playoffs until their 18th season, and while Red Miller was the coach to lead them there, the foundation was set before Miller arrived.

John Ralston was hired as head coach in 1972. He succeeded Jerry Smith, who had finished out the 1971 season after Lou Saban quit midway through the year. Ralston had never coached in professional football but had a highly successful career in college at Utah State and Stanford, leading the latter to back-to-back Rose Bowl wins in 1970 and 1971. "I thought it was exciting when John Ralston came in," said Broncos radio announcer Larry Zimmer. "He brought a college *rah-rah* thing to professional football. John was a great guy to work with. I don't think he gets his due for what he did for this organization."

Ralston certainly brought enthusiasm to the Broncos. He was a certified instructor for the Dale Carnegie Institute, which was built upon the power of self-improvement. Ralston believed in positive thinking, and he brought that to the Broncos. Ralston is actually quoted in the 1972 Broncos media guide, saying, "We will have a positive approach in everything we do."

He also had a remarkable ability to spot great players. "He just had an instinct about player talent," said the *Denver Post* sports writer Terry Frei, whose father, Jerry, was an offensive line coach under Ralston from 1972 to 1975.

The Broncos had good talent before Ralston arrived, with Floyd Little, Lyle Alzado, and Billy Thompson at the core. Ralston wasted no time in adding to it.

Ralston's first draft choice was tight end Riley Odoms, who became one of the top tight ends in team history. That first season, he also made trades that landed future Ring of Famers Haven Moses at wide receiver and Charley Johnson at quarterback. He also made a key trade for center Bobby Maples, a seven-year veteran who wound up playing seven seasons with the Broncos, most of that time as a starter. Little said the trades for Johnson and Maples were huge for Denver's road to success. "Two of the greatest players I had a chance to play with together," Little said. "They made a big difference, the two of those guys. What a joy to have two guys that knew how to win and did everything they could to win."

With free agency not yet instituted, the draft was extremely important, and Ralston may have been the best in team history at making his draft picks count. In 1973, he selected Otis Armstrong, Barney Chavous, Paul Howard, Tom Jackson, and Calvin Jones—all of whom spent several years in the starting lineup. The 1974 draft landed Ring of Fame linebacker Randy Gradishar and Claudie

Minor, who started all but four games for the Broncos from 1974 to 1981. "He was pretty much an elite offensive tackle and never got credit for being one," Frei said of Minor.

Ralston had a great draft in 1975, too, selecting corner Louis Wright, receiver/returner Rick Upchurch, nose tackle Rubin Carter, and safety Steve Foley. All four are considered among the best players in team history at their positions. Running back Jon Keyworth, obtained through a 1974 trade, was another significant acquisition for Ralston.

"He was willing to take chances on people like Randy Gradishar, who was viewed as damaged goods, and not listen to the conventional wisdom about players," Frei said. "They took players higher than anybody else would have taken them that turned out, guys like Randy Gradishar and Louis Wright."

In remaking the roster, Ralston guided the Broncos to their first winning season in 1973, as they finished 7–5–2. "That was the year they really gained credibility," Frei said.

Fred Gehrke

As a player, innovator, and general manager, Fred Gehrke had quite a career in pro football. A native of Salt Lake City, Utah, Gehrke worked with the Broncos from 1965 to 1981, first as director of player personnel and then as general manager. An NFL player, mostly with the Cleveland/Los Angeles Rams, Gehrke played in 1940 and from 1945 to 1950. While playing for the Rams, he thought the brown leather helmets were dull, so he painted them blue and put yellow horns on them. With that, Gehrke was credited for inventing the helmet logo. An art major, he hand-painted every one of the team's helmets in 1948. He also invented the face mask and the practice net that kickers and punters still use today on the sideline. His helmet design led the Pro Football Hall of Fame to honor him in 1972 with a Pioneer Award. With the Broncos, he was instrumental in bringing many top players to Denver, including Randy Gradishar, Floyd Little, Billy Thompson, and Tom Jackson.

The Broncos went 7–6–1 in 1974, 6–8 in 1975, and then had their best season yet in 1976, going 9–5. "That team was just one of the most motivated teams that I ever played on," Thompson said of those years.

By then, the Broncos were on the brink of something big, but Ralston wouldn't be the man to lead them to greatness. Expectations from the fans grew, and the players lost confidence in Ralston's ability to take them to the next level.

Denver had a championship-caliber defense in 1976, and many of the players believed all they needed to be a Super Bowl contender was a good quarterback. There wasn't much confidence in Steve Ramsey, who took over the starting job in 1975. Ralston had done virtually nothing to replace him. "He said, 'I know we need a quarterback,'" Thompson said. "Then he came back after he told us that he was going to do something and said, 'Okay, we've still got to go with Steve Ramsey because I can't find anybody better.' Everybody is going like, 'What? You mean, after you've seen it and we've seen it and you're telling us you can't find anything better than that?' It was a no-confidence vote. 'You mean to tell us you can't see that he's not the guy, and you're telling us that's the best you can do?'"

As far as Thompson is concerned, the final straw came in Week 5 of the 1976 season. The Broncos went to the Houston Astrodome with a 3–1 record, and the defense played yet another good game. The offense managed just a single field goal in the 17–3 loss. According to Thompson, offensive coordinator Max Coley missed the game after an emergency appendectomy, and that caused chaos. "Nobody could call the offense," he said. "[Ralston] couldn't. It was a mess. I'm going, 'Where are we going? If something happens, nobody can run it?' To me, that was very key. We lost that game to Houston in the Astrodome, and I knew then."

By the latter half of the season, Ralston's days were numbered. Dissatisfaction with Ralston ran throughout the organization, even among the players. A group of players labeled "the Dirty Dozen" gathered and led a revolt against Ralston. "My whole thing was that it was nothing personal," Thompson said. "I just wanted to win. All of a sudden, we were just stuck."

The player revolt wasn't the only reason Ralston was fired. Owner Gerald Phipps had decided to take away Ralston's role as general manager, so he could simply focus on coaching. Ultimately, however, Phipps and new general manager Fred Gehrke determined it was time for a change. "The player revolt was definitely part of it, no question about it," Zimmer said. "But the other part of it was that Gehrke convinced Phipps they need to make a change. That they were sort of spinning their wheels and not improving."

Ralston officially resigned on January 31, 1977, but it was clear he was pushed out. The next day, Miller was named the new head coach. It was an unfortunate end to Ralston's tenure with the Broncos. He was the first coach in team history to compile a winning record, going 34–33–3. He also set the stage for a magical 1977 season. "They always had some decent players under Lou Saban, but John Ralston's eye for talent and a pretty good coaching staff and some pretty good players got them around the corner a little bit during that era," Frei said. "He's not given enough credit for essentially assembling that team in '77 and moving the franchise forward."

Following his time in Denver, Ralston had several assistant coaching gigs before helping to get the United States Football League off the ground. He served as head coach of the USFL's Oakland Invaders. Ralston was inducted into the College Football Hall of Fame in 1992 and later returned to the sideline, coaching San Jose State from 1993 to 1996.

42 Tombstone

The 1960s and 1970s were a golden era for defensive ends. Hall of Famers Elvin Bethea, Fred Dean, Carl Eller, David "Deacon" Jones, and Jack Youngblood were among the fiercest quarterback hunters during that time. Rich "Tombstone" Jackson, who starred for the Broncos from 1967 to 1972, was as destructive as any of them. "He was unbelievable," Floyd Little said. "He's one guy that's overlooked for the Hall of Fame. He's certainly deserving. Deacon Jones, said outside of himself, [Jackson] was the best defensive end in the game."

A native of New Orleans, Jackson played offense and defense—and was also a National Association of Intercollegiate Athletics shot-put champion—at Southern University (Louisiana) before joining the Oakland Raiders in 1966. He was a backup linebacker with the Raiders. Prior to the 1967 season, Broncos coach Lou Saban worked out a five-player trade that sent receiver Lionel Taylor and starting lineman Jerry Sturm to Oakland in exchange for Jackson and two other players. Saban moved Jackson to defensive end, and he soon became a dominating force.

"I'm going to tell you something, that's a scary guy, because he came around not from the blind side, he came from the straight side," said Charley Johnson, who once faced Jackson and the Broncos when Johnson quarterbacked the Houston Oilers and then in practices when they were teammates in 1972. "So it was very difficult not to watch where he was going."

Jackson terrorized not only quarterbacks, but also opposing linemen with his powerful moves, such as the "halo spinner."

"He'd hit you upside your head and he'd spin around you and he was in there on the quarterback," Little said. "He changed the rules a lot because they had to protect their [heads] so much. He would whack you pretty hard."

There are actually stories of Jackson breaking opponents' helmets with his powerful head slaps. Because of Tombstone, the head slap became illegal in the NFL.

The 6'3", 255-pound Jackson suffered a knee injury seven games into the 1971 season. He was never the same after that, and four games into the 1972 season, Broncos head coach John Ralston traded Jackson to Cleveland. He played the final 10 games with the Browns but never played again. Unlike many of his defensive end peers, Jackson had a short career. He played just five dominating seasons, but few argue with how great he was.

"In his prime he was the very best run-pass defensive end the game has seen," *Sports Illustrated*'s Paul Zimmerman wrote in a 1992 article in which he named Jackson to his all-time Dream Team.

Those who played with or against Jackson will never forget the mark he left. "He was a tremendous athlete," Johnson said. "He belongs in the Hall of Fame."

Jackson lives with his wife, Kathrine, in New Orleans, where he works as a school administrator.

43 The Professor

He has master's and doctorate degrees. He's spent a dozen years as a professor in chemical engineering, preceded by 30 years in business. He's got a loving wife, a son, a daughter, and three beautiful granddaughters. Charley Johnson has a lot to be proud of, and some of the fondest memories were created during the four years that he quarterbacked the Denver Broncos.

Johnson was already 33 years old and 11 years into his NFL career when the Broncos sent a third-round draft pick to the Oilers in the summer of 1972 to obtain his rights. "I screamed so loud. I was very, very happy," Johnson said.

At the time, the Broncos had a new coach, John Ralston. In 1960, when Ralston was the head coach at Utah State University, he coached against Johnson in a loss at the Sun Bowl.

The pride of New Mexico State University, Johnson quarterbacked the Aggies to the best season in their history in 1960, leading them to an 11–0 record, capped by that win over Ralston and Utah State in the Sun Bowl. It was the second year in a row that Johnson led the Aggies to a Sun Bowl victory, earning game MVP honors both times. (New Mexico State hasn't been to a bowl game since.)

Johnson apparently made a lasting impression on the coach. "I was always super grateful to John Ralston for trading for me, because in two years in Houston, I had had three head coaches and surgeries five times," said Johnson, who had played nine years with the St. Louis Cardinals before going to Houston.

By 1972, Houston was moving on at quarterback, but Johnson still had the itch to play. "[Multiple surgeries] tend to ruin somebody's career and came awful close to ruining mine," he said. "But being reborn and getting to go to Denver was just awesome."

When he arrived in Denver, Johnson proved he still had something left in his tank. Steve Ramsey was the starting quarterback, but after the Broncos started 1–4, Ralston turned to Johnson, who then started 41 of the team's next 43 games. "It was one of those situations where I had a chance to go in there and get rid of the ball real fast and take the pressure off of the offensive line," Johnson said. "We wound up doing pretty well for a couple of years there."

The Broncos went 4–5 with Johnson under center in 1972, including back-to-back wins to close the season. In 1973, Johnson had one of the finest seasons of his career, throwing for 2,465 yards and 20 touchdowns. Most important, he guided the Broncos to their first-ever winning season, going 7–5–2. He led them to another winning season in 1974, as the Broncos finished 7–6–1. "I think we started to turn it around when we brought Charley Johnson in," Floyd Little said. "Charley had a grasp of the game unlike any quarterback that I had. There was something about Charley Johnson, that when he got up under that center or he called the play in the huddle, he knew it was the best play we had. The coach would send in the play and Charley would say, 'What the hell does he know? He never played.' I like that. I enjoyed playing with Charley. Charley got us right to the bubble. I liked that. I really did."

Johnson had a big impact on the Broncos, and not just in the wins column. He also gave the defense, for the first time, a veteran quarterback to test them in practice. "I thought Charley was the most analytical [quarterback], and he taught me how to read the quarterback," safety Billy Thompson said. "I had 40 interceptions in my career, and part of that was because of Charley."

Thompson, who joined the Broncos in 1969 as a rookie, had been through three losing seasons before Johnson arrived and, like Little, felt Johnson was an integral piece to the winning puzzle. "It was a team that didn't have a lot of weapons, but it was an up-and-coming team, and he could come in and manage it, which he did very well and won a lot of football games for us," Thompson said.

For all the successes in his life, getting the Broncos to win is near the top of the list for Johnson. "It's very satisfying," he said. "I was pretty sure I could do it if I could stay well."

He did stay healthy and took the Broncos to a new level. He was the first quarterback in Broncos history to start at least 20 games and finish with a winning record (20–18–3) and through 2015 was one of just six in team history with that distinction. Johnson also got the Broncos to start winning games on the road, in places such as Pittsburgh, San Diego, Kansas City, and Oakland. Johnson set the tone in his first start with the Broncos, on October 22, 1972, in Oakland. The Broncos had lost 14 straight games to the Raiders and in 12 previous trips to Oakland came away with just one win, in 1962. That day, Johnson completed 20-of–28 passes for 361 yards and two touchdowns in the Broncos' 30–23 win.

"We moved from being pretty much an also-ran and a taking-it-on-the-chin team to...all of a sudden, [opposing teams] couldn't just look at their schedule and say, 'Denver's coming to town. There's a win.'"

Although he didn't play long in Denver, Johnson's role in turning the Broncos into winners led to his induction into the Ring of Fame in 1986. "That was a wonderful thing," he said.

It's a sense of pride for him to have his name honored at the stadium, and he glances at it every chance he gets. "I can't resist," he said.

Johnson lost his starting job to Ramsey in the middle of the 1975 season and retired from pro football at the end of that season. From there, he spent nearly 30 years as a businessman in Houston before returning to New Mexico State University as a professor in chemical engineering. In January 2012, he revealed his desire to retire from teaching at the end of the school year. "I'm hoping it'll work out so I can spend a lot more time at Bronco reunions and all those weekends they make available to the Ring of Famers," he said. "I want to catch more fish, hit more good shots in golf, and spend time with my kids.

"I think it's time to relax."

He's certainly earned it.

44 To Do: Skiing

Denver is, without question, a Broncos town.

While the locals love their football team, Colorado is probably best known around the world for its winter playgrounds. There are surely some who believe Denver is buried in snow throughout the winter. The Denver metro area does get its fair share of snow, but it's also known for having 300 days of sunshine every year, and it's not uncommon for locals to play golf one day and go skiing the next.

Colorado's Rocky Mountains draw thousands of tourists every year, many of them looking to enjoy some of the greatest ski resorts in the world. Warren Miller Entertainment, which has produced dozens of ski and snowboard films, has its headquarters in Boulder, Colorado, and often debuts its films in Colorado.

Traveler's Digest lists two Colorado resorts among the top 10 in the world—Vail at No. 4 and Aspen at No. 10. NationalGeographic.com lists four Colorado locations among its top 25 ski towns in the world: Aspen, Crested Butte, Steamboat Springs, and Telluride. Those lists don't even include world-renowned resorts Winter Park, Copper Mountain, and Snowmass, the state's three largest resorts in terms of number of trails, skiable acres, and lifts. Then there's Wolf Creek, which is one of the smaller resorts but gets more snow than any of them on an annual basis.

Colorado's mountains feature everything from the posh resorts, such as Vail and Aspen—where there's a chance you'll bump into a celebrity or two—to the smaller, more budget-friendly resorts, like Howelsen and Eldora. Regardless of your choice, there's no shortage of places to visit. According to ColoradoSki.com, its

22-member resorts feature more than 1,700 trails, ranging from easy to difficult.

During the 2014–15 ski season, more than 7.1 million skiers visited the Colorado slopes. They all flock to the resorts for the same thing—to enjoy the fresh powder that dumps on the Colorado mountains throughout the winter.

45 The Reeves-Elway Feud

Dan Reeves has graced the cover of *Sports Illustrated* twice, and it's a good bet he doesn't have either one framed on his wall at home.

The first one, on November 6, 1967, showed him as a player with the Dallas Cowboys, arms folded, intense stare, and rain falling down upon him. The headline: The Unwanted Cowboy.

The second, on August 2, 1993, showed Elway on the left side of the cover, Reeves on the right, with a tear down the middle of the page and the words, Good Riddance. Grow Up. John Elway is ecstatic that he's still in Denver and his nemesis Dan Reeves is now in New York.

It was no secret during the latter part of their time together that Reeves and Elway weren't the best of friends, and the 1993 *Sports Illustrated* article portrayed a Broncos team that was thrilled to be out from under the iron thumb of Reeves, even if they did appreciate what he did for them. The comments by Elway, in particular, were biting.

"The last three years have been hell," Elway said in the article. "I know that I would not have been back here if Dan Reeves had been here. It wasn't worth it to me. I didn't enjoy it. It wasn't any fun, and I got tired of working with him."

Reeves, in the first weeks at his new job with the Giants, fired back.

"Just tell him it wasn't exactly heaven for me, either," Reeves said in the article. "One of these days I hope he grows up. Maybe he'll mature sometime."

The root of the problem between the two was Reeves' offense. He was old school in his approach, choosing to base his attack on the running game rather than Elway's rocket arm. During their 10 seasons together, Elway threw for 30,216 yards and 158 touchdowns. Fellow 1983 draft classer Dan Marino, under Miami's pass-oriented offense, threw for 39,502 yards and 290 touchdowns during that same time period. Another 1983 draftee, Jim Kelly, had more touchdown passes (161) in just seven NFL seasons during that time (he spent three years in the USFL). The dramatic disparity in numbers wasn't lost on Elway or anyone else.

"It's been frustrating," Elway said in that 1993 article. "People look at touchdown passes, and mine don't match up with Kelly or Marino or even Warren [Moon]. It was hard to argue with the first six years, but it got tough the last three or four years, when we just shut down the offense and played off our defense. I'd like to get the most out of what I do before it's too late. I mean, I'm no duckling anymore."

Karl Mecklenburg suggests there was more to the feud than just philosophical differences on offense. Reeves was a strong leader, which Mecklenburg believes was an asset to the team—and a young Elway—in the early 1980s. "John was fine with that until he got older and really wanted that leadership role," Mecklenburg said. "They got into a little bit of issues as he got older. John wanted to take over some leadership and wanted to make some decisions and wanted to be involved."

The other issue was Elway's close relationship with Mike Shanahan, who was a Broncos assistant coach from 1984 to 1987 and again from 1989 to 1991. Shanahan, a close friend of Elway, agreed with the quarterback's desire to open up the offense. Shanahan was fired after the 1991 season. "The relationship among those three had become somewhat dysfunctional by then," Denver talk show host Sandy Clough said.

Years later, Reeves said, "I didn't know I had a problem with John until I left and those things came out."

While Reeves understates the rift, it's probably true that their issues were exaggerated to a point. But there was no question it existed.

"Two very stubborn men butting heads and realizing how similar they were in a lot of ways," the *Denver Post* sportswriter Terry Frei said. "I don't think either one was right or wrong, it was just a butting of heads between very stubborn people."

Tommy Maddox Comes to Town

The last first-round pick Dan Reeves ever made for the Broncos was probably his most controversial draft selection. Going into 1992, the Broncos felt they were on the verge of another Super Bowl trip. They fell three points short of going to the Super Bowl the year before. Quarterback John Elway wanted a receiver. A running back or a top-notch defender would have helped, too. Instead, Reeves selected Tommy Maddox, a quarterback from UCLA. The move was viewed as Reeves planning for a future without Elway, and it certainly didn't help the relationship between the two.

Twenty years later, Reeves defended the choice. "No, I never regretted it because I felt like that was the right thing to do," he said. Reeves felt that, with the retirement of backup Gary Kubiak, he needed to get a young, talented quarterback who could learn for several years under Elway. "If we still had Kubiak, I probably wouldn't have done that. Here was a quarterback that I felt was going to be a good player in pro football and we could get him and he could learn from one of the best at the time."

In hindsight, Reeves admitted, "Yeah, if I had it to do over, I would go out and say, 'Okay, let's don't look for the future; let's go out and see what we can do for this next year, next two years.'"

Those stubborn people squared off in Elway's final game, as he led the Broncos to a 34–19 win over Reeves' Falcons in Super Bowl XXXIII. Elway won his second straight Super Bowl with Shanahan and earned game MVP honors. Reeves fell to 0–4 in the Super Bowl as a head coach. Years later, the two men have offered nothing but respect for each other publicly. Even as Reeves was asked about losing Super Bowl XXXIII, he praised Elway.

"He won it the year before, too, against Green Bay. He could have let me win one," Reeves joked. "I've got to hold that against him. He could have helped me win my only Super Bowl as a head coach. But I was thrilled to death for him. John played extremely well in both of those games."

Ultimately, Reeves and Elway did coexist for a decade of winning football. They won 98 regular-season games, qualified for the playoffs six times, and played in three Super Bowls. Losing all three Super Bowls only seemed to add fuel to the fire that drove them apart. "I'm sure John was frustrated with losing three Super Bowls; and I was frustrated with losing three Super Bowls," Reeves said. "But there's no way I could ever not have the greatest respect for him for giving me those opportunities. If I hadn't had Elway, I would never have been able to get another job somewhere else. I was able to go to New York and then able to go with Atlanta. John had a lot to do with that."

When Elway was elected to the Pro Football Hall of Fame in 2004, he personally invited Reeves, who made sure to attend. "I'm particularly glad to see my old coach, Dan Reeves, could be here," Elway said in his enshrinement speech. "Dan, I regret that we couldn't win a Super Bowl [together], but we went down fighting, that's for damn sure. I appreciate all the wins we did have together. And I want you to know that I fed off of your competitive spirit. Thank you."

46 Super Disappointments

On Monday, January 29, 1990, the Broncos boarded a plane home from New Orleans.

The night before, they had been dismantled by the San Francisco 49ers 55–10 in Super Bowl XXIV. It was the worst beating ever administered in Super Bowl history, and it was Denver's third Super Bowl defeat in four years on football's grandest stage.

On the plane, Elway sat quietly beside his wife, Janet. "I was sitting across the aisle from John and Janet," KOA radio's Larry Zimmer said. "He didn't want to talk to anybody. He was keenly disappointed. In a way, I think John thought that might be his last shot. I don't think he ever thought that eight years later he'd have the trophy in his hands."

We know, of course, that it wasn't Elway's last shot, but at the time, the loss to the 49ers, combined with the previous two Super Bowl defeats, took quite a toll.

"When you're a player, you wake up and it's like climbing all the way up a fourteener and getting to 13,999 feet and not getting there [then] going all the way back down and you've got to start at the bottom again," said Mecklenburg, who was a part of all three Elway-quarterbacked Super Bowl losses.

First off, let's give the Broncos their due. During the 1980s, no AFC team played in more Super Bowls than the Broncos. From 1983 to 1989, the Broncos had the best record in the AFC (73–37–1). During that seven-year period, Cleveland was the only AFC team to match the Broncos' five playoff appearances, and Broncos and 49ers were the only teams in the NFL to avoid a losing season. "It was an exciting time," Clough said. "John was coming into his own and was beginning to develop a reputation as a comeback quarterback. It was a very exciting time."

Getting there the first time with Elway, in 1986, wasn't as much of a surprise as it was in 1977. The Broncos had gone 13–3 in 1984 and then 11–5 in 1985. "We knew it was possible," said linebacker Tom Jackson, whose last season was in 1986. "I don't think anybody was shocked that we were there. The expectations were that we had won on and off, we were starting to create an environment of winning, and this was something we fully embraced."

As good as the Broncos were against their AFC foes, they were no match for the NFC. The Broncos got caught in the middle of a 13-game Super Bowl winning streak for the NFC. Most of the NFC's 13 wins came by blowouts; just two of them were decided by fewer than 10 points. The average margin of victory during the streak was 20.8 points. For the Broncos, though, it's not much of a consolation that they weren't the only AFC team to get pummeled during those years. "To this day, it still bothers me," Mecklenburg said. "That's part of being a competitor. I'd like to say that it doesn't, but it does."

Each one was different and painful in unique ways.

In Super Bowl XXI, on January 25, 1987, the Broncos met the New York Giants at the Rose Bowl in Pasadena, California. The Giants came out victorious, 39–20, as Phil Simms put on one of the greatest performances ever by a quarterback in the Super Bowl. He completed 22 of his 25 passes—accuracy that had never before and has not since been matched in an NFL championship game—for 268 yards and three touchdowns.

Often forgotten is that the Broncos were the better team in the first half. Elway had a great first two quarters, leading the Broncos into scoring position on four of five possessions. Had the Broncos been able to score on a first-and-goal-from-the-1-yard-line situation, and had Rich Karlis not missed two field goals, the Broncos would have gone into halftime leading at least 16–9, maybe even

Wide receiver Vance Johnson is less than celebratory after catching the final touchdown of Super Bowl XXI, a crushing 39–20 loss to the New York Giants.
Photo courtesy of Getty Images

20–9. Karlis, who had been 16-for-17 on field goals inside 40 yards that season, before his two misses, was hard on himself after the game. Truth is, though, the Giants were simply overpowering after halftime. Simms completed all 10 of his second-half passes, two of them for touchdowns, as the Giants became the first team to score 30 points in a single half during the Super Bowl.

New York's 30-point scoring barrage stood as a Super Bowl record for, oh, about a year.

The Broncos returned to the Super Bowl the next season, taking on the Washington Redskins on January 31, 1988, at Jack Murphy Stadium in San Diego. Heavy favorites this time around, the Broncos dominated early. Elway threw a 56-yard touchdown to Ricky Nattiel on the Broncos' first offensive snap of the game. Karlis added a 24-yard field goal later in the first quarter, and Denver was well on its way with a 10–0 lead. Washington then scored 35 second-quarter points en route to a 42–10 demolition of Denver. It was stunning, not just because of the 35 points, but because of who produced those points.

Doug Williams, the first African American quarterback to start a Super Bowl, didn't become the team's starter until rallying them to a win in the regular-season finale. From 1983 to 1987, Williams' only significant experience came as a two-year starter in the United States Football League. By 1990, he would be out of football. Timmy Smith rushed for all of 126 yards during the 1987 regular season and never got in the end zone. In his entire career, which lasted just three seasons, he ran for 602 yards and three touchdowns. On this day, Williams threw for 340 yards and four touchdowns. Smith rushed for two touchdowns and 204 yards, a Super Bowl record that still stands.

Those two painful defeats were at the front of everyone's minds when, two years later, the Broncos made that trip to New Orleans to face the 49ers. "They were dominant in the AFC," Clough said of the Broncos, "but they played the Eagles and the Giants from the NFC here in Denver and got pretty soundly thrashed in both games—not necessarily by big scores, but they lost both games. So there was still a sense that the NFC was dominant over the AFC and the Broncos were being led off to the slaughter.

"Everybody knew they were going to get killed. They probably knew."

Joe Montana threw five touchdown passes, Jerry Rice caught three of them, and the 49ers added three rushing touchdowns in the 55–10 beatdown.

Together, it was a collection of devastating defeats that put the Broncos in dubious company with the Minnesota Vikings as the only two teams, at that time, to go 0–4 in the Super Bowl. "It was crushing," Mecklenburg said. "I know it's disappointing as a fan. I grew up in Minnesota. I was a Viking fan. I know it's disappointing, but the next day you wake up and as long as you didn't bet the house on it, you get over it."

Still, Mecklenburg hasn't totally gotten over those losses, and neither has Reeves.

"If you don't play your best, you know, you're going to get beat," Reeves said. "The thing that eats at me is that I don't feel like [in] any of those three games we played our best. To me that's the coach's responsibility to get his team to play as well as they can. Apparently I came up short, because we didn't play our best."

During the first 50 years of the Super Bowl era, San Francisco's 55 points were the most by one team, and the 49ers' 45-point margin of victory was also a record. The Broncos were the only team to allow a 30-point half—and they did it twice. Nobody in the first 50 Super Bowls topped Washington's 602 yards gained in Super Bowl XXII.

Mecklenburg will never forget the pain of those losses, but he also doesn't forget the fact that the Broncos were the AFC's best team for a number of years. "Those years were special years,"

Mecklenburg said. "Those guys I played with are still some of the best friends I've ever made in my life."

Running back Sammy Winder, who played in all three losses, still considers those Super Bowls as his greatest memories from his playing career. "They were very exciting because that's the ultimate dream for any professional football player, to play in a Super Bowl," Winder said. "That's what you work for, that's what you go to camp for and [lift weights] for and train for. It was very exciting. You're on top of the world then.

"It was [frustrating] at the time, but today I don't have any regrets because there are so many guys playing nine, 10, 11 years and never get a chance to play in the Super Bowl. I feel fortunate that I was able to play in three."

47 Jason Elam

Kickers don't get drafted very often, so when a team invests in one via a third-round pick, that guy needs to be special. For 15 years in Denver, from 1993 to 2007, Jason Elam was special.

Taken in the third round of the 1993 draft from the University of Hawaii, Elam played in all but four games during his time with the Broncos. In 2007, he passed Elway for the most games played in a Denver uniform, with 236. Elam connected on a sensational 99.5 percent of his extra points (601 of 604) and 80.6 percent of his field goals (395 of 490). He made countless game-winning kicks and put himself into the NFL record books on October 25, 1998, when he drilled a 63-yard field goal against the Jacksonville Jaguars. That tied the NFL record for the longest field goal, a mark first set by Tom Dempsey on November 8, 1970. "The 63-yarder was obviously a highlight for me," he said at his retirement press conference on March 31, 2010. "It was just so fun."

He holds the Broncos' career record for points (1,786—a staggering 1,044 more than anyone else) and owns just about every major kicking mark in team annals. "Trust your swing," he said in 2010. "Really that's all I try to do is I try to just not get too fast, not make things too quick and just keep the normal rhythm of my swing. Fortunately more times than not they went through."

After the 2007 season, the Broncos and Elam parted ways. He was 37 years old, and the Broncos could save money by going with a younger kicker. "They had a salary cap that they had to fit people under and it just didn't work out," Elam said. It was odd for Elam and for Broncos fans, but he signed with Atlanta and played two seasons with the Falcons.

Record Breaker

Just before halftime on December 8, 2013, the Broncos trailed the struggling Tennessee Titans 21–17 at home. With just three seconds on the clock, Broncos kicker Matt Prater put all of his power into his right leg as he booted the ball, which flew through the frigid air before barely slipping over the cross bar for an NFL-record 64-yard field goal.

"By that time, my foot was numb, so I couldn't really tell [if it would be good]," Prater said. "It was so cold. I knew I hit it pretty good but I wasn't sure with the cold and everything it was going to get there. I saw the ref's hands go up and I can't even explain what I felt after."

Prior to that kick, four others in NFL history had nailed 63-yarders, including Denver's Jason Elam. Prater's record-breaker caused the Broncos to rush the field in celebration as they went to intermission. Riding that momentum, they blasted the Titans in the second half for a 51–28 victory.

For Prater, it was the highlight of his exceptional seven-year run in Denver (2007–13). One of the best kickers in team history, his .829 field goal percentage is a Broncos record.

Elam retired among the NFL's all-time leaders in extra points made (675), field goals made (436), and total points scored (1,983). He signed a one-day contract with the Broncos in 2010 so he could retire with the team that drafted him. "It was very important," he said of retiring as a Bronco. "You can't spend 15 years with one organization and not feel a special thought."

"Jason was everything you want in a player, everything you'd want in a kicker," Bowlen said at the retirement press conference. "He's definitely going into the Ring of Fame. I think he is a Hall of Famer, but kickers getting into the Hall of Fame is nearly impossible."

In the spring of 2016, Elam was elected to the Ring of Fame, joining Jim Turner as the only full-time kickers to receive that honor.

48 Nasty Nalen

Offensive linemen, by nature, have a bit of nastiness to them. So you know that when a lineman is considered particularly dirty, he's earned it.

Players who went up against Tom Nalen didn't like the guy much. In a 2004 *Sports Illustrated* players' poll, Nalen was listed as one of the dirtiest players in the NFL. Those who played with Nalen, however, remember an intense and dominating competitor who was one of the best centers to play the game from 1995 to 2007. "He was nasty. He was fearless," former teammate Alfred Williams said. "He was a guy who could at times dominate his position."

Nalen was selected to the Pro Bowl five times—more than any other offensive lineman in team history—and was the anchor of the offensive line that helped the Broncos win back-to-back Super Bowls in 1997 and 1998. "Tommy, he wasn't the tallest guy," safety Steve Atwater said. "He was about 6'2" and strong as an ox. If he'd get a hold of you, nobody would get off the block. We needed him because in the middle there, with the zone blocking scheme, you've got to have a good center who can get things going after getting the ball to the quarterback. He was a great center and he was a big asset for us."

Nalen was a seventh-round draft choice of the Broncos in 1994 and began that season on the practice squad. By 1995, he cemented his place in the starting lineup. By the time injuries forced him to retire in 2008, he had spent 15 years with the team, playing 194 games and starting 188 of them. Elway is the only player in team history with more seasons or more starts as a Bronco and Elway and Elam were the only players to suit up in more games.

"Tommy Nalen was the heart and soul of that offensive line," Williams said. "We called him 'Nasty Nalen,' and he did everything to make sure that blocks were finished. He didn't talk much, still doesn't. But when you look at his impact on the Denver Broncos, you see 1,000-yard rushers show up year after year after year while he's blocking. After he leaves that kind of goes away." The Broncos had a 1,000-yard rusher in 11 of Nalen's 12 full seasons as a starter. From 2007 (when Nalen played five games in his last season) to 2015, the Broncos had just two 1,000-yard rushers.

Nalen was a part of the Broncos line that was famous for not talking to the media, and he embraced that part of the job. He actually surprised many fans in February 2012 by spending two days cohosting an afternoon sports talk show on 104.3 The Fan in Denver. During that time, he explained why he didn't talk much as a player. "That's my lunch hour," he said. "I just felt like it was a waste of time. I'm half naked trying to get dressed for practice and you guys stick the microphone in my face and I know you're going to use anything I say, so I just clammed up. I loved it that way."

In addition to their reticence, the Broncos line was infamous around the league for their zone blocking schemes, which included cut blocks. The cut blocks, aimed at defenders' legs, angered players around the league and earned the Broncos—and Nalen—a reputation for being dirty. "We all did what we needed to do for us to win," Sharpe said. "If that meant crack-backs, cut blocks, whatever it is we needed for us to be successful, that's what we're willing to do. Sometimes you have to do those things, even though it might not be popular or if it was looked at as being illegal, we're trying to win ballgames. If that gave us the best chance to win, that's what we're willing to do. The offensive linemen were the spearheads of that."

Nalen used those blocks, but it was his nasty demeanor on the field that led him to success, and it's why he is still regarded as

Best of the Big Guys

Throughout their history, the Broncos have often featured great offensive linemen. The group that blocked for John Elway and Co. during the end of his career may have been the best, but Elway's line early in his career was good, too. Center Billy Bryan, guards Keith Bishop and Paul Howard, and tackles Ken Lanier and Dave Studdard were mainstays on the Broncos line for several years, along with valuable backup Mark Cooper. In later years, Keith Kartz and Doug Widell got in the mix. Bishop was the best of the bunch, becoming one of the few to make multiple Pro Bowls (or all-star games). The Broncos' linemen with multiple all-star selections (through 2015):

5 — Tom Nalen (1997–2000, 2003)
4 — Ryan Clady (2009, 2011, 2012, 2014)
3 — Gary Zimmerman (1994–96)
2 — Keith Bishop (1986, 1987)
2 — Eldon Danenhauer (1962, 1965)*
2 — Jerry Sturm (1964, 1966)*

* AFL All-Star Game

perhaps the best center in team history. "He's definitely as good as I ever played with," Sharpe said. "He was a great technician. He knew how to get his body in the proper position to be the most effective. He was definitely as good as I ever played with."

Many believe Nalen belongs in the Pro Football Hall of Fame, but he won't lose sleep over that.

"I never think about it unless someone asks me," he said on The Fan. "It's not important to me. It doesn't define me. The team I played for knows how I played. It's not that important."

In 2013, Nalen was inducted into the Broncos' Ring of Fame, making him just the second offensive lineman (along with Gary Zimmerman) to receive that honor.

49 A Major League City

The land that is now the parking lot for the Broncos' stadium has gone through quite a few changes over the years. Prior to becoming a parking lot, it was—as most Broncos fans know—Mile High Stadium. Before that, the land was actually a city dump. And prior to that, there was an old spring on that land. "My grandfather, Lee Howsam, used to go there and club bullfrogs and sell the frogs to the Brown Palace [hotel] for frog legs," said Robert Howsam, who is the son of the late Bob Howsam, the first owner of the Broncos.

Denver has come a long way since those bullfrog-clubbin' days. The city has gone through a dramatic transformation over the years, and it has grown up significantly since the Broncos' arrival in 1960.

Before the Broncos arrived, Denver's only professional sports team was the Denver Bears baseball club, a minor league affiliate of the New York Yankees. At the time, Denver was a much simpler place, a city that very much lived up to its reputation as a cow town.

Sports fans who wanted to keep up with big-time pro sports had to do it through newspaper accounts or the occasional television or radio broadcast. Denverites loved their Bears, though. In 1949, a total of 463,039 fans watched the Bears play, setting a minor league attendance record. The Bears had the highest attendance in minor league baseball for about 10 years. The Bears, which were later renamed the Zephyrs, played in Denver through 1992. They served as a farm club for several franchises, including the Yankees, Pittsburgh Pirates, Minnesota Twins, Montreal Expos, and Milwaukee Brewers.

The arrival of the Broncos gave Denver its first major professional sports franchise, and over time the city would grow to be a thriving sports town.

The Denver Rockets (later renamed the Nuggets) arrived in 1967 with the birth of the American Basketball Association. Like the American Football League, the ABA later would be dissolved, while some of its members—including the Nuggets—joined the more established National Basketball Association. Professional hockey came to Denver when the Colorado Rockies joined the National Hockey League in 1976. The team lasted just six years, but Denver was awarded another NHL team in 1995 when the Quebec Nordiques move to town and changed their name to the Colorado Avalanche. Denver hit the Major League Baseball scene in 1993—more than 30 years later than the Howsams hoped—when the expansion Colorado Rockies joined the National League.

Looking around Denver today, one would hardly recognize the town of the early 1960s.

Denver is one of just 12 cities in the country with teams in all four major leagues—NFL, NBA, NHL, and Major League

Baseball. Of those 12, just eight also have a Major League Soccer franchise. Denver also has professional teams in indoor and outdoor lacrosse.

In addition to being home to a host of professional sports franchises, Denver also boasts a winning tradition. Beyond the Broncos' three Super Bowl victories, the Avalanche have won two Stanley Cup titles, the Rockies reached the 2007 World Series, and the Nuggets made the playoffs an annual trip from 2004 to 2013. Even the Colorado Rapids have a Major League Soccer title to their credit.

It's probably not a stretch to say that Denver wouldn't be one of the country's top sports cities without the Broncos paving the way. "Without a doubt," former Broncos safety Billy Thompson said. "Without even the slightest bit of hesitation, I would say yes on that one."

The Broncos, as well as the Bears before them, showed the nation that Denver's fans love their teams and will support them. Even today, while attendance may waver a bit with performance, fans are there. "They have this innate thing about their sports teams that they embrace," Thompson said of Denver fans.

Denver, in general, has become a prominent city in the United States. That is, in part, because of its sports teams, but Denver is also home to one of the country's busiest airports, it has exploded with entertainment and nightlife options, and it has hosted such prominent events as political conventions and Pope John Paul II's arrival in August 1993.

Could all of this be traced to the Broncos in some way?

"I don't want to say that there weren't other factors that contributed," Tom Jackson said. "But leaning toward that, the city just took on more of a big-city feel to it. It became nationally known. I'd like to think a lot of that had to do with the Denver Broncos and their success. National prominence came to Denver, Colorado, and I think a lot of it was driven by the attention drawn by the football team."

To learn more about Denver, visit denvergov.org or denver.org.

50 "Heaven" Moses

Judging Haven Moses by statistics alone wouldn't be fair.

In 10 seasons with the Broncos, from 1972 to 1981, he never once led the team in receiving. Yet for 10 years he was one of the most consistent receivers the team has ever had, and his knack for making big plays in the clutch is nearly unmatched in team annals. "Haven was so smooth," quarterback Charley Johnson said. "I called him 'Heaven.'"

A first-round draft pick of the Buffalo Bills in 1968, Moses was in the middle of his fifth season with Buffalo in 1972. Out in Denver, the Broncos had a second-year receiver named Dwight Harrison. Harrison had had a solid rookie season in 1971, but during the 1972 season, he had an altercation with defensive lineman Lyle Alzado and brought a weapon into the team's facility. Shortly after that, the Broncos sent Harrison to the Bills for Moses. Harrison wound up playing eight more seasons as a productive defensive back. Moses, meanwhile, made an impact immediately on the Broncos offense.

"He came in at a time when the flanker position needed an extra guy," said Johnson, who threw passes to Moses from 1972 to 1975. "He didn't turn out to be an extra guy. He turned out to be *the* guy. For a new guy, he caught on so fast."

Although he played in just eight games for the Broncos in 1972 after the trade, he had five touchdowns. The Broncos closed the year with back-to-back wins, during which Moses had a combined six catches for 106 yards and four touchdowns. That was just the start of his special career in Denver. "He was one of the best receivers that I played with," running back Floyd Little said. "He helped make the Broncos what they are."

Although he never did lead the Broncos in receiving, Moses is in select company in team history with those who compiled at least 300 catches (302) and at least 5,000 receiving yards (5,450). His 44 touchdown receptions tied a team record that has since been broken.

"Haven Moses, he can be put right up with the greatest receivers ever," said Craig Morton, Denver's quarterback from 1977 to

Bill Van Heusen

On the field, Bill Van Heusen was a key player for the Broncos for nine years, from 1968 to 1976. He joined the Broncos as a rookie free agent from Maryland in 1968 and became the team's starting punter—a job he held for his entire nine years with the Broncos—and a backup wide receiver. Through 2015, his 574 career punts were the second-most in team history (Tom Rouen had 641), and he still shared the team record for most punts in one game, with 12 against Cincinnati in 1968. His 41.7-yards-per-punt average ranks eighth in team history. On December 2, 1973, he booted a 78-yard punt, which was the longest in team history at the time and has been topped just once since then (Chris Norman had an 83-yarder in 1984). Van Heusen also proved to be a valuable receiver, catching 82 passes for 1,684 yards and 11 touchdowns. His 20.5-yards-per-catch average is still a team record.

For all the good Van Heusen did, his lasting impression on the Broncos came off the field. He was one of the ringleaders of "the Dirty Dozen," the group that rallied to get head coach John Ralston fired after the 1976 season. Although others were involved in that revolt, it is believed that Van Heusen was made the scapegoat by management. He was cut before the 1977 season and, at the age of 31, his career was over.

1982. "He could read defenses better than anybody—in the holes, getting into zones. He knew exactly where to be."

Moses was often at his best when the Broncos needed him most, which he proved during those final two games in 1972. In 1973, he had at least one touchdown in five of the team's seven wins. He caught at least one touchdown pass in six of the Broncos' nine wins in 1976. Moses had perhaps the best game of his career in the 1977 AFC Championship Game, catching five passes for 168 yards and two touchdowns. He then had his best season in 1979, with career highs in catches (54) and yards (943) as the Broncos got to the playoffs for the third season in a row.

Johnson had other weapons but always relied on Moses when he needed a big catch. "He was running a lot faster than it looked like," Johnson said. "He fooled everybody. Certainly one of the best, you bet. You just counted on him. He was a go-to guy a lot more than you would think."

When Morton arrived in 1977, he discovered the same thing, and fans called them the "M&M Connection."

Quarterbacks weren't the only people in Denver to appreciate Moses. The fans adored him, and Moses gave countless hours of his time to the community. After retirement, Moses became the director of development for the Denver Police Activities League. "What a wonderful person," Morton said. "He's the best person and he's also one of the best teammates."

In 1988, the Broncos inducted Moses into the Ring of Fame, fittingly in the same class as Morton.

51 Lionel Taylor

The Broncos were in the midst of a three-game Eastern road trip at the start of their inaugural season of 1960 when Lionel Taylor showed up to try out for the team.

At 6'2" and 215 pounds, Taylor became the first player from New Mexico Highlands University (NMHU) to play professional football in 1959 when he played linebacker for the NFL's Chicago Bears. Trying out with the AFL's Broncos, Taylor made the team as a defensive back. Almost as quickly as he signed his contract, Taylor was moved to receiver—and he never looked back. "First game, he caught five or six passes," safety Goose Gonsoulin said.

With six catches for 125 yards and a touchdown in his debut, Taylor became the star attraction the Broncos needed during their first season. The Broncos proved to be what Taylor needed, too. "I was in the NFL and I didn't think the AFL would make it, but I thought if I went over to the AFL and made a name for myself, I could come back to the NFL and make some money," Taylor told DenverBroncos.com. "As it turned out, it was the greatest thing that ever happened to me because I never went back to the NFL."

For seven seasons, from 1960 to 1966, Taylor was the best receiver in the AFL. In fact, he may have been the best in all of pro football. He caught 543 passes for 6,872 yards and 44 touchdowns. Every one of those numbers stood as team records until Shannon Sharpe and Rod Smith came along more than 30 years later.

"In practice we could tell he had great hands," Gonsoulin said.

Taylor led the AFL in receptions five times from 1960 to 1965 and posted four 1,100-yard seasons. In 1960, he caught 12 touchdown passes, which remained the team's single-season record for 21 years.

For a first-year team that lacked talent, Taylor was a welcomed addition to the squad, and for several seasons he and quarterback Frank Tripucka formed a lethal duo. It wasn't just great hands that made Taylor a star, though. He was a multisport athlete growing up in West Virginia and carried that into his career at NMHU, where he was a three-time letterman in basketball. It showed during his time in Denver. "Lionel had the moves more like a basketball player than a football player," Gonsoulin said. "He was good at getting open quickly. He would slide, and if you threw the ball close to him, he could get it. He had real strong hands and he could catch real good."

For his accomplishments in high school, Taylor was inducted into the West Virginia Sports Hall of Fame. He is also in the NMHU Hall of Honor and, in 1970, was inducted into the Colorado Sports Hall of Fame. In 1984, he was part of the inaugural class for the Broncos' Ring of Fame. Taylor was traded to Oakland in 1967 but never played for the Raiders. He played two more seasons, with minimal success, with the Houston Oilers. After his playing days, Taylor went on to a successful coaching career and was on Super Bowl–winning staffs with the Pittsburgh Steelers. He now lives in Albuquerque, New Mexico.

Since Taylor left, the Broncos have had many great receivers, but through 2015, he still ranked third in team history in career receptions and career yards and was tied for fifth in touchdown receptions. "We needed some help on offense at that time, and Lionel fit the bill," Gonsoulin said. "Lionel had that natural talent for catching the ball. Thank goodness we got him."

52 Raider Week

It doesn't matter if the Broncos are Super Bowl contenders or AFC doormats. When the Oakland Raiders are the next team on the schedule, a newfound passion flows through the fans and players.

"I put a checkmark by it," said former Broncos safety Billy Thompson, who faced the Raiders 27 times during his 13-year career. "It was one of those kinds of games. The Raiders were the bad boys. They were the bullies. And they were very vocal about it. That was a team you wanted to shut up."

There are years when the Broncos' other AFC West division rivals—the Kansas City Chiefs, San Diego Chargers and, for a number of years, the Seattle Seahawks—were the cream of the divisional crop, and those games have been known to rile up the fans. When it's "Raider Week," however, everybody knows it. The fans get a little more juiced, and the players do, too.

"Boy, I tell you, we got ready for that game," former running back Floyd Little said. "We hated the Raiders. Everybody would try to get ready to play in that game because that was a game we had to win."

For years, it wasn't much of a rivalry. From 1965 to 1971, the Raiders won all 14 meetings. It was during that time, however, that the Raiders began building their reputation as the bad boys of professional football. The Broncos, more than most teams, saw that up close and personal. "I don't know if they had bounties on us, because they tried to get you out of the game," Little said. "There's no question in my mind there was some incentive to get me out of the game. One time I got hit so hard that my shoe came off. [Raiders safety] Jack Tatum saw me going off the field and he was jubilant to see me going off. I just went to get my shoe and came back, and he was like, 'Damn, he's back.' You just had a feeling that there was some sort of incentive to keep me out of the game."

Since the mid-1960s, the Raiders have embodied the spirit of their longtime owner Al Davis. A pioneer in the American Football League, Davis, who passed away in 2011, was a hated man by Broncos fans, some of whom call him "Darth Raider"—or worse. Davis, however, was respected by many Broncos players because he ultimately had one objective. "I mean it with respect that there was nobody that tried harder than him to win every game," said Goose Gonsoulin, an original Bronco.

Gonsoulin and the Broncos saw that before Davis even became a Raider. Davis was an assistant coach with the Chargers from 1960 to 1962. During the AFL's inaugural season of 1960, Gonsoulin led the league with 11 interceptions. Late in that season, the Broncos played in Los Angeles against the Chargers. Davis always admired Gonsoulin, but Gonsoulin didn't know Davis at the time.

AFC West Rivals

There's no question the Broncos' biggest rival over the years has been the Raiders, but they've had some heated affairs with the Kansas City Chiefs and San Diego Chargers as well. They also had some memorable games with the Seattle Seahawks, who were AFC West rivals from 1977 to 2001. Here's how the Broncos have stacked up against their AFC West foes (records through 2015):

- Kansas City Chiefs (formerly Dallas Texans): 54–57 in the regular season, 1–0 in the playoffs. Broncos are 35–21 at home against the Chiefs.
- Los Angeles/Oakland Raiders: 49–60–2 in the regular season, 1–1 in the playoffs. Broncos are 24–29–2 against them in Denver.
- Los Angeles/San Diego Chargers: 62–49–1 in the regular season. Broncos are 38–17–1 against them at home.
- Seattle Seahawks: 34–19 in the regular season, 0–2 in the postseason. Broncos were 32–17 against the Seahawks when they were division rivals and have a 21–5 record against them in Denver.

"After the game is over with, I go into the dressing room and this guy walks over and he hands me a piece of chalk," Gonsoulin said. "He said, 'How about you draw the hardest play for you to cover up there on the blackboard?' I thought, *That's kind of weird.* So, I got the chalk out and I started drawing something that was easy to cover, rather than hard. The general manger of the Broncos, Dean Griffing, walks over and says, 'Al, get your ass out of here!'"

Davis wasn't always so bold, but he was always relentless in his pursuit of victory, and so were his players. Davis joined the Raiders as a coach in 1963 and became their owner in 1966. From that point on, the Raiders embraced Davis' attitude, and it always showed on the field. They are often the most penalized team in the NFL, frequently because of numerous personal foul calls.

"They were as predictable and obvious of a team as you'd ever want to meet," said Karl Mecklenburg, a Bronco from 1983 to 1994. "They would line up in a formation and there was one thing they were going to do. You knew it, they knew you knew it, and they didn't care. They just said, 'We're bigger, badder, and tougher than you and we're going to jam it down your throat.' That kind of challenge was exhilarating. I'd wake up on Sunday morning before the Raider game and it felt like Christmas morning as a kid."

The fans felt the same way and often took their passion to a new level during those games. "Our fans didn't like them; they didn't like us," Little said. "There were always fights in the stands when they would come to a game or we would go to a game. It was a rivalry unlike any in the National Football League, I think."

During Mecklenburg's years, the Broncos and Raiders took turns beating each other up. Of the 25 games they played during Mecklenburg's years, 14 were decided by a field goal or less.

From John Madden and Ken Stabler to Lester Hayes, Jack Tatum, and Steve Wisniewski, the Raiders have always had players with the ability to crawl under the skin of the Broncos. And often it wasn't just one player—it was the whole group.

"They were dirty," Little said. "They tried to hurt you. They were more physical than any team we played, so it made us physical and took us out of our element. We were trying to play at their level of being tough and being dirty. So many penalties are hidden after the play. They still today are the same old Raider team."

53 Smooth Smitty

You know those people at the office who show up every day, don't say much, and always get their work done? Paul Smith was that guy for the Broncos. From 1968 to 1978, he was a quiet standout on the defensive line.

"One of the few guys that I think never got credit for what he had done," said Thompson, who played with Smith from 1969 to 1978. "Paul was the quiet one that didn't say much but just did it on the field. He didn't ask for anything. He just played. But one of the greatest linemen we've had, and nobody even knows about him."

Smith came in quietly, as a ninth-round draft choice from the University of New Mexico in 1968. The Broncos pegged him as a linebacker, but he quickly proved to be a better fit on the defensive line, where he played in college. He earned his way into the starting lineup on a part-time basis as a rookie. With great feet and exceptional quickness, not to mention toughness, the 6'3", 255-pound Smith became a regular in the lineup. Smith registered at least 10½ sacks four straight years from 1970 to 1973, with a high of 12 in 1971. He finished his career with 55½ sacks. Although injuries hampered him late in his career, he was a force whenever he got on the field. "If you go back and look at the linemen during his time, he was always in the top of whatever it was—whether it be tackles, whether it be sacks," Thompson said. "He factored. He wasn't just there. He made an impact. Always came ready, always played hard, always gave you everything he had."

Known by his teammates as "Smooth Smitty," Smith was the first to play 10 years for the Broncos, and he helped lay the foundation for the Orange Crush defense. As Smith got older, the Broncos added several young players, including Rubin Carter, Barney Chavous, Tom Jackson, Randy Gradishar, and Louis Wright, who would all become significant members of the Orange Crush. "There were certain guys that when I got there—Smooth Smitty, Lyle Alzado, Pete Duranko—guys who embodied the right spirit of how to play defense and had done it in the midst of losing for a long time and still maintained that," said Jackson, who was drafted in 1973. "That was the thing that struck me about those guys. They didn't allow the losing to in any way undercut the things they were as football players. So when we came in, even though they hadn't won, there was a foundation to build on."

Smith, who finished his career with two seasons in Washington, was elected to the Broncos' Ring of Fame in 1986. He passed away from pancreatic cancer in 2000.

54 Jim Turner

Jim Turner was one of the finest kickers in professional football during the 1960s and 1970s. Following seven great seasons with the New York Jets, Turner was traded to the Broncos in 1971. Never missing a game, he kicked for the Broncos for nine seasons, drilling 151 field goals.

It is a play in which Turner didn't kick the ball, however, that may be his most memorable.

On October 16, 1977, the Broncos were in Oakland to play the hated Raiders. Denver had a good team, bringing a 4–0 record into the game. But this was the Raiders. Oakland was also 4–0 and the reigning Super Bowl champion. In fact, the Raiders had won 17 straight games dating back to the previous season. They had won the AFC West division five years in a row. They also owned the Broncos, going 24–2–2 against them from 1963 to 1976. This day, however, belonged to Turner and the Broncos.

Denver already led 14–7 when they lined up for a second-quarter field goal. Turner was set to boot a 42-yard kick that would have put the Broncos up by 10. Instead, the Broncos stunned the Raiders. Backup quarterback Norris Weese was the holder on the play. After receiving the snap, he kept the ball and rolled to his right. Turner ran to the left. Weese set his feet, looked to the left, and lobbed the ball to Turner, who caught it near the 15-yard line and jogged into the end zone untouched for a touchdown.

"It's football's ultimate surprise play," Turner told the *Colorado Springs Gazette-Trail* after the game. "Every team has it in their playbook, but you never see it. Teams don't like to put their kickers in that position, where they're susceptible to injury. You see, defenses don't care much for kickers who try to do anything but kick. So the play is used only once in a...well, I've never seen it before, and this is the first time in my 14-year career that I've tried it. It was just logical that it would work. Realistically now, who's going to cover me, a 36-year-old kicker who still wears high-topped shoes?"

As memorable as that play was, it wasn't the reason Turner became a member of the Broncos' Ring of Fame in 1988. Until Jason Elam came along in the 1990s and 2000s, Turner held team records for career points (742) and career field goals made (151).

A quarterback at Utah State University, Turner had himself a whale of a pro career as a kicker. Between his time as a Jet and his time as a Bronco, he kicked 304 field goals and scored 1,439 points. At the time of his retirement, he ranked second in pro football history in both categories. Turner's career included a

Standout Punters

During their history, the Broncos have had some very good punters come through town, including a pair of Pro Bowlers. Some of the best:

Jim Fraser (1962–64): The only Broncos punter to earn All-Star honors more than once, he made the AFL All-Star game in 1962, 1963, and 1964. He had a career gross average of 44.1 yards per punt, ranking among the best in team history. He also had two of the five punts of 75-plus yards in team history.

Tom Rouen (1993–2002): He never achieved Pro Bowl recognition but averaged 43.9 yards on a team-record 641 punts. In four different seasons, he averaged at least 45 yards per punt.

Britton Colquitt (2010–present): Through 2015, he was still playing and carving out perhaps the best career of any Broncos punter. He was the team's career leader in gross average (45.2) and net average (39.2). He also held single-season team records in both categories.

Bob Scarpitto (1962–67): He served as the team's punter for just three years (1965–67), but his 44.3 career average was third in team history and he made the AFL All-Star game in 1966. Also a receiver during his seasons in Denver, he caught 145 passes for 2,439 yards and 24 touchdowns.

Mike Horan (1986–92): A Pro Bowler in 1988, Horan's 42.5-yard career average is sixth in team history through 2015. He also had several of the top single-season and single-game performances.

Luke Prestridge (1979–83): The first Bronco punter to go to the NFL's Pro Bowl, in 1982, Prestridge averaged 41.8 yards per punt for his career and tied the team record with 12 punts in one game.

Super Bowl championship with the Jets in 1968 and a Super Bowl runner-up finish with the Broncos in 1977.

After retirement, Turner became an academic tutor at Denver's Jefferson High School and was active in the NFL's Play It Smart program. Longtime Broncos fans will never forget Turner's contributions to their winning teams in the 1970s. And few will forget the play that helped the Broncos clobber the hated Raiders in 1977. "He left no doubt as to who the slowest player on the team was on that play," former Broncos quarterback Craig Morton once said. "But he got into the end zone."

55 To Do: Coors Brewery

Few things go better with football than beer, and Colorado is legendary for its beer.

Since 1873, Coors has been brewed in Golden, Colorado, located just west of Denver. Adolph Coors was born in Germany and it was there that he learned the art of brewing. He later immigrated to the United States and sought to own a brewery. Seeking the best water to use for his beer, he made his way to Golden. He opened up a brewery, utilizing the cold spring waters of the Rocky Mountains.

Coors made it through prohibition and the Great Depression and in the 1950s developed the first all-aluminum can in the United States. That changed how beverages were packaged, as it eliminated the taste of steel in the drinks. To this day, Coors claims to remain true to its formula from 1873. Not only does it still use the cold Rocky Mountain water, it features high-country barley that is farmed just a few miles away.

Free tours of the brewery are available during business hours for those interested in learning more about the brewing and packing process of Coors beer. At the end of the tour, those who are at least 21 years old are allowed to sample Coors products. For information on the tour, call (800) 642-6116 or visit millercoors.com.

Even if you're not a fan of Coors, Colorado is the place to be for beer drinkers. It is home to dozens of breweries, including the Anheuser-Busch facility in Fort Collins, less than an hour from Denver.

In addition, downtown Denver features several microbreweries, including the Wynkoop Brewing Co., which is a popular brewpub in town. Another popular destination right in the heart of Denver is the Chop House and Brewery, where many of the Broncos went to celebrate their Super Bowl victory in 1998.

56 Happy Returns

From 1975 to 1983, Rick Upchurch was not only one of the most popular players in Denver, he was one of the best punt returners the National Football League had ever seen.

A 5'10", 175-pound receiver from the University of Minnesota, Upchurch was an electrifying player who still holds many of the Broncos' punt-return records. During his career, he had 3,008 yards on 248 returns, taking eight of them back for touchdowns. At the time, no player in NFL history had more punt returns for touchdowns, and going into 2016 he still ranked in the top four. "He was awesome," said Dan Reeves, who coached Upchurch from 1981 to 1983. "I've had some pretty good returners, but without question Rick Upchurch was the best. He had eyes in the back of his head. He made moves and did things you didn't teach. You don't teach somebody to have the skills that he had."

Upchurch had four touchdown returns in 1976 alone—still tied for the NFL single-season record—and was selected to the Pro Bowl four times during his career. "He's the greatest punt returner ever," Morton said. "When he wanted to really do it, he was amazing."

Billy Thompson held most of Denver's punt-return records until Upchurch came along, and even he admits that Upchurch was "very explosive."

"He was exciting. I enjoyed watching him," Thompson said.

Although most prolific on punt returns, Upchurch was also exceptional on kickoff returns. He was the Broncos' primary kick returner for just three seasons (1975–77) yet still ranks among the team's all-time leaders in kickoff-return yards, with 2,355. He had 1,084 of those in 1975, one of only two players to hit the 1,000-yard mark during the Broncos' first 35 seasons. Upchurch's play on special teams alone made him one of the team's all-time best players, but he was more than a returner.

In his first game as a pro, he had 153 receiving yards, 90 of those on a touchdown pass from Charley Johnson. He also had 118 return yards that day, giving him one of the best debut performances in team history. During his career, he caught 267 passes for 4,369 yards and 24 touchdowns. He had his best year in 1979, catching 64 passes for 937 yards and seven scores. In 1983, he became the first player to catch a pass from John Elway. "He was just a great return guy, and therefore he became a valuable receiver for us because you knew if you [got] him the ball in his hands he was going to make some catches," Reeves said.

Another claim to fame for Upchurch is that he once dated Condoleezza Rice, who was an undergraduate student at the University of Denver before becoming U.S. Secretary of State years later.

Despite all of the flash that came with Upchurch, for years, he was viewed as the best Bronco not included in the Ring of Fame. How was Upchurch overlooked for that honor?

"I think the problems he had off the field...kept him from getting that kind of recognition, because he was a great player," Reeves said. "He could have been a greater player and a better player if he hadn't had the problems he had off the field."

During his career, Upchurch battled marijuana use. He even spent 28 days in a Minnesota rehabilitation center during the summer of 1983. "I'm clean," he said after his stay and after a meeting with Reeves. "They evaluated me and said I was clean as a hound's tooth. The Broncos have been behind me 100 percent and are continuing to help, giving me drug-screening tests every week...."

Darrien Gordon

Had Darrien Gordon stayed in Denver long, he might have set every punt-return record in team history. Signed as a free agent in 1997, his two seasons as a Bronco were electrifying. He averaged a team-record 12.46 yards on punt returns and took three to the end zone for touchdowns in 1997. Those three were the second-best single-season totals in team history, and Rick Upchurch is the only Bronco with more career punt-return TDs. Gordon and Upchurch are also the only two Broncos to ever return two for TDs in the same game. On defense, he was just as valuable, starting all 39 games (including playoffs) at cornerback for the two-time Super Bowl champs. In those two seasons, Gordon intercepted eight passes, returning two for touchdowns during the regular season. In seven postseason games, he averaged 14.7 yards on punt returns and picked off five passes (a team postseason record). He had two interceptions in the 1998 AFC Championship Game and then two more in the Super Bowl two weeks later. Gordon left for Oakland after the season and played four more years. His 3,601 career punt-return yards rank among the all-time best in NFL history.

He said at the time that he used marijuana socially and to help him sleep after games. He said giving it up wouldn't be easy. "It's going to be tough, I admit, because marijuana was something I enjoyed."

Although the Broncos stood behind their star, there was controversy later that week, during training camp, when an article in the *Denver Post* quoted Upchurch as saying, "I'm not saying I haven't or won't touch any more of it. As long as I don't do it on the football field or in public or distribute it, I think it's all right."

The Broncos publicly stated at the time that Upchurch's comments could damage his future with the team. Upchurch denied those statements and wound up staying with the team. Despite that controversy, Reeves had nothing but praise for a player widely regarded as one of the most exciting to ever wear a Broncos uniform. "I had some situations where I had to stay on top of him and keep my eye on him and make sure we tested him and make sure he knew we were going to have him walk a straight line, but he did a good job for me," Reeves said.

Upchurch retired in the summer of 1984 because of nerve damage in his neck. Although he had the condition for years—in fact, Purdue and Iowa both passed on him because of it—he played for many seasons. In 1984, though, Upchurch told the media, "My doctors and the Broncos' doctors are in agreement—it's too dangerous for me to continue playing. I won't be going to any other team. It's time to go, time to move on."

Following retirement, Upchurch, who is married with four children, got into a career in coaching. He coached at Tabor College in Kansas for a while and in 2005 became the head coach at Pueblo East High School in southern Colorado.

Finally, in 2014, Upchurch was inducted into the Ring of Fame—along with Reeves and Gene Mingo.

"It's an honor to be up there with all the other guys that are up there already," he said. "To look back and feel slighted and all of that stuff, I really didn't feel that way or look at it. I often looked at statistics and wondered why it took so long for me to get there…but once again, I don't have control of that. I'm glad that this particular time they chose myself to go in with Dan and with Gene Mingo."

57 The Go-To Guy

Two years into his NFL career, Steve Watson hardly had the look of a Pro Bowl player.

A free agent from Temple, he caught six passes for 83 yards as a rookie in 1979. In 1980, he caught six more passes, for 146 yards. The 6'4" 195-pounder spent much of that time watching Rick Upchurch, Haven Moses, and Riley Odoms catch the majority of the team's passes. Even then, however, Broncos quarterback Craig Morton saw something special. "I remember Steve Watson when he was a rookie," Morton said. "Fran Polsfoot was our receivers coach and Steve Watson was this big ol' white guy that could run and just kind of hung around Haven. He was like Haven's shadow. I said, 'Fran, whatever you do, you've got to keep this kid because he's going to be great.' I'd say that to him every day. And he was."

In 1981, the Broncos brought in a new coach, Dan Reeves, and Watson's career took off. Watson caught 60 passes for a career-best 1,244 yards and 13 touchdowns that season, with most of those passes coming from Morton. He made the Pro Bowl that year. "Steve was a free agent, and I kind of always had a feeling for free agents because I was one myself," Reeves said. "Steve did exactly what the free agent is supposed to do: he came in there and made the best of his opportunity and continued to get better."

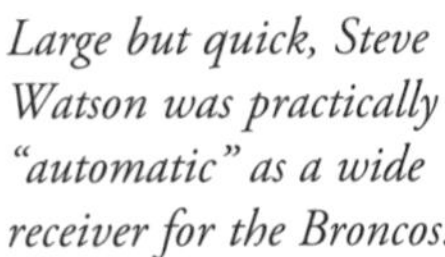
Large but quick, Steve Watson was practically "automatic" as a wide receiver for the Broncos.

The 1981 season was the only year in which Morton was able to utilize Watson as a primary weapon, but Watson had the full trust of his veteran quarterback. "He wasn't afraid to try little things," Morton said. "I would always make sure he was the guy because he was so tall. I'd tell him, 'Be 30 yards on the markers and I'll throw the ball there and be there and we'll get it.' He was there and he got it."

From 1981 to 1986, Watson was Denver's top receiver, catching 330 passes for 5,716 yards and 35 touchdowns during those six seasons. Three times he finished with more than 1,000 yards. "He and Craig Morton originally had that great rapport with each other, and he had a super year my rookie year," Reeves said. "When John [Elway] came in, he became John's go-to guy."

He was certainly a go-to guy for Elway during the 1986 AFC Championship Game in Cleveland. Watson had a big 12-yard catch during the Drive that tied the game at the end of regulation and then had a 28-yard catch in overtime that set up Rich Karlis' game-winning field goal.

Watson finished his nine-year career with 353 catches for 6,112 yards and 36 touchdowns, ranking among the top 10 players in Broncos history in all three categories. "He was a big target, great hands, very knowledgeable," Reeves said. "He ran great routes and was just a tremendous competitor. He was not afraid to catch the ball over the middle. He was a tough guy. He blocked as well as anybody I've ever seen. He was just a smart, tough receiver."

Watson later became an assistant coach with the Broncos, working under Mike Shanahan for eight seasons, from 2001 to 2008.

58 To Do: Fourteeners

If being a mile above sea level isn't enough elevation for you, don't worry. Colorado is home to 53 mountain peaks that rise above 14,000 feet.

From Sunshine Peak, at 14,001 feet above sea level, to Mt. Elbert at 14,433, Colorado's fourteeners are popular destinations for climbers, hikers, and outdoors enthusiasts. Located throughout the Colorado Rocky Mountains, the fourteeners are convenient for those living in various parts of the state.

The Sawatch Range, just a couple of hours west of Denver and Colorado Springs, is home to many of the peaks, boasting 15 of them, including Mt. Elbert. The most famous of the fourteeners is Pikes Peak, located about 10 miles west of Colorado Springs and visible from Denver on a clear day. Named for Zebulon Pike, a U.S. solider and explorer, Pikes Peak is among the top tourist attractions in Colorado. The summit can be reached by foot, vehicle, or railway.

Another popular peak along the Front Range is Mount Evans. It features the highest paved road in North America and offers tourists some of the majestic views in the state. The Mount

Evans byway is open from Memorial Day to Labor Day. It was named for John Evans, who was the second territorial governor of Colorado. He also founded Evanston, Illinois, and the University of Denver.

Because it ranks at the top of the list in terms of elevation, Mt. Elbert is often a crowded place on the weekends, but it's worth the trek. Named in 1873 for Samuel Elbert, who was a territorial governor of Colorado and the son-in-law of Evans, the peak had its first recorded summit by H.W. Stuckle in 1874. The near-two-hour drive to Mt. Elbert from Denver is enjoyable in itself. Once there, Mt. Elbert is a nine-mile climb from the trailhead to the summit. In those nine miles, there's a whopping 4,700-foot elevation gain. Although those numbers may seem daunting, Mt. Elbert is one of the easiest of the peaks to ascend.

North Maroon Peak may be the most difficult of the fourteeners to ascend. It features 12 miles and a 4,800-foot elevation gain over much more difficult terrain than that of Mt. Elbert.

Grays Peak and Torreys Peak, located near each other, are also among the easier fourteeners to climb, and at approximately 50 miles from Denver, they're also some of the easiest to get to. The peaks were named in 1872 for two famous botanists, Asa Gray and John Torrey. The peaks have been referred to as "the Ant Hills" by local Indians and "Twin Peaks" by 19th-century miners.

While climbing 14,000-foot mountain peaks may not be for everyone, the sites of many of the peaks feature camping options, as well as other outdoor activities nearby. For information on any of the peaks, including how to get there, how to prepare for your trip, and statistical information, visit 14ers.com.

59 Eddie Mac

No. 87 has been a special number in Broncos history.

Receiver Lionel Taylor became the Broncos' first big star, and he did so while wearing 87. Fittingly, he was traded for defensive end Rich "Tombstone" Jackson, who did the number justice in another way. Taylor and Jackson are both Ring of Famers.

Living up to those standards isn't easy, but Ed McCaffrey did it with class. A Broncos receiver from 1995 to 2003, he is still one of the most popular players in recent Broncos history.

"In the last 20 years that I have had the honor of owning this football club, he is going to be remembered by me, and I think by most of the fans and the people here, as the bravest and the most courageous player to play for the team," owner Pat Bowlen said at McCaffrey's retirement press conference on March 2, 2004. "I know that it'll probably be a long time before we get another player—another wide receiver—like Eddie Mac who will do the things that he did to take this team to championships."

During the latter part of Elway's career, McCaffrey was one of his most trusted receivers, catching a combined 109 passes for 1,643 yards and 18 touchdowns during the Super Bowl–championship seasons of 1997 and 1998.

McCaffrey, who starred at Stanford University, was a third-round pick of the Giants in 1991 and had three solid seasons with them before hooking on with San Francisco in 1994, where Mike Shanahan was an assistant coach. Although McCaffrey had never been a starter, when Shanahan took Denver's head coaching job in 1995, one of his first free-agent signees was McCaffrey. "My contract was up and I didn't have much game film for coaches to evaluate," McCaffrey told DenverBroncos.com. "Luckily, as fate

Ed McCaffrey does what he does best, laying himself out across the middle for hard-earned yardage. Photo courtesy of Getty Images

would have it, Coach Shanahan saw me battling Deion Sanders every day in practice and thought enough of me to bring me with him to Denver when he was named head coach. The rest is pretty much a dream come true."

In nine seasons with the Broncos, he caught 462 passes for 6,200 yards and 46 touchdowns. All of those numbers ranked among the top five in Broncos history at the time of McCaffrey's retirement.

McCaffrey had his best season in 2000, when he caught 101 passes for 1,317 yards and nine touchdowns. He broke the team record of 100 set by Taylor, of course. That mark has been tied or broken four times since. Also during that season, he and Rod Smith became just the second set of teammates to reach the 100-catch mark in the same season. He was looking for another great season in 2001 when disaster struck in the opener. Playing the New York Giants on *Monday Night Football*, McCaffrey broke his leg. It was a gruesome injury that ended his season.

In typical Eddie Mac fashion, he came back and had another great year in 2002. Throughout his tenure in Denver, McCaffrey was known for his toughness. He took hit after hit after hit because of his willingness to go across the middle. He also delivered big hits as one of the best blocking receivers in the league. "This sport is tough," he said upon his retirement. "People are tearing muscles, breaking bones, and getting knocked out every week. That's never kept me from playing, and that's not the reason I'm retiring. It's part of the reason. I like being healthy, I like my health. I feel very accomplished. I feel I've had a very rewarding career.

"I've taken a beating, but I would never retire just for that reason, because I would have never made it through one season if that were the case."

He not only made it through; he carried on the great tradition of the No. 87. In retirement, McCaffrey, his wife, Lisa—whose father was an Olympic sprinter—and four sons have continued to live in Colorado, and McCaffrey stays active in football through various camps he runs. He also has a line of foods, including McCaffrey's Rocky Mountain Horseradish Sauce and various types of mustard, and can be seen in commercials for "Good Feet." In 2012, McCaffrey joined KOA radio as the color analyst for Broncos games, working alongside Dave Logan.

McCaffrey's oldest son, Max, went on to play receiver at Duke University. In 2015, his second son, Christian, was runner-up for the Heisman Trophy as a star running back and returner at Stanford.

60 One of a Kind

Muhammad Ali had plenty of epic fights during his illustrious boxing career. His bout at Denver's Mile High Stadium on July 14, 1979, wasn't among them, but it was certainly among the most *interesting* "fights" of his career.

Ali's opponent that day was a legendary figure, but certainly not the type of legend he was used to fighting. Instead of Joe Frazier or Sonny Liston, Ali's opponent in Denver was none other than Broncos defensive lineman Lyle Alzado. Although Ali's career was nearly over, he had won the heavyweight title just 10 months earlier against Leon Spinks. Alzado had been a Golden Gloves champ years earlier but wasn't exactly at Ali's level. "It was unbelievable," said Broncos Hall of Fame running back Floyd Little. "I didn't realize that Lyle was pretty good."

Alzado trained hard for the fight, although it really was just an exhibition. Alzado took the bout a little more seriously than Ali, which surprised Ali a bit. "We saw it and go, 'Lyle can't be serious!'" Billy Thompson said, recalling his first reaction to the fight. "It was a big publicity stunt. Then he hit Ali, and Ali responded after that."

Ali took care of Alzado, but Alzado hung in there. "Lyle went out there and did pretty good," said Little, who was in Alzado's corner for the fight. "I think he lost by two points. He stood toe to toe with Ali and did a good job."

That was the last performance Alzado ever had at Mile High Stadium as a Denver Bronco, but it certainly was a memorable one for a man who may be the most complex player the team has ever employed. "He was one of a kind," Thompson said.

Alzado was born in Brooklyn, New York, and went to tiny Yankton College in South Dakota. Yankton closed its doors in 1984, and Alzado was one of only four Greyhound players to ever reach the NFL. He was—at various times and sometimes at once—intense, braggadocios, driven, kindhearted, loyal, and charitable. For eight years, from 1971 to 1978, Alzado played with the Broncos, and his teammates saw all sides of him.

"He always wanted to be a superstar," Little said. "He used to ask me, 'What do I have to do to be an All-Pro player?' He was quite talented, but he always had an inferiority complex. He didn't ever think he was good enough."

Alzado, however, was a phenomenal player. He was among the Broncos' team leaders in tackles every year except 1976, when he was injured and played just one game. His 64.5 quarterback sacks were a team record when he left Denver and still rank him among the top handful of players in team history. Yet simply playing well wasn't enough for Alzado. A deep desire to become a star made him a larger-than-life figure during his 15 years in the National Football League. "He always wanted to be out there," Thompson said. "He wanted to be in lights."

A fourth-round draft choice of the Broncos in 1971, Alzado had to fight to make the team that season. He did, and he became

Costa Gains National Attention

Throughout his pro football career, Dave Costa played for four different teams and was a top-flight defensive lineman for all of them. From 1967 to 1971, he starred for the Broncos, making the AFL All-Star game three years in a row. He had 37½ sacks during that time. In 1969, the Broncos faced the defending Super Bowl–champion New York Jets at Mile High Stadium. During that game, Costa leveled Jets quarterback Joe Namath. A photo of that hit shows a grimacing Namath flying to the ground and Costa towering over him. *Life* magazine named it the Sports Photo of the Year in 1969.

a popular teammate; he was also well known around Denver for his charity work. Street-smart and book smart, Alzado obtained a degree in special education. In Denver, he spent countless hours and dollars helping others. In 1976, he was given the NFL Players Association's Byron "Whizzer" White NFL Man of the Year Award.

As a teammate, he was intensely loyal. "Great guy, big heart," Thompson said. "He gave you everything he had. He'd give you the shirt off his back."

In many ways, Alzado achieved his dreams. He became an NFL star and dominated opponents for 15 years. Following his eight years in Denver, he played three years in Cleveland and four more with the Los Angeles Raiders. Along the way, he helped many others through his kindness and charity. He even got to Hollywood, with several acting credits to his name.

Alzado's life story, however, has a tragic conclusion. In 1969, when Alzado was still at Yankton, he began using steroids and continued to do so throughout his NFL career—including his eight years in Denver—and after his retirement. Thompson said he never knew but in hindsight probably should have. "During the time Lyle was here, I never saw him do that," Thompson said. "All I knew was that he was very emotional all the time. That was probably the reason."

The more Alzado used steroids, the more he changed, Little said. "He became a changed person when he wound up in [Los Angeles]," Little said. "He was even different when they traded him to Cleveland."

In 1991, at the age of 42, Alzado was diagnosed with brain cancer. It was caused, he believed, by his years of steroid abuse, although doctors at the time said there was no proof of that. "Everyone knows me as a tough, tough guy," he wrote in a *Sports Illustrated* piece months after his diagnosis. "And I've never been afraid of anything. Not any human, not anything. Then I woke up in the hospital last March and they told me, 'You have cancer.' Cancer. I couldn't understand it. All I knew was that I was just so weak. I went through all those wars on the football field. I was so muscular. I was a giant. Now I'm sick. And I'm scared."

Alzado's health deteriorated rapidly. He was a mammoth, 6'3" and 275 pounds, as a player but dropped to less than 200 pounds before dying of pneumonia on May 14, 1992. "The last time I saw him…I didn't recognize him," Thompson said. "He was a shadow of himself. When I saw him, it shocked me."

Alzado's death was a wake-up call for many players who were using steroids, and it hit close to home for those who played with him in Denver. Yet nobody who knew him in Denver will ever forget him. He was a fantastic player, but nobody ever knew what he'd do next. Typical of Alzado, it was that fight against Ali that led him out of Denver. Just weeks after the bout, he was in training camp with the Broncos. Alzado had a great relationship with the team's public-relations guru, Jim Saccomano, in part because the two cohosted a radio show together. So during camp in 1979, Alzado confided in Saccomano, telling him he felt he could pursue a boxing career. Finally, Alzado told Saccomano one day that he had decided to leave football for boxing.

Within a few days, the Broncos traded Alzado to Cleveland. He never did get into boxing.

61 Disaster in Denver

The Broncos were Super Bowl champions in 1997 and 1998, and when asked which team was better, defensive end Alfred Williams didn't hesitate with his answer.

"The [1996] team that got beat by the Jacksonville Jaguars the year before," he said. "You look at the talent that we had on that team, that team was a great team that got caught being flippant and was enjoying everything too much."

The Broncos were every bit as good in 1996 as they were in 1997 and 1998. Had it not been for a stunning 30–27 loss to Jacksonville in the playoffs that year, the Broncos might have been the only team in NFL history to win three straight Super Bowls. Denver finished the regular season at 13–3, with two of the losses coming after a 12–1 start that clinched home-field advantage throughout the AFC playoffs. To some, that was a ticket to the Super Bowl, considering the Broncos were 8–0 at Mile High Stadium that year and 8–1 in home playoff games during their history, to that point. After a first-round bye, the Broncos hosted the Jacksonville Jaguars in the divisional playoffs on January 4, 1997. Jacksonville was in its second year of existence, went 9–7 in the regular season, and upset Buffalo in the wild-card round the week before. With the No. 1 offense in the NFL and the No. 4 defense, the Broncos were 14-point favorites. The only question was whether the New England Patriots or Pittsburgh Steelers would be coming to Denver for the AFC Championship Game a week later.

Fifteen minutes into the game, the Broncos led 12–0 because of a pair of touchdowns. Then a not-so-funny thing happened on the way to the next round. Jaguars quarterback Mark Brunell, who led the NFL in passing yards, found a rhythm and began chipping away at the Denver lead, while the Broncos offense stalled time after time. The Jags got a field goal, forced a Broncos punt, and then marched 80 yards for a touchdown. After another Broncos punt, Jacksonville got the ball back with 57 seconds to go in the first half. A 44-yard pass from Brunell to Jimmy Smith set up a Mike Hollis field goal. The 75,678 fans at Mile High Stadium were stunned as the Broncos went into intermission trailing 13–12. The Broncos never led again. Brunell threw a third-quarter touchdown pass. Early in the fourth, Hollis booted his third field goal of the day for a 23–12 Jacksonville lead. Denver rallied, and when John Elway hit Ed McCaffrey with a 15-yard touchdown pass with 1:50 to play, the Broncos were within three points. The ensuing onside kick was recovered by Jacksonville, though, and the Jags ran out the clock.

"You just shake your head, shrug your shoulders, and understand that the team who was better prepared beat us," Williams said. "I don't know. I can't even explain how it happened. I've never gone back and looked at the game."

Aside from the Broncos' four Super Bowl losses, this was likely the most difficult defeat in team history. "It was by far the most painful loss I've ever experienced, and I lost a national championship game [at the University of Colorado]," Williams said.

After the game, some players said it would take a while to get over the loss. Fifteen years later, Williams said, "I don't know when that's going to happen, because it hasn't happened yet."

At least on the field, the Broncos recovered. They went 12–4 the next season and, in the first round of the playoffs, did what many thought they'd do in 1996, crushing the Jaguars 42–17. The Broncos went on to win their first Super Bowl. In 1998, they went 14–2—including a blowout win over Jacksonville—and won yet another Super Bowl.

The championships were celebrated and enjoyed, but that loss to the Jaguars on January 4, 1997, will forever be a thorn in the side of the Broncos who were on the field that day. "No, winning two Super Bowls in a row doesn't make up for that loss," Williams said. "The guys that were a part of this team will always remember this."

Romo

Bill Romanowski was one of those guys that people loved having on their side and hated having against them.

Romanowski was already a very good NFL linebacker by the time he signed with the Broncos in 1996. He had played six seasons in San Francisco and two in Philadelphia, establishing himself as a heavy hitter who shined through his intensity. It wasn't until he got to Denver that he became a lightning rod. "There, my stature grew, my salary increased, my game elevated, and my antics acquired a following they never before had," he wrote in his book, *Romo: My Life on the Edge*. "I fed off it."

So did the fans, who quickly embraced him as one of their favorite players. Including the playoffs, he played in 105 games as a Bronco from 1996 to 2001 and was in the starting lineup for every single one of them. In each of his six seasons, he was one of the team's top three tacklers. He also registered 23 quarterback sacks, 11 interceptions, and nine fumble recoveries as a Bronco. He made the Pro Bowl twice, in 1996 and 1998.

On top of his statistical contributions, Romo was an emotional leader that Denver's defense lacked before his arrival. "Romo was a great teammate," Williams said. "He really was. He was always looking to improve everybody around the facility and he wanted the new types of ways to look at everything. He brought a refreshing energy to the NFL while I was a part of the Denver Broncos. He wanted to know the best treatment, the best way to do every part of the job. He was intelligent, he was a great reactionary linebacker, but the thing that made him special was his competitiveness. I think that is the signature of Bill Romanowski: how competitive he was."

That competitiveness is what drives people to love him or despise him, and it has gotten him in trouble on the field. He was fined for a helmet-to-helmet hit that broke the jaw of Carolina Panthers quarterback Kerry Collins in 1997. Later in his career, he punched a Raiders teammate, tight end Marcus Williams, during a scrimmage, damaging Williams' eye socket and ending his career. In 1997, during a crucial game in San Francisco on *Monday Night Football*, Romanowski's fire gained national attention. Here's how he describes the scene in his book:

"At the bottom of the pile, I tried to rip the ball out of wide receiver J.J. Stokes' hands. I didn't get the ball, but I got his testicles in my hand, and I became a human nutcracker. I squeezed them and twisted them with all my anger. He jumped up, woofing: 'That's bullshit, Romanowski! That's dirty!' And for some reason, I was like, 'Who the hell are you?' And, without thinking, just spit in his face. *Splat!*"

No big deal, he thought, since spitting happened all the time. But the *MNF* cameras caught this one. It was a turning point, of sorts, for the Broncos. They were in the midst of a great season, but the 34–17 loss to the 49ers was their second straight humbling defeat, dropping them to 11–4 with one regular-season game to play. "It was an embarrassment for the team more than anything else," Williams said. "It's not the way you want to be known as a football club, as a team." It could have divided them, but the Broncos didn't let that happen. "We had a team meeting and we talked through it and Romo apologized and we moved on," Williams said. "It was that quick."

The Broncos pounded the Chargers 38–3 the next week and then went 4–0 in the playoffs to win their first Super Bowl—with Romo playing a key role along the way.

Off the field, Romo's fire was just as intense. He always strove to be the best he could be and did so by meticulously taking care of his body. He lived off of supplement pills and powders that he carried around in a tackle box. "Romo had the tackle box everywhere he went," Williams said.

His burning desire to find the latest and greatest supplements got him in some hot water when he was investigated for prescription- drug fraud. Eventually the charges were dropped. As much as fans loved him in Denver, Romanowski became Public Enemy No. 1 when he signed with the hated Raiders before the 2002 season. At the age of 36, he starred for the Raiders in 2002 and then kept

Dominating Defense for the Champs

Bill Romanowski was the most visible player in the Broncos' defensive front seven during their two Super Bowl runs. That group, however, was filled with standout players.

Linebacker John Mobley led the team in tackles both seasons, with 294 total in that time. Allen Aldridge and Glenn Cadrez also stood out at linebacker. On the defensive line, Neil Smith, Alfred Williams, and Maa Tanuvasa were three significant free-agent signings. Williams was a Pro Bowler in 1996 and Smith in 1997. Smith, a five-time Pro Bowler with Kansas City from 1988 to 1996, was a rock for that line.

The best of that group wound up being Trevor Pryce. Denver's first-round pick in 1997, he didn't play much that year but led the team with 8½ sacks in 1998. He then made four straight Pro Bowls from 1999 to 2002, and by the time the team let him go after 2005, he ranked sixth in team history with 64 sacks. Pryce signed with Baltimore and played five more good seasons in the NFL.

it going into the 2003 season until a concussion sidelined him after three games. Up to that point, he had never missed a game in his 16-year 243-game career, but after Week 3 of the 2003 season, he never played again.

63 To Do: Red Rocks

Thousands of fans, many of them teenage girls, tossed jelly beans on the stage and screamed with excitement during every song. The mop-topped boys from Britain wowed the crowd at Red Rocks Amphitheatre on August 26, 1964. It was the only stop on the Beatles' first tour of the United States that didn't sell out, yet that night kicked off a great tradition at the now-world-famous outdoor concert venue.

Although Red Rocks opened in the early 1900s, The Beatles' visit was the first rock 'n' roll performance of note at the venue located in Morrison, just minutes from Denver. It has since become quite famous for its rock 'n' roll shows. Jimi Hendrix, U2, Stevie Nicks, Neil Young, Tom Petty, the Grateful Dead, Willie Nelson, and many others have played memorable shows there. U2's June 5, 1983, show produced a top-selling live album titled *Under a Blood Red Sky*, along with a video that became a best seller.

For many of music's top acts, the remarkable natural acoustics at Red Rocks, an open-air amphitheatre featuring two 300-foot monoliths of sandstone, are considered to be second to none. And for many music lovers in Colorado, there's no better place to see a show, where the sounds are marvelous and the views majestic. "It makes your hair just stand up when you think about the artists who've been here," Erik Dyce, who has done marketing work for

Red Rocks for nearly a quarter century, said to the *Denver Post.* "This place is a temple. It's overwhelming when the venue overpowers the artist."

A truly unique venue, Red Rocks' official website claims the venue as "the only naturally occurring, acoustically perfect amphitheatre in the world."

Red Rocks is much more than just a concert venue, however. More than a million visitors each year enjoy the natural beauty of the area through hiking, biking, and other recreational activities.

64 Otis Armstrong

When Otis Armstrong was healthy, he was one of the best running backs ever to come through Denver. Problem was, good health and Armstrong rarely went hand in hand.

"Had he not had the injuries, he probably would have broken a lot more records," Billy Thompson said.

An All-American at Purdue, Armstrong was the No. 9 pick in the 1973 draft. The Broncos still had future Hall of Famer Floyd Little, but with the fragility of running backs, insurance was necessary. In fact, the Broncos drafted 21 other running backs and acquired eight others through trades in the nine seasons during which Little was in Denver.

Armstrong turned out to be much more than just insurance. Armstrong played eight seasons in Denver, from 1973 to 1980. In that time, he gained 4,453 yards—ranking fourth in team history through 2015—scored 25 touchdowns, and dazzled teammates and fans alike. "Great running back," Thompson said. "He really made an impact on the team, no doubt. He made his presence felt."

At 5'10" and 196 pounds, Armstrong was listed at the exact same size as Little and often displayed the same type of Hall of Fame skills. "I called him 'the Rook,'" quarterback Charley Johnson said. "When the Rook would really pin his ears back and really run, he could *run*."

He was a popular man in the locker room, too. Craig Morton called Armstrong "Mr. Cool" and described him as "a wonderful player, great guy, and a lot of fun. He had a great sense of humor."

Little was still an elite running back in 1973, finishing in the top 10 in the NFL in rushing. Armstrong ran the ball just 26 times for 90 yards as a rookie. When Little injured his Achilles' tendon during training camp in 1974, it opened the door for Armstrong. Little didn't miss any games but was never fully healthy, so the Broncos relied on the young legs of Armstrong. That season, Armstrong led the NFL with a team-record 1,407 yards and set a single-game team record with 183 yards in a win over the Houston Oilers. (Both records have since been broken several times.) A hamstring tear limited him to four games in 1975, but he came back to rush for 1,008 yards in 1976.

In the first 30 years of Broncos history, Armstrong was the only running back to compile two 1,000-yard seasons. Through 2015, Terrell Davis, Clinton Portis, and Little were the only players in team history with more 100-yard games than Armstrong's 13. Had Armstrong managed to stay healthy, he likely would have had more 100-yard games and 1,000-yard seasons, but after 1976, his best year netted just 489 yards. Various injuries to his legs, neck, and back limited him throughout his final four seasons.

Despite the injuries, Armstrong still had great moments in those final seasons, including a pair of 100-yard games late in his final season. The last of them, on October 26, 1980, he had 106 yards and a touchdown in a 14–9 win against the New York Giants. The following week, at home against Houston, he hurt his neck and got a concussion. Doctors discovered problems with his spine and warned him that if he continued to play, he could become paralyzed. On that advice, he retired with four games to go in the season.

Three years after his playing career ended, Armstrong filed a $24 million lawsuit against the Broncos for medical malpractice, alleging that team doctors concealed the injury to his spine. The Broncos argued it was a congenital condition. The two sides came to a settlement, and Armstrong also wound up with NFL disability benefits. No amount of money could make up for the toll on Armstrong's body, however. Maintaining a home in Denver, Armstrong has dealt with pain since he left football.

In 2007, however, he told the *Denver Post* that he remained upbeat, knowing that his fate could have been worse. One of his best friends and former Purdue teammates, Darryl Stingley, was a starting receiver for the New England Patriots when a hit by Oakland Raiders safety Jack Tatum in a 1978 preseason game left him paralyzed for life. Stingley passed away in 2007 at the age of 55.

"I've gotten a lot of strength from him," Armstrong told the *Post*. "I guess that's the way I deal with it. I'm happy. I'm in pain and I have trouble sleeping, but I'm doing pretty good, thank God. A lot of people are worse off than I am."

65 Defensive Wizard

The Broncos' Ring of Fame includes nine players who starred on defense under the direction of Joe Collier. That says a lot about Collier.

"He is probably still one of the greatest minds I've ever been around in football," said Billy Thompson.

From 1969 to 1988, Collier worked as the Broncos' defensive coordinator. He was the architect of the 3-4 defense that defined the Orange Crush in the 1970s. He is also credited for putting players such as Thompson, Karl Mecklenburg, and Randy Gradishar in positions to become stars. Those who played for Collier hold him in high regard as a defensive mastermind. "A lot of the defenses they play now are things that we were playing back in the '80s," Mecklenburg said. "[Collier] was an innovator. To me, the best coaches are guys that can look at their personnel and build their system around them. That's what Joe was able to do with us."

Collier was the first defensive coordinator in the NFL to use the 3-4 defense full-time. He did it to take advantage of his stable of talented linebackers—Randy Gradishar, Tom Jackson, Joe Rizzo, and Bob Swenson—in the 1970s.

As players changed, so did Collier. He set his defense to utilize the intelligence of players such as Jackson, Mecklenburg, Rick Dennison, and Jim Ryan in the 1980s. "We had probably one of the smartest linebacker crews to ever play the game," Mecklenburg said. "[Collier] was able to do all these innovative things. Everybody knew at least two positions, a lot of guys three positions. We were able to really have some fun with game planning and scheming based on the other team. Joe came up with all that stuff by looking at us and saying, 'You know what? We've got guys who can handle this. Let's take advantage of that.' I'm sure if we had all been 6'5", 260-pound guys that were just thugs on the field, he would have figured out a system that would have taken advantage of that."

No matter what the scheme, Collier's approach to defense was that every player on the field had a job—and every player was held accountable. "To me, that's the way you play defense," Thompson said. "I didn't want to be the one [singled out]. To me, I hated to be the one to walk in that room and they say, 'Hey Billy, this is your assignment. What are you doing?'"

Originally hired by Lou Saban, Collier wound up also working for head coaches Jerry Smith, John Ralston, Red Miller, and Dan Reeves in Denver. "He was awesome," said Reeves, who became the head coach in 1981 and leaned heavily on Collier

Camping in Greeley

Since 2003, the Broncos have held their annual training camp at their Dove Valley headquarters in Englewood. It's not so much of a camp as it is extended practices. Prior to 2003, the Broncos held actual camps, where players would get away from family and concentrate on football for several weeks. From 1960 to 1981, they held camp in several different locations, including the California Poly–Pomona campus from 1972 to 1975. No site has seen more Broncos camps than the University of Northern Colorado. Located in Greeley, about an hour north of Denver, UNC hosted Broncos camp from 1982 to 2002. "I still get the willies when I drive by Greeley," linebacker Karl Mecklenburg said at the thought of those camps, which were more demanding than NFL camps are today. "It was as physically, emotionally, and mentally challenging a thing as I've ever done. I can't say I liked it."

Mecklenburg does admit, though, that camping in Greeley had its benefits, particularly for fans and the city. Every year, the Broncos' arrival was a big deal to the people and economy of Greeley. Broncos fans came to practices in droves at the wide-open facility because it was fairly easy to get autographs. Back then, the players had to walk past a sea of fans to get to their locker room. Today, the crowds are limited, and the players don't have to walk past any of them if they don't want to.

"I think it was good for Greeley," Mecklenburg said. "I think it was good for the fans. There wasn't as much control with keeping the players and the fans separate. That was a good thing for the fans. [For the players] there was a bonding that went on when you're living in a dorm room, you're away from your family. You had the once-a-week visits [from family], but the rest of the time it was just your team. You're all living together. To me, I think there was an advantage to Greeley in that you came closer together as a team."

from the start. "For me, here's a coach that had tremendous experience and he also knew our football team well. When you come in, one thing you don't know is your players. It was invaluable to me for the knowledge he had. Then he was just a great person to work with."

Collier's influence stuck with Reeves throughout Reeves' career. It was Collier who persuaded Reeves to let the offense and defense go at each other at full speed in practices—something that wasn't done in Dallas, where Reeves had spent his whole career before coming to Denver. Reeves also put a heavy emphasis on goal-line defense during the latter part of his career, because that's what Collier did and, "[the Broncos] were the most difficult short-yardage team I had ever seen."

Although he had a short stint as the head coach of the Buffalo Bills from 1966 to 1968, Collier was perfectly content focusing his attention on one side of the ball with Denver for 20 years. Of course, he doesn't take full credit for the success or for producing eight Ring of Famers. "I don't think anyone thought of me as a genius until we got all those good players," he once told the *Denver Post*. "There must have been a correlation."

The players and Reeves know what he meant to the Broncos, though. "Joe was a great football coach," Reeves said. "Very loyal and would do anything you would ask him to do." Well...except for one thing.

After the 1988 season, a rare down year for the Broncos defense, Reeves wanted to make changes on the defensive staff. Collier wouldn't do it. "He didn't feel comfortable firing one of his coaches, so I had to make a change to the whole staff," Reeves said. "That's the reason we had to part ways. The toughest thing in the world to do is to let somebody go, and to let them go really with no reason, as far as Joe was concerned...that was one of the more difficult things I ever had to do."

Collier's final chapter in Denver did nothing to tarnish the legacy he built as a defensive mastermind. "He was a tremendous football coach and a tremendous person," Reeves said.

66 To Do: Black Hawk/ Central City

The historic mountain towns of Black Hawk and Central City were founded by people looking to get rich. Today, they thrive with people looking to get rich.

Located about 40 miles from Denver, the neighboring towns are full of history, but it is the casinos that keep them hopping.

John H. Gregory located there in May 1859, staking the first mining claims in the area. Word quickly spread, and on June 11 of that year, the *Rocky Mountain News* reported: "When we entered the diggings on the 20th of May, there were about twenty men in that vicinity, only two quartz leads had been opened and but three claims on one of those and two on the other. In two weeks from that time more than 3,000 men were at work, at least thirty leads satisfactorily prospected, and several hundred claims opened and profitably worked."

More than 20,000 people were living in the area by July, all of them looking to get in on the start of the gold rush. The Colorado Central railroad reached the area by 1872.

Although the mining towns went through tough times in later years, the restoration of the Central City Opera House in 1932 sparked a bit of resurgence in the area.

Heading into the late 20th century, Black Hawk and Central City still had plenty to offer tourists in terms of the opera house and historical landmarks. The rest of the state had plenty of options, too, so the mountain towns needed an economic boost. A November 6, 1990, election approved legalized gambling in Central City, Black Hawk, and Cripple Creek.

Today, history is alive and well in all three towns. Historic landmarks have been preserved and offer tourists a glimpse into the past. Among it all are the ever-busy casinos and hotels, kept alive by people looking for the same thing gold miners sought in 1859.

Getting to the casinos is easy, too. While it's a short drive up the mountain on Interstate 70, several shuttles are available in the Denver metro area to take patrons to and from the popular mountain towns.

67 McDisaster

Want to get Broncos fans riled up? Ask them what they think of Josh McDaniels.

Even the die-hard fans could debate just about any topic in Broncos history. Best running back? Best receiver? Best player not in the Ring of Fame? Biggest win? All lend themselves to healthy debate.

There are two things most every Broncos fan would agree upon:

1. They love John Elway.
2. They hate Josh McDaniels.

The level of hatred for the man who coached the Broncos from 2009 to 2010 may vary. Some argue he ruined the franchise for years to come. Some simply say his tenure was a bad two years.

Either way, the McDaniels era can really only be classified one way.

"Pretty much a disaster," said Denver radio talk show host Sandy Clough, who added it "was not entirely his fault, because he was given power he wasn't ready to assume."

Following the Broncos' epic collapse at the end of 2008, Mike Shanahan was fired by owner Pat Bowlen. At that time, the Broncos had an offense full of bright young stars, featuring quarterback Jay Cutler, receiver Brandon Marshall, tight end Tony Scheffler, and, to a certain degree, running back Peyton Hillis. They also had a defense that was historically bad in 2007 and 2008. It seemed obvious to most, Shanahan included, that if the defense got an overhaul, the Broncos could contend for the playoffs right away. "We've got [the offense] going in the right direction," Shanahan said during his final press conference.

The fan favorite to replace Shanahan was New York Giants defensive coordinator Steve Spagnuolo, a 49-year-old with an extensive background as a defensive coach. If not Spagnuolo, surely Minnesota Vikings defensive coordinator Leslie Frazier would get the job. Like Spagnuolo, he was 49 years old with years of experience coaching defense. Regardless of who the next coach would be, it was highly unlikely he would have the power Shanahan had. In addition to being the head coach, Shanahan handled general manager duties; ultimately, that's what did him in. The popular saying around the media was that Mike Shanahan the general manager got Mike Shanahan the coach fired. When Shanahan was fired, Bowlen said, "I don't anticipate that the next coach will have both jobs."

On January 12, 2009, Bowlen introduced the 32-year-old McDaniels, who had been the offensive coordinator in New England, as the next head coach. Although fans wanted a defensive coach, it was tough to dispute McDaniels. He had coordinated New England's explosive offense, which set an NFL record with 589 points in 2007. He was praised, perhaps even more so, for what he did in 2008. After star quarterback Tom Brady was hurt in the season opener, McDaniels got career backup Matt Cassel to play at a high level in guiding the Patriots to an 11–5 mark.

If the Broncos didn't hire McDaniels as their head coach that month, somebody else would have. Yet from day one, McDaniels' age and offensive background made him a target for fans.

Then it quickly became clear that, contrary to Bowlen's comments earlier in the month, McDaniels was in charge. Brian Xanders may have been the general manager, but there was no question that McDaniels made the final decisions on personnel moves, just as Shanahan had. That put the McDaniels era in jeopardy from the start. "He didn't turn it down when they offered it to him, but at the same time, it was a mistake to offer him that kind of authority," Clough said.

McDaniels ultimately sealed his fate with one of his first moves in Denver. He explored the possibility of trading Cutler, the Broncos' 25-year-old Pro Bowl quarterback, to Tampa Bay in a deal that would have also landed Cassel in Denver. Cutler was offended, and the soap opera began. Despite several attempts at reconciliation, the damage was done. On April 2, the Broncos traded Cutler to the Chicago Bears for quarterback Kyle Orton and a collection of draft picks. Many fans still haven't forgiven McDaniels for that one.

Still, he seemed to get a measure of redemption once the 2009 season began. Several of the players he signed in free agency—Brian Dawkins, Andre Goodman, Renaldo Hill, Correll Buckhalter—played key roles in helping the Broncos get out to a 6–0 start in 2009. That, however, proved to be what Clough described as "fool's gold." The Broncos went 2–8 the rest of the way and missed the playoffs yet again.

The Broncos never regained the winning edge with McDaniels. They were 3–9 in 2010 when he was fired. Following that 6–0 start, McDaniels went 5–17 in his final 22 games.

The final straw came during 2010 when the Broncos were found guilty of illegally videotaping a San Francisco 49ers practice prior to their game in London. Although there was no evidence McDaniels viewed the film, he and the team were each fined $50,000 by the NFL. "McSpygate," as it became known (a nod to the Patriots' 2007 progenitor "Spygate," which had occurred during McDaniels' tenure with that team), provided further embarrassment to the organization. About a week after the punishment came down, the Broncos fell to 3–9 with a loss in Kansas City, and Bowlen fired his once-promising young coach. Broncos chief operating officer Joe Ellis said at the time that the videotaping incident "was one of several factors, and it was just a culmination of factors that led to Mr. Bowlen's decision."

McDaniels likely would have survived McSpygate had he won more games and been able to avoid the series of disastrous personnel moves he made. By the end of the 2009 season, he had alienated Hillis, Marshall, and Scheffler, trading all three of them in the spring of 2010. Barely more than a year into his tenure, McDaniels had run off all four young offensive stars who Broncos fans were eager to see grow up together. "The fundamental mistake he made was that he tried to fix something that wasn't broken, specifically the offense," Clough said.

Even one of McDaniels' best moves didn't pan out. Defensive coordinator Mike Nolan, the first man McDaniels hired for his staff, vaulted Denver from 29th in total defense in 2008 to seventh in 2009. McDaniels ran Nolan off after 2009, as well, and the 2010 defense was one of the worst in franchise history.

In addition to those decisions, McDaniels' tenure was marked by a series of puzzling draft-day moves, including:

- Ignoring the glaring holes on defense and taking running back Knowshon Moreno with the 12th pick of the 2009 draft. By 2011, Moreno was a backup and by 2014 he was no longer with the Broncos.

- Trading a 2010 first-round pick to Seattle to get cornerback Alphonso Smith in the second round in 2009. After one season in Denver, Smith was traded for a backup tight end.
- Trading two third-round picks to get tight end Richard Quinn—projected by many as no better than a fifth-round pick—in the second round. Quinn lasted just two years in Denver and retired in 2014. During his NFL career, Quinn had just one catch—11 fewer than he had during his college career.
- Sending three draft picks to Baltimore to get into the first round and draft quarterback Tim Tebow in 2010—a move hotly debated throughout Tebow's two seasons in Denver.

Even Ellis admitted the Broncos made a mistake in handing the keys to the kingdom to McDaniels in 2009. "It's fair to say that we probably burdened him with too much of that and we were unfair to him in that respect," Ellis said.

Had McDaniels been hired simply to coach, this chapter might read a little differently. He was rehired by New England at the end of the 2011 season to run the Patriots offense, and he is still regarded as one of the top offensive minds in football.

Great coach or not, McDaniels remains one of the most reviled figures in team history, and his short stay in Denver will forever be looked upon as some of the darkest days the Broncos have ever seen.

68 Tebow & the Magic of 2011

Heading into the 2011 NFL season, the Broncos appeared to be an easy team to figure out.

Coming off a franchise-worst 4–12 record in 2010, another tough year was in store. They had a rookie in charge of football operations; of course, that rookie was John Elway, but it *was* his first year on the job. They had a new head coach, John Fox, who was fired after going 2–14 in Carolina. And, to top it all off, the Broncos had a quarterback controversy on their hands—and it was no ordinary situation.

Kyle Orton was a veteran who had quarterbacked the Broncos for two years, but he had never endeared himself to Denver fans, despite putting up solid numbers. Behind Orton was Tim Tebow, a former Heisman Trophy winner from the University of Florida who possessed high character that fans loved.

Logically, it didn't make sense to go with Tebow. Throughout training camp and the preseason, Orton was clearly the best quarterback on the roster, while Tebow showed plenty of limitations as a passer. Even veteran Brady Quinn had passed Tebow on the depth chart. Tebow was a mega star who had yet to prove he could play well in the NFL, but fans—some of them, anyway—were vocal about wanting him under center. Some Denver fans even put up the cash for a roadside billboard that read: Broncos Fans to John Fox: Play Tebow!!

Fox stuck with Orton, but the theme of the Broncos season was quickly becoming, "Suck for Luck." Stanford University quarterback Andrew Luck was shredding college defenses and was widely regarded as the surefire No. 1 draft pick in 2012. Some die-hard fans actually believed the best thing for the Broncos was to lose as much as possible in 2011 in order get the first draft pick and pin their future on Luck.

Four games into the season, the Broncos were predictably in the running for Luck, at 1–3. Orton was struggling and demands for Tebow grew louder. When the media asked Orton about the situation, he said, "[Fox] is the only one that I'm going to listen to. I'd rather you guys not waste my time with the questions, because I'm not going to answer them."

Orton's terse replies and poor play made him less likeable to the public, and in Game 5, he buried himself for good. Orton played a horrible first half and the Broncos went into halftime trailing the visiting San Diego Chargers 23–10. Fox benched Orton and inserted Tebow into the lineup. In the fourth quarter, Tebow ran for a touchdown and then threw a touchdown pass. The Broncos lost 29–24, but Tebow had given them a chance and that was enough. The Broncos sat at 1–4 and had Luck on the mind, but for better or worse, Tebow would be the QB for the remainder of the season. Orton never played for the Broncos again.

"I think they put [Tebow] in so that you, the fan, could see what they saw every day: that the balls weren't accurate, that he had trouble delivering a spiral from time to time, that reading progressions of defense was really something that he struggled with," Tom Jackson said.

Fans saw all of that, but they saw something else, too.

"As soon as he got in, he started to win," Jackson said.

Tebow's first start came on October 23 in Miami, where the Broncos had never won (0–10, counting the preseason). With three minutes to play in this one, they trailed 15–0. No team since the AFL-NFL merger in 1970 had ever rallied to win with that big of a deficit in the final three minutes. This hardly seemed to be the day to change that, given that Tebow was a dreadful 4-for-14 for 40 yards prior to Denver getting the ball with 5:23 to play.

In the final 5:23, however, Tebow completed 9 of 13 throws for 121 yards and two touchdowns. With his feet, he scored the game-tying two-point conversion with 17 seconds left. A Matt Prater field goal in overtime gave the Broncos an 18–15 win.

After getting crushed at home by Detroit, the Broncos revamped their offense to fit what Tebow ran at Florida. In the new offense, Tebow threw for 124 yards and two touchdowns and ran for 118 yards in beating the Raiders in Oakland, 38–24. The next week, they somehow came out of Kansas City with a 17–10 win.

Four days later, Tebow pulled off another miracle against the New York Jets in front of a national television audience on *Thursday Night Football.* The Broncos trailed 13–10 when they got the ball back with 5:54 to go. Tebow was playing poorly again, but led a 96-yard, game-winning touchdown drive. He ran or threw the ball on 11 of the 12 plays, capping it with a 20-yard touchdown run with less than a minute remaining, to give Denver the win.

A few days later, Orton was released, and he later signed with the Chiefs. Meanwhile, during the next two weeks, Tebow and the Broncos rallied to beat San Diego and Minnesota, both on the road. Tebowmania was taking the NFL world by storm.

"It was like this vicious circle, an up-and-down emotional roller coaster of the likes we have never seen," Jackson said. "But it wasn't just Denver. It was the entire country."

Andrew Luck? *Please.* The Broncos were in a playoff race, and it kept getting more insane. The Broncos sat at 7–5 when the Chicago Bears came to town on December 11. Chicago led 10–0 with three minutes to play. Enter Tebow…again.

Tebow threw a 10-yard touchdown pass to Demaryius Thomas with 2:08 to play to cut the deficit to 10–7, but Chicago recovered the ensuing onsides kick. At ESPN headquarters in Bristol, Connecticut, Jackson and his colleagues knew that all the Bears had to do was keep the ball in bounds and run out the clock. "Everybody was getting ready to walk away [from the TV]," Jackson said. "The game's over."

On second down, Bears running back Marion Barber inexplicably ran out of bounds, stopping the clock. "Everybody came back and sat down," Jackson said.

Chicago was forced to punt. Tebow had just 56 seconds and no timeouts, but he moved the Broncos 39 yards down the field to set up Prater's game-tying 59-yard field goal. In overtime, the Bears got the ball and marched downfield—until a stunning Barber fumble. Nine plays later, Prater's 51-yard field goal gave the Broncos their sixth straight win. In Bristol, Jackson, Chris Berman, and Trent Dilfer prepared for ESPN's postgame show, which was to begin minutes after Prater's kick.

"Boomer looks at Trent and [me] and goes, 'Okay, since you guys are experts, explain to me what just happened,'" Jackson said. "I had said it to Trent before we ever went on, I said, 'I'm going to let you explain this one. You're the quarterback. Tell me what happened.' He goes, 'I don't know,' and I said, 'Well, I don't know either, so I'm sure our national viewership will enjoy our commentary.'"

Few people could explain exactly what was happening, but considering Tebow's public expressions of religiosity, divine intervention seemed logical. He began virtually every press conference or interview with expressions such as, "First and foremost, I'd like to thank my Lord and Savior, Jesus Christ," and ending them with "God bless."

Tebow's religious views earned him fans and detractors, and so did his play, but every time he was hit with criticism, he just smiled. "I'm just so blessed to have an opportunity to be the quarterback for the Denver Broncos and play a game in front of such great fans and with great teammates, and I'm just very thankful for the platform that God has given me," he said.

In reality, Tebow didn't play that well—except when it mattered most. He made a habit out of digging a nearly insurmountable hole and then finding a way to climb out.

"It was the most intriguing thing I saw all year," Jackson said. "ESPN started taking polls and found out the majority of the country thought it was divine intervention and that God really is taking a hand in Tim Tebow's three hours on a field on a Sunday. I talked to professional football players unable to explain what they were looking at."

It was tough to explain, but Tebow was the main attraction in a simply fascinating show. He was a *Sports Illustrated* cover boy, the subject of a *Saturday Night Live* skit, and the unintentional creator of a cultural phenomenon called, "Tebowing." He often celebrated big plays or big wins by Tebowing—kneeling down, elbow on his knee, head resting on his fist, and praying. Both in honor of the QB and in mockery, people around the world posted photos and videos on social-networking sites of themselves Tebowing. Opposing defenders would often break into a brief moment of Tebowing upon sacking the young quarterback.

"Everybody was kind of living the wave of his life during the season, whether it was because of his performances or what he does outside of football," Broncos receiver Eric Decker said at the end of the season. "It's been the first time I've seen somebody that is so polarizing, such an icon, and has so much following. But [there are] a lot of positives that come with it."

The positives, of course, were the wins. He played ugly football, but there was no denying it: the Broncos found ways to win with Tebow under center.

"You had to do a double take and say, 'Okay, there's something special here,'" Jackson said. "Underneath all of the fundamental mechanics, there's something very special. There's a special human being."

After beating the Bears, the Broncos lost their last three games—including the finale against Orton and Kansas City—but even at 8–8 they won the AFC West division and went to the playoffs for the first time in six years.

In the first round of the playoffs, Tebow found another bit of magic. He threw for a career-high 316 yards and two touchdowns and capped the night with an 80-yard touchdown pass to Thomas on the first play of overtime to beat the Pittsburgh Steelers 29–23. "I was running pretty fast, chasing [Thomas]—like I could catch up to him," Tebow said of the winning play. "Then, I just jumped in the stands—first time I've done that; that was fun."

The ride came to an end the next week with a 45–10 loss in New England during the division playoffs, but that was not the enduring memory of 2011. Fox did a great job in his first season as head coach, linebacker Elvis Dumervil was great once again, and first-round draft pick Von Miller was named the NFL's defensive rookie of the year. The 2011 season will always be remembered for Tebow, however.

Tebow completed a league-worst 46.5 percent of his passes and his 72.9 quarterback rating was near the bottom of the league. Yet for the first time since Elway retired in the spring of 1999, the Broncos had a quarterback who fans embraced, and he took them on an amazing journey. Former Bronco Shannon Sharpe, who was then an analyst for CBS, said, "I've never seen anything like that in the history of sports."

He may never see it again. Just a few weeks after the season ended, the Broncos signed future Hall of Fame quarterback Peyton Manning and traded Tebow to the New York Jets. He failed to recapture what he had in Denver, though, and was cut after one year in New York. Despite tryouts with the Patriots and Philadelphia Eagles, Tebow never played a game after 2012.

Tebowmania was short-lived, but for Broncos fans, it was a thrilling and unpredictable ride.

69 Alex Gibbs

You'd be hard-pressed to find an offensive line coach more highly regarded than Alex Gibbs.

At every stop along his career—and there have been a lot of them—Gibbs has produced great results. Throughout his career, he has worked for every team in the AFC West, as well as the Indianapolis Colts, Atlanta Falcons, Houston Texans, Seattle Seahawks, and several college programs. The North Carolina native is best known, however, for what he did in two separate stints with the Broncos. Gibbs coached the Broncos offensive line from 1984 to 1987 and then again from 1995 to 2003.

He is regarded as the "godfather of zone blocking," a philosophy that allows linemen to work together to block an area, rather than each lineman being assigned to a specific defender.

With Gibbs leading the Broncos' offensive line, Sammy Winder rushed for 3,397 yards from 1984 to 1987 and went to the Pro Bowl in 1984 and 1986.

When Mike Shanahan was hired as Broncos head coach in 1995, he brought Gibbs back to Denver. In Gibbs' first season, a rookie sixth-round pick named Terrell Davis gained 1,117 yards behind Gibbs' line. Davis gained a remarkable 6,413 yards from 1995 to 1998, running behind a small, athletic line that had mastered zone blocking. Thanks in large part to Gibbs' work, the Broncos became famous for their running game. No team in the NFL gained more rushing yards from 1995 to 2005. As good as Davis was, the zone blocking scheme paved the way for several rushers to succeed, even after Gibbs left:

- Olandis Gary: 1,159 yards in 1999

- Mike Anderson: 1,487 yards in 2000 and 1,014 yards in 2005
- Clinton Portis: 1,508 yards in 2002 and 1,591 yards in 2003
- Reuben Droughns: 1,240 yards in 2004
- Tatum Bell: 1,025 yards in 2006

Running backs loved playing in Denver, and linemen loved playing for Gibbs. "He taught an old player like myself how to grab a few more years in the league by playing smarter," former Broncos tackle Gary Zimmerman said in his Hall of Fame induction speech in 2008. "Alex was hard on us, expecting perfection—and that made us better. He taught us to read coverage and understand how defenses worked. It was a lot easier to play when you had a good idea what your opponent might do. He, too, gave some awesome motivational speeches, but it would not be appropriate to repeat them here. Thanks, Alex, for making me a smarter player and instilling the proper mind-set to play the offensive line position."

As a testament to Gibbs' contribution to the Broncos' success, Houston head coach Gary Kubiak, the Broncos' offensive coordinator from 1995 to 2005, hired Gibbs to coach the Texans' line from 2008 to 2009. "I'm not sure how long we'll have him, but whether it's one year, two years, or longer, we've got to soak up his knowledge of the game," Kubiak told the *Houston Chronicle* when Gibbs was hired in 2008. After a long coaching career, Gibbs retired in 2010.

70 To Do: 16th Street Mall

On any given day or night, Denver is a bustling place full of shopping, dining, and people hustling to and from the office. At the heart of it all is the 16th Street Mall, a tree-lined, mile-long district that is among the most popular destinations for visitors and residents.

The transit mall was designed and laid out by I.M. Pei and Partners, the same architectural firm that designed the Rock and Roll Hall of Fame in Cleveland and the Pyramide du Louvre in Paris. It features 16 blocks of shopping, dining, and entertainment options for thousands of visitors each day.

If it's shopping you want, there's no shortage of locations, such as the Virgin Records Megastore, Niketown, Gap, H&M, and a host of other locations selling clothing, jewelry, souvenirs, and more. Hungry? The Hard Rock Café, Rock Bottom Brewery, Maggiano's, and a host of smaller cafés and restaurants provide plenty of options, in addition to some fast-food joints.

The mall also offers entertainment, such as a bowling alley and a movie theater. Many people choose to walk the mall and take in all the sights, but for those who aren't interested in walking, there is a free shuttle bus, bike taxis, and horse-drawn carriages.

While the 16th Street Mall has plenty of entertainment options on its own, it is also centrally located near many of Denver's other great landmarks, including the Denver Performing Arts Complex, Colorado Convention Center, Coors Field, and the Pepsi Center.

71 "Al" Leader on Defense

Throughout their history, the Broncos have had a lot of great players and great leaders on defense. Goose Gonsoulin, Lyle Alzado, Randy Gradishar, Tom Jackson, and Karl Mecklenburg are among the best in that regard.

Al Wilson wouldn't take a backseat to any of them. For eight seasons, from 1999 to 2006, Wilson was the Broncos' starting middle linebacker. He made the Pro Bowl five times, was seemingly always around the ball, and provided an immeasurable amount of leadership for the Denver defense.

Emotional, hard-hitting, and technically sound, Wilson proved more than worthy of being the 31st overall pick in the 1999 draft after a great career at the University of Tennessee. He earned his way into the starting lineup as a rookie in 1999 and maintained that spot throughout his career. A hard hitter, he finished six of his eight seasons with more than 100 tackles. He also accumulated 21½ sacks and five interceptions, one of which he returned for a touchdown.

Nobody ever questioned Wilson's role as a leader on the defense; and it was often he who got the team fired up in pregame huddles. He once told DenverBroncos.com that being a leader simply came naturally. "I think leaders are born, so it's hard to think of one particular thing," he said. "I just go out and play hard and try to make the other guys understand about who I am, my personality, and where I'm coming from."

Wilson was in the midst of another Pro Bowl season in 2006 when he injured his neck against the Seattle Seahawks on December 3. As he was carted off the field, fans at Invesco Field at Mile High chanted, "Wil-SON! Wil-SON! Wil-SON!" He returned the next week and remained in the starting lineup until the season finale when his sore neck kept him on the sideline. Wilson's neck injury wound up ending his career. After the 2006 season, the Broncos had a deal that would have sent Wilson to the New York Giants. The Giants' medical staff wouldn't clear Wilson to play, however, and the deal fell through. The Broncos released their defensive captain, in part to clear up salary-cap space in moving forward. It was a decision that coach Mike Shanahan described as "very, very tough."

Wilson, who was just 29 years old at the time, still hoped to play. "I think I have several more years left in me," he said.

Wilson never did play again, however, retiring in 2008. "He meant so much to this organization," Shanahan told ESPN.com at the time. "I really enjoyed all the years he spent with us—hate to see him go. He gave it everything he had every day."

Wilson later filed a suit against the Broncos for how they handled his injury but lost his case. Regardless, he will forever be remembered as one of the greatest defensive players in team history and could one day find himself in the team's Ring of Fame. "I have no regrets," he told the Associated Press in 2007. "I gave them all I had. I can walk away with my head held high."

72 Holding His Own

Quarterbacks always know how good the cornerbacks are on other teams. And when quarterbacks prepared to face the Broncos defense in the mid-to-late-1970s, they knew Louis Wright was the man to avoid. Wright was a five-time Pro Bowler who was one of the best cover corners in the NFL.

Playing opposite Pro Bowl corner Louis Wright, Foley had a lot of passes thrown to his side. He was up to the challenge and then some, a punishing force in the Denver secondary.

In order to throw the ball, quarterbacks often looked to the other side of the field, manned by Steve Foley. "A lot of quarterbacks took their chances against me rather than Louie Wright on the side," Foley told the *Denver Post* in 2009. "I've always been competitive by nature. When you have 12 brothers and sisters, you learn to be that way."

True to his nature, Foley answered the challenge every day, making life difficult for opposing quarterbacks in his own right. "Steve meant a lot to us," former teammate Billy Thompson said. "He was very intelligent, a very hard worker. He gave you everything he's got."

Foley never made it to the Pro Bowl, but he spent 11 seasons in the Broncos' defensive backfield, from 1976 to 1986. During his first four seasons, at the height of the Orange Crush defense, Foley played cornerback. In 1980, he moved to safety and played seven seasons there. "He was very critical on that defense for the

'77 team," Thompson said. "He didn't make any mistakes. He was a very important piece. I worked with Steve every day. He had a big heart. I love him like a brother, and he just gives you everything. I can't say enough good things about Steve."

Foley's path to the Broncos' defensive backfield included some bumps. A star quarterback at his Louisiana high school, Foley played quarterback at Tulane University, suiting up with his brothers, Rob and Mike. The Broncos had no interest in him as a quarterback, however, and selected him in the eighth round of the 1975 draft as a defensive back. For 11 years, he proved himself a valuable member of the defense and intercepted 44 passes—a number that still ranks as the best in team history.

"He had great hands," said Dan Reeves, Broncos head coach during Foley's final six seasons. "He could have been a receiver. That made him dangerous as a safety, because he was going to make some interceptions and make some big plays and get you in the right coverages. He was just extremely bright and had great hands. Not the biggest safety in the world, but he got the job done."

73 To Do: The Cherry Cricket

Peanut butter belongs with jelly, and it's a natural fit when paired with chocolate.

Visit one of Denver's most popular restaurants and you can actually get the stuff on top of a juicy hamburger. Throw a fried egg on top of that, and you've got one of the more popular burger concoctions that Denver has to offer: the Goober Burger.

The Cherry Cricket has been voted numerous times as having one of the best burgers in the country and is routinely voted the top burger joint in Denver—quite the compliment in a city known for its beef.

Places to Eat

Aside from the Cherry Cricket, here are a few other top dining options in Denver.

Brooklyn's: A classic sports bar located next to Sports Authority Field. There's another Brooklyn's near the Pepsi Center, home to the Denver Nuggets and Colorado Avalanche.

Buckhorn Exchange: Denver's original steakhouse, it opened in 1893 and claims to have served five U.S. presidents: Theodore Roosevelt, Franklin Roosevelt, Dwight Eisenhower, Jimmy Carter, and Ronald Reagan. Just five minutes from downtown, the Buckhorn is known for serving steak and less traditional meats, such as rattlesnake, yak, ostrich, elk, and quail.

Casa Bonita: Known more for the experience than the food, Casa Bonita has a menu of good Mexican dishes. Mainly, it's a popular destination for families, who can watch cliff divers while they eat, listen to live musicians, and take in the arcade.

Denver Chop House & Brewery: Located near Coors Field, it's got a great combination of excellent food and a laid-back atmosphere. You might also spot a player or two there.

Elway's: You've got to get one of Denver's best steaks at the restaurant named for the Broncos' greatest player, right? There's one location in south Denver, one located within the Ritz-Carlton Hotel in downtown Denver, and a third in Vail.

Shanahan's Steakhouse: Not to be outdone by Elway, the legendary Broncos coach has his own restaurant, which opened in 2009 and is already known for its steaks and fine wines. Shanahan's two Super Bowl trophies and rings are on display, which provides a special treat for Broncos fans.

By themselves, the succulent half-pound burgers are among the best you'll ever taste, but that's not why most people come to the Cherry Cricket. As the Goober Burger exhibits, this is not your usual ketchup, mustard, and onion burger joint—although those toppings are certainly available, too.

The Cherry Cricket prides itself on its long list of available toppings for its delicious burgers. Peanut butter, cream cheese, salsa, and jalapeños are just a few of the 20-plus toppings you can get at the Cherry Cricket. Having a hard time deciding which toppings you want? No worries. The Cricket has a dartboard, with each spot representing a different topping. Grab the darts and take your chances.

Located in the Cherry Creek shopping district, one of the metro area's most popular shopping destinations, the Cricket opened in 1945 in the living room of original owner Mary Zimmerman. In 1950, Zimmerman moved the restaurant to its current location. Through the years, restaurant ownership has changed hands several times. The identity of the restaurant has changed as well, and the building itself has gone through several additions. The Cricket has gained quite a following in Denver, though.

National exposure hasn't hurt, either. The Cricket has been featured on *Man vs. Food* and *The Best Thing I Ever Ate.*

Of course, the Cricket has plenty more on the menu, from wings and fries to all sorts of sandwiches, as well as Mexican entrees and salads. Yet it's the burgers that keep the crowds hopping. It's a must-stop for anyone who craves a juicy hamburger—or peanut butter.

74 Hurricane

Together, the members of the Orange Crush defense of the 1970s made 23 Pro Bowl appearances and account for almost one-quarter of the 22 spots on the Broncos' Ring of Fame. Yet the key to that entire defense didn't earn either of those honors.

For 12 years, from 1975 to 1986, Rubin Carter was one of the most dominating defensive tackles in football, and he may be the most underappreciated Bronco in team history. "The guy that I thought that was most underrated and didn't get the credit a lot was Rubin Carter," said Thompson, a three-time Pro Bowler. "One of the greatest nose tackles to ever play the game."

Lyle Alzado, Randy Gradishar, Tom Jackson, and Thompson were all already in place before Carter arrived. The 1975 NFL Draft brought Louis Wright, Steve Foley, and Carter into the fold. Running a 3-4 defense, the Broncos needed a nose tackle, and the 6'0", 256-pound Carter fit the bill. He was nicknamed "Hurricane" because of his style of play and the fact that he was a University of Miami Hurricane. (Carter is not to be confused with the middleweight boxer of the 1960s who was framed for murder, who shares the same name and nickname with the Broncos lineman.)

Carter began his brilliant career in 1975. "Rubin Carter turned out to be the catalyst for everything we did because you can't play that 3-4 without having a great nose tackle," Jackson said.

Carter had very good numbers, registering 960 tackles and 30 sacks during his first 11 seasons (by his 12th season, in 1986, he had been relegated to a backup role), but was never the playmaker that others on the defense turned out to be. There was a reason for that. The 3-4 defense is designed for the big plays to be made by linebackers and defensive backs. The Broncos had plenty of players

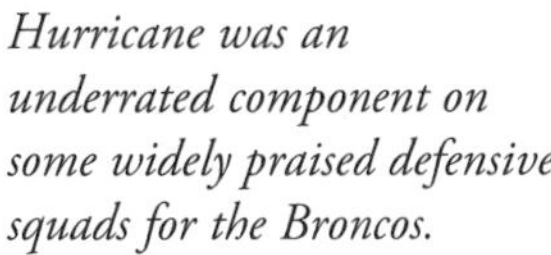
Hurricane was an underrated component on some widely praised defensive squads for the Broncos.

capable of doing that, but prior to Carter's arrival, Jackson said the Broncos "couldn't control the middle of the field." That changed when Carter got into the lineup.

"When Rubin came in, getting double-teamed and often times triple-teamed, he became the guy who controlled the center and both guards," Jackson said. "When we saw him throwing the Raiders away like little kids, we knew that we were going to be able to control the middle of the field, people weren't going to be able to run on us, and everything else was going to feed off that."

Thompson said he and his teammates were in awe at how powerful Carter was in the trenches. "One center couldn't stop Rubin," Thompson said. "If there was a center by himself, it was over. They knew that, so most of the time Rubin was double-teamed. Most of the times we played, Rubin Carter was double-teamed and he still made plays."

Carter did earn one distinction that no other defender in Broncos history has earned—gracing the cover of *Sports Illustrated.* His intense eyes peered out of his face mask on the cover of the October 17, 1977, edition with the title, The Case for the 3-4 Defense.

"A nose tackle has to be able to endure the pounding," Carter said in that edition of the national magazine. "On most plays, a 250-pound center and a 260-pound guard hit me. That's 510 pounds each play."

On most plays, Carter handled both. So why didn't he ever make it to the Pro Bowl? A logical reason is that the 3-4 defense was not widely used in the NFL, so most of the Pro Bowl linemen were traditional 4-3 defensive tackles. New England's Ray Hamilton, who was also an elite nose tackle, never made it to a Pro Bowl, either. "They said they couldn't figure out how to find a spot for a guy who played the nose tackle, as opposed to playing one of the conventional two interior tackle positions," Jackson said. "My thought always throughout my career and after has been they would have seen something great if they ever lined Rubin Carter up on one guy. If they had ever sent Rubin to the Pro Bowl and seen what he looked like on one guy, it would have been overwhelming. Whoever they put in front of him, he would have destroyed."

Jackson recalls the Hall of Fame speech given by former Washington Redskins offensive line great Russ Grimm. "He said, 'There's nothing more satisfying in football than moving another man against his will,'" Jackson said. "And that's what Rubin was able to do. He was able to move two or three guys against their will.

"That ability, it made us the Orange Crush."

75 Simon Fletcher

Rubin Carter may be the most underappreciated Bronco of all time, but he's got competition for that claim from Simon Fletcher.

From 1985 to 1995, Fletcher was a dominating force on a defense that helped the Broncos get to three Super Bowls. A second-round draft choice from Houston in 1985, Fletcher was among the best pass rushers in football throughout his career. "Simon was an unbelievable athlete," former teammate Karl Mecklenburg said. "He could have been an Olympian in the 400 [meter dash]. He was just a great, great athlete and a guy that was as good of a pass rusher, as far as a speed pass rusher, as anybody."

Fletcher's statistics were sensational. The 6'5" 240-pounder is the Broncos' all-time sacks leader with 97½, nearly 20 more than anyone else. His 16 sacks in 1992 was a team record until Elvis Dumervil recorded 17 in 2009. Fletcher held the NFL record for most consecutive games with a sack, recording at least one per game in 10 consecutive games between the 1992 and 1993 seasons (Minnesota's Jared Allen eclipsed the mark in 2011 with 11). Fletcher did it all while playing in a team-record 172 consecutive games, never missing a game during his 11 seasons.

"If he would have actually tackled everybody he hit, he could have had double the sacks he had," joked Mecklenburg, whose 79 sacks rank second in team history. "He was always in the backfield, he was always harassing the quarterback. The number of sacks I got were because Simon would chase them to me because he didn't tackle them. He was just a thorn in the side of a defense."

As dominating as he was, Fletcher was curiously ignored when it came time for individual honors. He never did get selected for a Pro Bowl. About the only honor Fletcher did get was the AFC Defensive Player of the Month award in December 1991.

For many years, Fletcher was viewed as perhaps the best defensive player in team history who was not in the Ring of Fame. That changed in the spring of 2016, when he was finally recognized and elected.

How Fletcher went about his career without much recognition is a mystery to Mecklenburg, who believes Fletcher was similar to another dominating sack artist of that era, Derrick Thomas from Kansas City. "Derrick Thomas is in the Hall of Fame, and Simon was every bit of the threat that Derrick was," Mecklenburg said. "Every team we played had to game plan and try to figure out a way to try to block Simon. Even though they would make those adjustments, they still couldn't do it. He was a tremendous, tremendous pass rusher."

76 The Judge

The best tight end in Broncos history? That's a no-brainer.

Or is it?

The easy answer is Shannon Sharpe, a member of the Pro Football Hall of Fame and the Broncos' Ring of Fame. Sharpe retired with just about every NFL receiving record for tight ends. He has, by far, caught more passes for more yards and for more touchdowns than any other tight end in Broncos history. Yet Sharpe isn't the only option.

"I love Shannon Sharpe, but the greatest tight end that ever played football here was Riley Odoms," said Thompson, who played with Odoms from 1972 to 1981.

"The Judge" got it done on the field.

Odoms was the fifth overall pick in the 1972 NFL Draft, one of just four top-five picks in team history through 2015. A native of Luling, Texas, Odoms played 12 seasons for the Broncos, from 1972 to 1983. In those 12 years, he caught 396 passes for 5,755 yards and 41 touchdowns. Sharpe is the only tight end in team history with better numbers, and there are only a few wide receivers who topped those marks.

Four times Odoms led the Broncos in receiving, and all four times he was selected to the Pro Bowl. "Riley had probably the softest hands of anybody I ever saw," said Charley Johnson, who was Odom's quarterback in Denver from 1972 to 1975. "He could catch the ball and you'd think he was catching a powder puff. He was excellent at his position. He was as good as anybody that ever played it."

Craig Morton, who threw dozens of passes to Odoms from 1977 from 1982, said, "There's not a better tight end. He was great."

Thompson takes that a step further, saying Odoms, nicknamed "the Judge," might be the best of the bunch in any day. Not only was Odoms a prolific pass catcher, he was a tremendous blocker and was asked to block more often than not. Perhaps most impressive, Odoms did his work primarily on low-scoring, run-oriented offenses, and he never did play with a quarterback who made the Pro Bowl.

"Shannon was very critical in the history of the Broncos and what he and Elway accomplished," Thompson said. "But I guarantee you if you put Riley Odoms in that situation...I've never seen a tight end block and catch and run like Riley Odoms. One of the best tight ends I've ever seen, and he never got credit because he did a lot of the dirty work."

77 To Do: Elitch Gardens

Needing some thrills to fill your football off-season?

Since 1890, Elitch Gardens Theme & Water Park has been a main attraction in Denver. Located adjacent to Sports Authority Field, and a popular destination for some of the Broncos players, Elitch Gardens is visited by thousands every year.

Originally, the park opened as one of the first zoos west of Chicago, as John and Mary Elitch converted their farm into an attraction for local residents. Through the years, Elitch's has hit several milestones, including claims to be the home of Denver's first symphony orchestra, its first botanical garden, it's first children's museum, and its first motion-picture theater.

The original park was located in northwest Denver, but it moved near downtown in 1995.

While filled with thrilling modern rides, the park is also full of history. The park's original carousel—which opened in 1928 and took three years to carve—and the original Ferris wheel, from 1936, are both still in operation.

Today some of the more popular rides include:

- **Tower of Doom**—This ride offers a spectacular view of the city and mountains, but look quick. Once you're at the top, you plummet 200 feet at a rate of about 60 mph.
- **Twister II**—A famous wooden roller coaster, it stands 10 stories high and includes a 90-foot drop and a pitch-black tunnel. It is the park's longest roller coaster, at 4,640 feet.
- **XLR8R—**Elitch's claims it is "the largest free-fall swing in Colorado." Those who dare to ride are taken 150 feet in the air before being dropped in a free-fall that mixes bungee jumping, hang-gliding, and skydiving.
- **Half Pipe—**A unique aspect to the park, Elitch's claims the half pipe is "Colorado's most thrilling snowboard ride around."

In addition to these rides, Elitch Gardens, opened from May through October, features plenty of things for those a little less daring, as well as for little kids. There's a water park, concerts and special shows and plenty of kid-friendly rides.

78 No Shoe, No Problem

The 1986 AFC Championship Game proved to be the coming-out party for Broncos quarterback John Elway. It was he who engineered "the Drive," tying the game with Cleveland at 20 and sending it into overtime.

It was Rich Karlis, however, who graced the cover of *Sports Illustrated* the next week—a memorable shot of him and backup quarterback Gary Kubiak leaping for joy after Karlis' field goal in overtime won the game. In part because of that kick, which sent the Broncos to the Super Bowl, and in large part because he kicked all his field goals with a bare right foot, Karlis is still to this day a beloved figure in Broncos history.

Part of a 478-person tryout in 1982, Karlis made the team as a rookie and went on to play seven solid seasons in Denver. He still ranks in the top four in team history for field goals made (137), field goals attempted (193), extra points made (244), and extra points attempted (254). He's one of only five kickers in team history to hit at least 70 percent of his field goals. After his time in Denver, Karlis played for the Minnesota Vikings in 1989 and for the Detroit Lions in 1990 before retiring. During one game as a Viking, he tied an NFL record with seven field goals. The mark stood until 2007.

Getting Their Kicks

Finding a reliable kicker isn't easy in the NFL, yet the Broncos have made it seem that way. Gene Mingo started the tradition in the Broncos' inaugural season of 1960. In addition to playing running back and returning kicks, Mingo twice led the AFL in field goals made, with his 27 in 1962 standing as the team's single-season record for 27 years.

Gary Kroner, Bob Humphreys, and Bobby Howfield kept the tradition going throughout the rest of the 1960s, and then Jim Turner starred from 1971 to 1979, making 65.1 percent of his field goals, breaking Mingo's record. Since then, the Broncos keep getting better:

- Fred Steinfort (1979–81): 67.2 percent accuracy on field goals
- Rich Karlis (1982–88): 71.0 percent
- David Treadwell (1989–92): 78.0 percent
- Jason Elam (1993–2007): 80.6 percent
- Matt Prater (2008–13): 82.9 percent

No one can forget Karlis' unusual barefoot kicking style, nor can one argue with his results.

Several of Karlis' kicks with Denver had great significance. His overtime winner in the 1986 AFC Championship Game was the most important, but he won several games with his right foot, and his 48-yard kick in Super Bowl XXI was, for many years, the longest in Super Bowl history.

What made Karlis unique, though, were not the kicks themselves, but how he went about his job. He was the last kicker in the NFL to kick with a bare foot. Self-taught, Karlis didn't start kicking until his senior year of high school. He learned to kick barefoot when he saw someone on television doing it. Karlis tried it out and felt he had more control of the ball with his bare foot. Of course, kicking a football with no shoe did create some problems. He had to watch where he was walking on the sideline, especially during the two years he played with lineman Tom Glassic, who was infamous for vomiting on the sideline.

Cold, snowy games—which were all too common in Denver—presented a challenge, too, although he did wear a warm boot on the sideline when he wasn't kicking. In truth, he was only barefoot for a few moments during the kick.

In addition to those challenges, he had little margin for error. "When I hit it right, the ball went great, and when I didn't, it hurt like hell," Karlis told the *Denver Post* in 2007.

Despite the difficulties of kicking barefoot, Karlis always stayed true to his form. Well, almost always. "Last year, when there was a 28-below-zero wind chill in Kansas City, I wore a thin sanitary sock and made a 24-yard field goal," Karlis told *Sports Illustrated* in 1984. "But later, a woman stopped me in a Denver bank and told me I was a wimp."

79 KOA Radio

Bob Martin's voice boomed through the airwaves on January 1, 1978, as the Broncos closed in on a 20–17 victory over the Oakland Raiders in the AFC Championship Game.

"They don't have to run another play!" Martin exclaimed, with the Mile High Stadium crowd of 74,982 roaring in the background. "Somersaulting, Haven Moses comes out! The Broncos on the field! It is over with 19 seconds to go! The miracle has happened! The Broncos are going to the Super Bowl!"

Since 1970, KOA Radio, located on 850 AM on the dial, has been a part of Broncos history. The 50,000-watt station has delivered Broncos games to fans throughout Colorado, as well as through affiliates in Montana, Nebraska, New Mexico, North Dakota, South Dakota, and Wyoming.

Through most of those 40-plus years, Broncos fans have become comfortable with the distinct voices of Martin, Larry Zimmer, and Dave Logan.

During KOA's first season with the Broncos, Joe Finan and Joe McConnell called the games. In 1971, Martin and Zimmer were paired and spent 19 years together, taking Broncos fans through the end of the Floyd Little era to four Super Bowls and the first years of the John Elway era. "Bob had already been doing the Broncos for a few years [at KTLN 1280 AM]," said Zimmer, who moved to Denver after broadcasting University of Michigan games, "but I just felt we were on the ground floor of something big."

Martin, who passed away in February 1990, and Zimmer developed close relationships with many of the players and coaches throughout the 1970s and 1980s, and they earned the respect of the Broncos. "Bob Martin was one of the greatest all-time announcers for the Broncos," said Ring of Famer Billy Thompson. "He and Larry Zimmer were excellent commentators."

During their 19 years together, Martin and Zimmer became friends in and out of the broadcast booth. They had many of the same interests and, of course, shared their passion for the Broncos. "I obviously enjoyed working with Bob," Zimmer said. Their calls and analysis of many of the Broncos' greatest moments, including the 1977 AFC Championship Game, the 1986 AFC Championship Game, and more, still live in the minds of many fans.

Martin and Zimmer stayed together literally until Martin couldn't do it anymore. They traveled to New Orleans for Super Bowl XXIV, which was played on January 28, 1990. Martin battled cancer throughout the season but kept doing his job. "He seemingly was able to pull himself up and get those broadcasts done and you'd never know he was sick," Zimmer said. "Bob was a very private person. He didn't want people to realize how sick he was." Zimmer said Martin "was determined he was going to do that Super Bowl." At their New Orleans hotel, Martin taped the pregame interview with head coach Dan Reeves days before the game. After that taping, he went back to his hotel room. "He never left it again until we took him to the hospital the night before the game," Zimmer said.

As it turned out, Martin's last game on the air was Denver's 37–21 win over Cleveland in the AFC Championship Game. He passed away within weeks of the Super Bowl, leaving a hole in the Broncos family. "Bob was a very good friend of mine," Floyd Little said. "He was one of the greats."

Fortunately for KOA, it replaced Martin with another great—Dave Logan. A Denver-area prep sports star as well as a star athlete at the University of Colorado, Logan was a receiver for the Cleveland Browns from 1976 to 1983 and with the Broncos in 1984. "When the opportunity presented itself, obviously he wanted to do it and I wanted him to do it," said Zimmer, who spent many years pulling double duty by covering University of Colorado football on Saturdays and the Broncos on Sundays.

Zimmer and Logan teamed for seven seasons before Zimmer left the Broncos to concentrate on Colorado football. "To me, Dave Logan is the best analyst I've ever worked with," Zimmer said. "He was just terrific. I really enjoyed those seven years that we worked together."

Since Zimmer left, Logan has been the rock on Broncos broadcasts. He has teamed at various times with former NBA player and longtime Denver broadcaster Scott Hastings, former Bronco lineman David Diaz-Infante and, most recently, former Broncos quarterback Brian Griese and receiver Ed McCaffrey. Like Zimmer, Logan has pulled double duty during his time at KOA, as a high school football coach. Considered the top high school coach in Colorado, he has led Arvada West, Chatfield, Mullen and Cherry Creek to state championships. In state history, he ranks second among coaches with seven championships and is among the top 10 in career wins. "He really enjoys [broadcasting]," Zimmer said. "It keeps him a part of pro football that, unless he became a coach, he probably wouldn't be."

It is from the radio that fans know Logan best. His experience as a player and coach brings instant credibility to his broadcasts, and his hometown roots make fans feel like he's one of them. One of Logan's most memorable broadcasts came on January 25, 1998. His raw emotion came through the speakers of radios throughout the Rocky Mountain region when the Broncos defense batted down a Green Bay pass to secure the team's first Super Bowl title.

"Denver's going to win it!" Logan exclaimed. "Oh baby, they're going to win this thing!"

Whether it was Martin and Zimmer or Logan, fans have come to depend on KOA to bring them the sounds of their beloved Broncos. And there's no sign of Logan changing that anytime soon. "I think Dave will continue to do it as long as he can," Zimmer said.

80 To Do: National Western Stock Show

For years, Denver has had a reputation for being a cow town. In many ways, the city has shed that image.

Yet for about two weeks every January, Denver embraces its heritage during the National Western Stock Show. The event celebrates agriculture and the cowboy way of life through educational activities, interactive exhibits, and live shows, including daily rodeos.

During the early 1900s, stockmen wanted a place to meet and show off their animals and buy more livestock. Subsequently, from that need, the Stock Show was born in 1906. That livestock convention turned into the National Western Stock Show, which has been a favorite event in the Mile High City for more than a century.

Prior to 1980, the show was primarily for those involved with the agricultural and livestock industries, although many patrons did attend. The event took a big financial hit during January 1978, however, when attendance suffered during the Broncos' Super Bowl XII loss to the Dallas Cowboys. It was after the 1980 show, however, that the National Western Stock Show began to develop into the event it is today, incorporating more events and activities for the average citizen. It is now home to the world's largest horse show and one of its most lucrative professional rodeos. The National Western Stock Show is also Colorado's largest trade show. More than 600,000 patrons pass through the gates each year, with a record of 726,972 during the 100th anniversary in 2006.

While the event is tailor-made for country-and-western lovers, it's hardly just for cowboys and cowgirls. Once inside, there's no shortage of things to do, for folks of all ages and backgrounds, from taking in the live shows to passing by the 300-plus vendors' booths. Jewelry, household products, Western wear, farming and ranching products, and even tractors, trailers, and trucks keep the registers busy every day. Of course, typical fair cuisine—hot dogs, burgers, corn dogs, chicken fingers, and funnel cakes—prevents the masses from going hungry.

Despite all the items available for purchase, it doesn't take a full wallet to enjoy yourself during a day at the National Western grounds. You can get lost for hours simply touring the facilities and getting up close with all sorts of animals, including cattle, horses, sheep, rabbits, and chickens. Education is a big part of the Stock Show. Children, in particular, have opportunities not only to learn about animals, but about all sorts of agricultural practices.

The live events are always a popular part of the Stock Show. PRCA Rodeo, the Mexican Rodeo Extravaganza, and Wild West Show are among the highlights.

"It truly was just a convention, a trade show for people within the livestock and horse industries," said Chuck Sylvester, general manager of the National Western Stock Show from 1978 to 2003. "I set about changing that and trying to have events that drew more urban people. Now the public is invited to come in and participate, be entertained and educated."

81 Sports Authority Field at Mile High

Since 2001, the Broncos have played their home games at a state-of-the-art stadium in the middle of Denver.

Originally named Invesco Field at Mile High—naming rights were sold to Sports Authority in 2011—the massive, steel structure is an impressive site to commuters who drive through the heart of Denver on Interstate 25.

For 41 years, Mile High Stadium was the home to memorable games, memorable players, and some of the loudest fans in professional football. Yet even as the Broncos were hitting their peak on the field in the late 1990s, owner Pat Bowlen began looking into plans for a new home. For all of its charm and nostalgia, Mile High Stadium, which opened in 1948, was approaching its 50th birthday and had been through several remodels. In May 1997, Roger Goodell, who was the NFL's senior vice president for league and football development, went before the Denver Metro Football Stadium District Board to discuss the issue at hand. "The number one thing I would say that we look at is a long-term solution," Goodell, who later became NFL commissioner, told the board, as quoted in the *Rocky Mountain News*.

Remodeling Mile High Stadium was not the preferred long-term solution. About two months later, a site for the new stadium (just to the east of the old one, but on the same general site) was determined.

All that was left was for Denver-area voters to approve a tax that would help pay for the hefty price tag of building a new stadium. The tax amounted to one penny for every $10 of retail sales in a six-county area of Denver—or roughly $15 per year for those earning $39,000. It was a heated and controversial issue for months in Denver, and on November 3, 1998, residents went to the polls and agreed to back the new stadium. By approving the tax, residents became responsible for 75 percent of the cost, which ultimately amounted to about $400 million.

The timing of the vote could not have been better for the Broncos, Bowlen, and the pro-stadium backers. The Broncos were defending Super Bowl champions, and two days before the vote they defeated the Cincinnati Bengals to improve to 8–0 en route to a second consecutive world title. The team's success likely played a significant role in the tax being approved. "I just think it's a great thing for Denver, a great thing for all the communities, really, and great for the organization of course," Broncos linebacker Bill Romanowski told the *Denver Post*. "I definitely think it's time to build a new stadium. I really enjoy playing in Mile High Stadium, but…I really don't have any sentimental attachment to it. More than anything I enjoy playing in front of the Denver fans, so hopefully when they get a new stadium, they'll be a lot more comfortable and we can all enjoy it even more."

Romanowski may not have had sentimental feelings toward Mile High Stadium, but the fans sure did. It was tough for them to say good-bye to the old place, and for many fans the corporate attachment to the new place didn't sit well. The stadium was named for Invesco Funds Group, yet many fans continued to call the new place "Mile High Stadium."

Construction on the new stadium, located right next to Mile High Stadium, began in the summer of 1999. For two seasons, fans that attended games at Mile High got a close-up look at the progress of the building. When it was done, fans couldn't deny the awesome site it had become. The stadium covered more than 1.7 million square feet and took more than 4.8 million man hours to complete. It was built with, among other things, 85,000 cubic yards of concrete, 12 million pounds of reinforced steels, 12,000 tons of structural steel, and 130,000 bricks.

Invesco Field was unveiled on August 11, 2001, with a concert by the Eagles. The Broncos made their debut with a preseason game against the New Orleans Saints two weeks later. On September 10, 2001, the stadium was put on display for the nation, as the Broncos hosted the New York Giants on *Monday Night Football* in the regular-season opener. One popular Bronco (running back Terrell Davis) returned from injury, another popular Bronco (receiver Ed McCaffrey) broke his leg and was lost for the season. But the Broncos beat the Giants 31–20 and made it a grand opening for their $400 million home.

In the spring of 2016, Sports Authority went out of business and the name of the stadium was in question that summer. Regardless of the name, some fans argue that the new stadium is not as loud as Mile High Stadium. And it was a somber time for many in the spring of 2002 when old Mile High was completely demolished. While the old days of Mile High Stadium are missed, the new stadium has carried on the tradition of sold-out crowds, memorable moments, and thunderous noise when the Broncos are winning.

82 The Heir Apparent

The Chicago Bulls went through nearly a decade of futility after the departure of Michael Jordan. NBC lost a measure of appeal without *Cheers* and *Seinfeld* filling primetime hours. Heck, even Van Halen was never the same during its split from lead singer David Lee Roth.

So it was in Denver, where, from 1999 to 2011, the Broncos struggled to find a suitable long-term replacement for its own legend, John Elway.

"Nobody is going to ever follow him," said Craig Morton, who had the good fortune to play quarterback in Denver before Elway.

In the dozen years after Elway's retirement, Brian Griese, Jake Plummer, Jay Cutler, and Kyle Orton all took turns trying to fill the Hall of Famer's shoes and escape his shadow. Truth is, each one of them was talented and did good things in Denver, but for one reason or another, none of them were embraced by QB-starved Broncos fans.

When Griese, a third-round draft pick in 1998, drew the assignment of replacing Elway, his pedigree seemed solid. His father, Bob, was a Hall of Fame quarterback. Oh, and head coach Mike Shanahan compared him to Hall of Famer Joe Montana. No pressure, right?

Taking over in 1999, Griese spent four years as Denver's primary starter and by most standards would have been considered a success. He posted a winning record (27–24) and threw for 11,763 yards, 71 touchdowns, and 53 interceptions. Until Peyton Manning came along in 2012, Griese had the two best seasons in team history in terms of completion percentage. His 102.9 passer rating in 2000 is the best by a Broncos quarterback not named Manning.

The constant pressure of being compared to three Hall of Famers—Montana, Elway, and his dad—proved to be his undoing, however.

He didn't help himself off the field, either. In three separate incidents, he was arrested for driving while impaired, hit his head after running and falling in Terrell Davis' driveway, and sprained an ankle by, according to him, tripping over his dog at home. The constant criticism on and off the field led Griese to withdraw publicly, earning himself a sour reputation among the media and fans. By the end of the 2002 season, the fans were ready to move on, and so was Shanahan.

In the spring of 2003, several quarterback-needy teams had their eyes on Jake Plummer, a free agent who had quarterbacked the Arizona Cardinals for six years. In 1998, he ended a 60-year drought for the Cardinals with a playoff win. Shanahan and the Broncos won the sweepstakes, signing Plummer to a seven-year, $40 million deal.

Plummer delivered, too. Three seasons into his contract, he had led the Broncos to a 32–11 record, three playoff appearances, an AFC West title, and the only postseason win the Broncos had from 1999 to 2010. He also piloted the Broncos to the 2005 AFC Championship Game. Plummer was terrible in that game, though, throwing two interceptions and losing two fumbles in a 34–17 loss to Pittsburgh.

Was Plummer the long-term answer? Uh, not quite. Three months after the AFC championship loss, Shanahan traded up in the 2006 draft to select Vanderbilt quarterback Jay Cutler with the 11th overall pick.

Plummer played poorly in 2006, but kept winning, taking the Broncos to a 7–2 record while Cutler watched from the sideline.

Perhaps the most talented quarterback in Broncos history, Cutler was on the verge of stardom before Josh McDaniels came along. Photo courtesy of Getty Images

Then Plummer and the Broncos lost back-to-back games to fall to 7–4; Shanahan turned to Cutler.

"He's our future, he's our present," Shanahan told the Associated Press on the day he made the switch.

Plummer wound up with a .722 winning percentage (39–15), second-best in team history. His 27 touchdowns in 2004 tied Elway's team record, and he holds team marks for passing yards in one game (499) and most consecutive passes without an interception (229). He also was somewhat popular among the fans (although not so much with the media), extremely generous with his time and money, and a team-first player in the locker room.

Without the support of Shanahan, though, Plummer got a ticket out of town. After the 2006 season, he was traded to Tampa Bay but never reported to the Bucs. Always known for doing things his way, Plummer elected to retire and moved on to a quiet life away from football.

With that, the Cutler era began. Cutler not only embraced the comparisons to Elway, he attacked them. "I have a stronger arm than John, hands down," the brash quarterback told *The Sporting News* in 2008. "I'll bet on it against anybody's in the league. Brett Favre's got a cannon. But on game days, there's nobody in the league who's going to throw it harder than I am at all."

Strong-armed and arrogant, Cutler held the job through 2008. It was enough time to both frustrate and tantalize Broncos fans desperate for a star quarterback to fill Elway's shoes. Cutler was respected by his teammates but was aloof and arrogant around the media and never did get fully embraced by the fans, many of whom despised his on-field demeanor and his habit of throwing costly interceptions at the wrong time.

During his short time in Denver, Cutler set several team records, including posting the best career passer rating in team history (87.1) to that point. He threw for 9,024 yards and 54 touchdowns and was selected to the Pro Bowl in 2008. But he also lost more games than he won (17–20) and never took Denver to the playoffs.

Shanahan still believed in him and, despite the fact that Cutler didn't exactly have a warm personality, the fans were eager to see him progress.

Just 25 years old when the 2008 season ended, Cutler was well on his way to a brilliant career in Denver. But the Broncos' inability

The new man in Denver: Peyton Manning—alongside Broncos owner Pat Bowlen and vice president of football operations John Elway—arrives.
Photo courtesy of Getty Images

to win their last three games of the 2008 season—in some respects because of Cutler's mistakes—cost them a shot at the playoffs. It also wound up costing Shanahan his job.

Shanahan's replacement, Josh McDaniels, wasn't quite sold on Cutler and even discussed trading him to Tampa Bay. McDaniels had his eye on a quarterback he worked with in New England, Matt Cassel. Once word of that leaked, Cutler's days in Denver were numbered. "I'm upset," Cutler told the *Denver Post* at the time. "I mean, I'm really shocked at this point."

Cutler's relationship with McDaniels, although still new, was damaged for good. Several weeks later, with no signs of a change in that relationship, the Broncos traded Cutler to the Chicago Bears for Kyle Orton and some draft picks.

Orton was no Elway, for sure, but that wasn't his biggest problem. Bitter at losing Cutler, fans spit venom at McDaniels and, therefore, Orton.

Like his predecessors, Orton had great moments. He got the Broncos off to a 6–0 start in 2009 and his numbers from 2009 and 2010 were very good—7,455 yards, 41 touchdowns, and 21 interceptions. After that 6–0 start, though, Orton was 6–21 as the Broncos' starter.

Doomed from the start of the 2011 season, with Tim Tebow looking over his shoulder, Orton got off to a miserable start. He was benched midway through the fifth game and never played for Denver again. He was released a few weeks later, and came back as Kansas City's starter in the final game of 2011, helping the Chiefs beat the Broncos.

The Broncos moved on to Tebow, who won games and, most important, was embraced by fans like no Denver quarterback since Elway. He also struggled mightily with throwing the ball, leaving many to question his ability to succeed. Elway, the Broncos' executive vice president of football operations, and head coach John Fox both gave lukewarm support of Tebow in public.

Two months after the 2011 season ended, so did the Tebow "era." The Broncos jumped at a chance to sign future Hall of Famer Peyton Manning and traded Tebow to the New York Jets.

Manning, finally, became the man to fill the void left by Elway in 1999.

83 D-Will

Shanahan stood at the podium and beamed as he spoke about Darrent Williams, recalling some of the great moments Williams had delivered to the Broncos on the field.

When he was done, Shanahan closed his remarks by saying, "D-Will, we love ya. We'll miss ya. Your spirit will always be with us."

Then he pointed toward the casket, where the body of the once-promising young star lay.

"You meant a lot to us D-Will. Love ya."

Around 2:00 AM on January 1, 2007—just a few hours after the Broncos' season came to a crushing end with an overtime loss to San Francisco, a loss that cost the team a playoff spot—Williams, a 24-year-old starting cornerback, was riding in a limousine when another vehicle pulled up beside it and opened fire. Williams was hit in the neck with a bullet, dying almost instantly.

After the December 31 loss to San Francisco, Williams and some friends, including Broncos teammates Brandon Marshall and Javon Walker, went out to celebrate New Year's Eve. They went to the Safari Club in Denver. Inside the club, the group with Williams got into an altercation with another group, which included Willie Clark, a Denver gang member. The club closed at 1:30 AM, and afterward, outside in the cold and snow, there was another altercation, which allegedly involved Willie Clark and his friends against Marshall and his cousin, Blair Clark.

Willie Clark headed for his SUV, a Chevy Tahoe, apparently to get a gun. Marshall and his cousin headed for their limousine to flee. Williams and his group, in another limo, left the scene as well. Minutes later, Willie Clark's SUV pulled up next to Williams' limo, which carried 17 people, including the driver. At least 15 shots were fired at the limo. It is believed that Willie Clark's shots were meant for Marshall, whom Clark believed to be in Williams' limo. Three of the shots hit passengers, including the shot that hit Williams in the left side of his neck and exited out the right side of his neck. Inside the limo, Walker held on to his teammate, the only fatality from the altercation.

Within hours, word spread to Broncos players, coaches, and administrators.

Six days after their disappointing loss to the 49ers, the Broncos found themselves in a Fort Worth, Texas, Baptist Church mourning a teammate. It was the first time in team

Gone Too Soon

On January 1, 2007, Darrent Williams became the first active Bronco to lose his life. Unfortunately, he hasn't been the last.

Just 53 days after Williams' death, backup running back Damien Nash collapsed during a charity basketball game. Nash, who played just one season with the Broncos, died of apparent heart failure. The basketball game was designed to raise money for heart transplant research. Nash's brother, Darris, had received a heart transplant.

On September 20, 2010, wide receiver Kenny McKinley, who was on the injured-reserve list with a knee injury, was found dead at his home from a self-inflicted gunshot wound. McKinley, in his second season, was depressed because of injury as well as from deep financial trouble before taking his own life.

history that an active Denver Broncos player had passed away. Owner Pat Bowlen arranged for a charter flight to take the entire team to the funeral. Everyone on the team attended, except for Walker. "Javon is struggling," Shanahan told the press after the funeral. "He's going through some very heavy grief right now."

Williams, who starred at Oklahoma State University, was a second-round draft choice of the Broncos in 2005. Despite being just 5'8" and 188 pounds, he made an impression right away. He earned a starting job at cornerback, playing on the opposite side of the field from All-Pro Champ Bailey. With teams shying away from Bailey, Williams was often busy, but he responded. He picked off two passes as a rookie, returning one of them 80 yards for a touchdown. He intercepted four more—including another one for a touchdown—in 2006. He also returned punts and kick-offs for the Broncos.

In addition to his play on the field, Williams made a long-lasting impression on his teammates for his will to succeed, his kind heart, his infectious smile, his stylish outfits, and his ever-changing hairstyles. Although just two years into his career at the time of his death, Williams was one of the Broncos' most popular players. "We can't thank you enough for bringing Darrent into our life," Broncos safety John Lynch said to the Williams family during his eulogy at the January 6, 2007, funeral. "We are so blessed to have had the opportunity to be in his presence. That smile, he was something special."

Immediately following his death, the Darrent Williams Good Guy Award was created. Voted upon by media that covers the team, the annual award goes to the Broncos player who best displays Williams' enthusiasm, cooperation, and honesty when dealing with the press.

More than three years after the shooting, Willie Clark was convicted of first-degree murder and 16 counts of attempted murder of the other passengers in the limousine. He was sentenced to life in prison without parole, plus an additional 1,152 years in prison—72 years for each of the 16 attempted murder counts.

84 2005 AFC Championship Game

The Broncos had been building up to something big.

Although they hadn't won a playoff game in the six seasons since John Elway's retirement, they had been to the playoffs three times, including in 2003 and 2004.

Going into the 2005 season, there was plenty of optimism. Jake Plummer was entering his third season as the starting quarterback. Mike Anderson and Tatum Bell were a solid one-two punch at running back. Rod Smith was still one of the game's elite receivers.

Defensively, the Broncos had built a squad, led by All-Pro cornerback Champ Bailey and third-year defensive coordinator Larry Coyer, that could clamp down on the opposition. Two trades with Cleveland landed the Broncos three big defensive linemen—Ebenezer Ekuban, Michael Myers, and Gerard Warren—who were counted on to make the defense even better.

The season started in disastrous fashion, with a 34–10 loss at Miami on opening day. But after that, the Broncos put together their best season in the post-Elway era. Several players, including Plummer, Anderson, Bell, Smith, and Bailey, had exceptional seasons as the Broncos finished 13–3 to easily win the AFC West title. They then hosted two-time defending Super Bowl champion New England in the divisional playoffs.

Patriots quarterback Tom Brady had never lost a playoff game in his career, coming in to the game with a 10–0 mark. Brady's win streak came to a close against the red-hot Broncos, though. Anderson scored a pair of touchdowns, Smith caught a TD pass from Plummer, and Bailey had a remarkable 100-yard interception return to set up a touchdown. Bailey's play came late in the third quarter, at a time when the Broncos led 10–6. Brady had the Patriots poised to score when Bailey stepped in with the longest non-scoring interception return in NFL postseason history. Anderson's one-yard touchdown on the next play gave Denver a 17–6 lead, and they would go on to win 27–13.

Next up was the AFC Championship Game at home against the Pittsburgh Steelers. Everything pointed to a Broncos win. They had won 11 straight home games. They were 4–0 all-time at home in AFC Championship Games. Pittsburgh, on the other hand, was the first No. 6 seed to even get that far, let alone to the Super Bowl. The Steelers had already won two playoff games on the road, and no team in 20 years had won three.

So what happened? Well, the Broncos played poorly and the Steelers rolled to a 34–17 victory behind young quarterback Ben Roethlisberger and veteran running back Jerome Bettis. Plummer, who had lost two fumbles all season, lost two more against the Steelers. He had thrown seven interceptions all year but threw another two against the Steelers. All those turnovers made the afternoon much easier on the Steelers, who led 24–3 by halftime. "Even without turnovers, if we lose, I'm taking the blame," Plummer said after the game. "That's my job as the quarterback. As the quarterback I've got to lead this team to a win, and I didn't get that job done. I fought all year and all through this game, but [I] had a couple poor decisions, and in a game like this you can't do that."

For a pair of veterans, both of whom helped the Broncos win back-to-back titles in 1997 and 1998, the loss was a devastating blow. "Bottom line is that there were a lot of guys who were brought in here to win the Super Bowl," linebacker and special teams standout Keith Burns said after the game. "You can pick out a few bright spots of the season, but to me it is a complete failure. Anything less than hoisting that Lombardi Trophy is a failure."

Smith, who had his eighth career 1,000-yard season that year, agreed. "This is all you work for," Smith said in the postgame locker room. "You work to be in this situation and win, and we didn't get it done. It wasn't a great season. The only way it's great is if you go all the way. There's only one team that has a great season, and that's the team holding the Lombardi Trophy at the end of the year."

Pittsburgh went on to beat Seattle in the Super Bowl, won another one in 2008, and went back again in 2010. As for the Broncos, that loss kick-started an off-season of change and would be their last playoff game for six years. Longtime offensive coordinator Gary Kubiak left after the season to take the head coaching job in Houston. Plummer, despite his stellar won-lost record, was benched in favor of a rookie the next season. Anderson was released after the season in a money-saving move.

Within two years of that season, tremendous team leaders, such as Smith, Burns, center Tom Nalen, and linebacker Al Wilson, were gone. The 2005 AFC Championship Game did prove to be a turning point for the Broncos—just not the one they hoped it would be.

85 Elvis Is in the Building

If he were four or five inches taller, Elvis Dumervil never would have been sitting around waiting for his name to be called on the second day of the 2006 NFL Draft.

At the University of Louisville in 2005, Dumervil led the country in sacks, with 20—the second-best single-season total in NCAA history—forced an NCAA-record 11 fumbles, and earned the Bronko Nagurski Award, which annually goes to the top defensive player in the nation. Despite his achievements at Louisville, he sat as 125 other players, including seven other defensive ends, were drafted. Heck, even a kicker—a kicker!—was drafted while Dumervil waited. Finally, late in the fourth round, with the 126th pick, the Broncos took him. "I didn't watch the draft the second day," he told DenverBroncos.com in 2006. "I was lifting weights when Coach Shanahan called. Whenever I get frustrated, I lift weights."

At 5'11" and weighing just more than 250 pounds, Dumervil was considered too small to play defensive end in the NFL. The Broncos felt Dumervil's ability to make big plays was difficult to ignore and took a chance on him. "The biggest factor [in drafting him] is his ability to make and create plays," Broncos general manager Ted Sundquist said on DenverBroncos.com after the draft. "If he is not making the tackle, he's forcing the quarterback into somebody else."

After the 2006 draft, Dumervil made the Broncos look brilliant and the rest of the league look foolish. Dumervil had a team-high 8½ sacks as a rookie, despite being declared inactive for three games and never cracking the starting lineup. The next year, he became a full-time starter and notched 12½ sacks and a career-high 56 tackles.

When the Broncos changed coaches in 2009 and switched to a 3-4 defense, many wondered whether Dumervil would have a spot on the team. He changed his body—adding muscle while dropping some weight and increasing his speed—and became a Pro Bowler. He recorded 17 sacks to break Simon Fletcher's 17-year-old single-season team record of 16. That breakout season landed Dumervil a six-year, $61.5 million contract prior to the 2010 season. Unfortunately for Dumervil—known by Broncos fans as "Doom"—he tore his pectoral muscle in training camp and sat out the entire season.

Healthy again in 2011, he had to readjust to another new coaching staff and a return to the 4-3 defense but still finished with 9½ sacks and was selected to the Pro Bowl. After being told he was too small, Dumervil, who led the Broncos in sacks his first four years, was considered one of the best pass rushers in the NFL.

Despite switching positions and playing for five defensive coordinators and three head coaches in six years, Dumervil proved that a little guy can dominate. "I've worked extremely hard," he said. "[Playing for so many coaches], it's a lot of adversity, but you still have to compete and work hard. Just to be in the league this long, with a couple of Pro Bowls, a playoff win finally, it's special."

Dumervil's time in Denver came to a close after the 2012 season. He and the Broncos could not reach agreement on a contract, and Dumervil left to sign with the Baltimore Ravens. During his time with the Broncos, Dumervil recorded 63½ sacks, ranking among the best in team history. In Baltimore, he continued to terrorize quarterbacks and in 2014, he tied his career high with 17 sacks for the Ravens.

86 Sammy Winder

For nine years, Sammy Winder lined up in the Broncos' backfield —despite management's best efforts to find someone else to take his spot.

Winder was a fifth-round draft choice from Southern Mississippi in 1982, and he was hardly a lock to make the team. After all, San Jose State's Gerald Willhite was Denver's first-round draft choice that year, and head coach Dan Reeves loved the thought of Willhite's speed in the lineup for years to come. The Broncos also already had veterans Rick Parros and Dave Preston—who combined to rush for 1,389 yards in 1981. "I had some wishful thinking," Winder said. "Everybody wants to play eight or 10 years. I believed it in my heart that if I made the team I was going to be able to stick [around] that long. I believed it, but I don't know if everybody around me believed it."

The 5'11", 203-pound Winder made the team and wound up splitting time with Willhite and Parros in the strike-shortened 1982 season. A preseason injury to Willhite opened the door for Winder in 1983. He led the team in rushing that year and again in 1984—when he posted a career-high 1,153 yards.

Following his great 1984 season, Winder watched as Denver selected Steve Sewell in the first round of the 1985 draft. Once again, the Broncos were looking for another starter. "I really didn't have the breakaway speed that they were looking for," Winder said. "Willhite did and Sewell did, but that was the only thing they were displeased with [about me] or trying to improve. I won't say they were trying to get rid of me from the team, but just trying to get me out of the lineup and get some speed in the lineup."

Winder is one of the most recognizable players from the Broncos' Super Bowl teams of the late 1980s.

In 1988, the Broncos tried again, trading for future Hall of Famer Tony Dorsett. "Dorsett came to town and I'm thinking I'm going to get the pink slip, and they ended up moving me to fullback," said Winder, who still ran for 543 yards and had nearly as many carries as Dorsett that season.

Despite all those challenges, Winder maintained his starting role and carved out a nice career in Denver. Whether it was injuries to Willhite or Sewell, a seamless move to fullback in 1988, or his own God-given ability, Winder found his way into the starting lineup 83 times in 127 games as a Bronco. "My career was really one of those careers [where] I was in the right place at the right time," he said.

While he never did have that breakaway speed, Winder made up for it in other areas. "I think just my determination to get positive yardage," he said. "I was one of those guys that, the tougher the better. That's the way I felt. When we played a team that had a high-ranking defense, I looked forward to that game to try to get positive yards. I tried to get as many as I possibly could."

He led the team in rushing five years in a row from 1983 to 1987. Hall of Famer Floyd Little is the only other player in team history to lead the team in rushing five years in a row. By the time

Winder was done, after the 1990 season, he had 5,427 yards and 39 rushing touchdowns—numbers that still rank among the best in team history. Winder was selected to play in two Pro Bowls, in 1984 and 1986. "I lived for playing football during that time," he said. "That was something I could have done a couple times a week. I wanted to hit and I wanted to be hit. Football was my life."

Winder even made a name for himself with a patented touchdown dance—the Mississippi Mud Walk, in which he would slowly high step in the end zone, as though he was walking through thick mud. "It was a spontaneous thing I did in the end zone [as a rookie in 1982]," he said. "It was nothing really planned. I think Dan [Reeves] gave it the name 'Mississippi Mud Walk' on the coaches' show one night, and it just took off from there."

It wasn't until 1989 that Winder lost his starting role. The Broncos drafted rookie Bobby Humphrey that year and Winder went to the bench. "Finally Bobby Humphrey got me out of there," said Winder, who retired after the 1990 season.

Humphrey gained 2,353 years in his first two seasons, but a contract dispute led to Humphrey being shipped out of town after the 1991 season, during which he played only four games after holding out. Once again, the Broncos were searching for a running back.

"I should have hung around, huh?" Winder joked.

Following his playing career, Winder moved to Jackson, Mississippi, and still owns Winder Construction.

Winder also still owns a place in the heart of Broncos fans, and he will always look back with pride at a career that included three Super Bowl appearances. "I loved it," he said. "I had a great time with the Broncos. I have no regrets whatsoever. It would have been nice to win a Super Bowl, but it was great. The people there treated me nice. It was an all-around plus for me."

87 The Three Amigos

Out from the smoke, they emerged. Three men, donning cowboy hats, black overcoats, and bandannas; their expressions signaled they were ready for battle.

Mark Jackson, Vance Johnson, and Ricky Nattiel will forever be known in Broncos lore as "the Three Amigos"—a trio of wide receivers with similar skill sets, contrasting personalities, and one heck of a catchy nickname. Not to mention a memorable poster and video to go with it.

Together, they were John Elway's primary targets for a brief period in the late 1980s, and during the Broncos' 1987 Super Bowl run, they enjoyed their fame.

All three were fast, had good hands, and were about the same size, with Jackson and Nattiel both listed at 5'9" and 180 pounds and Johnson listed at 5'11" and 185. Naturally, they came to be linked together, and during the 1987 season, their popularity boomed.

Johnson joined the Broncos as a second-round draft choice in 1985. He was the longest-tenured Bronco of the three, playing in Denver from 1985 to 1993 and again in 1995. He was the second player in team history with at least 400 career catches and the fourth with at least 5,600 receiving yards. He led the Broncos in receiving three years in a row from 1987 to 1989. Off the field, he was a complex man who had numerous run-ins with the law, both during his career and for years after. With fancy cars and unique hairstyles, he was the flamboyant member of the trio.

Jackson, known for his smile and upbeat attitude, came aboard in 1986 as an unheralded sixth-round draft pick, yet he put together seven memorable seasons as a Bronco. He caught at least 26 passes and had at least 436 yards in each of his seven seasons in Denver. He was on the receiving end of Elway's game-tying touchdown pass in the final moments of regulation in the 1986 AFC Championship Game. In the 1987 AFC title game, he hauled in four passes for 134 yards, including an 80-yard touchdown.

Nattiel was Denver's first-round draft choice in 1987 but never lived up to that first-round billing. He was the quiet member of the group, both off the field and on. He played six seasons for the Broncos, from 1987 to 1992, but caught just 121 passes for 1,972 yards. Nattiel was at his best in his first two years, catching a total of 77 passes for 1,204 yards. He became a minor part of the offense after that, but he did catch a 56-yard touchdown pass early in Super Bowl XXIV, giving Denver a 7–0 lead. Of course, Washington then went on to crush the Broncos 42–10.

As individuals, each one of them could have been a go-to receiver for Elway. But collectively, they were tough to stop and fun to watch. In 1987, they combined for 99 catches. In 1988, their best year together, they combined for 160 catches and more than 2,300 yards.

During the height of their popularity, they drew big crowds wherever they went and delighted fans with an "Olé!" celebration whenever one of them scored a touchdown.

They weren't the greatest receivers in team history. In fact, none of them ever made it to a Pro Bowl. Yet along the way, they provided Denver fans with fun times and left everlasting memories of their time together. Their music video, which featured them dressed as cowboys on horseback, emerging through smoke into an old saloon and doing the Olé at Mile High Stadium, was both comical and entertaining for fans. The video included a mariachi

The Three Amigos celebrate with an end-zone dance during Super Bowl XXII against the Washington Redskins. Photo courtesy of Getty Images

band, a brief appearance by then–Denver mayor Federico Peña, and a set of catchy lyrics, excerpted below.

In the city of the Mile High
The battle, it is drawing nigh
Let the Rocky Mountain thunder roar
Send the Amigos off to war

Hey, who are those guys?
Three Amigos! Touchdown banditos!
One amigo turning on a dime
Another tightropes down the sideline
The last one slices through the heart
The next thing that you know,
They are dancing in the end zone
Olé!
Hey, who are those guys?
Three Amigos! Touchdown banditos!
Ol' great John and his shotgun
Put the Redskins on the run,
His bullets flying everywhere
No one is safe with him out there
You can bet he'll take a chance
Go deep to Ricky, Mark, or Vance!
40, 30, 20, 10
Amigos they will strike again
And you will hear the war cry
Echo down from fans on high
Olé!

The video truly is a sight to behold and, thanks to YouTube, it lives on. The Broncos have had better individual receivers come through the ranks, but they've never had a collection quite like the Three Amigos.

88 Ring of Fame

Anyone who has ever attended a game at old Mile High Stadium or at Sports Authority Field has seen the names of Broncos greats on display.

The most significant figures in Broncos history are honored in the Ring of Fame, which is displayed around the Level 5 facade at the Broncos' home field. The Ring of Fame was conceived by Broncos owner Pat Bowlen in 1984, the year he purchased the team. Establishing the Ring of Fame was one of the first, and perhaps the most significant, move Bowlen made in terms of demonstrating his loyalty to the Broncos' past.

Earning a spot in the Ring of Fame is the highest honor given to a Broncos player, and it's an exclusive club. From 1994 to 2011, only seven players were added to the Ring of Fame.

The Ring of Fame, in fact, is a popular topic of debate for Broncos fans—not so much about who is in, but who isn't. Past greats Rubin Carter and Barney Chavous are among the most hotly debated players not included.

There's not much debate over the guys who are honored. The first class of Ring of Famers included Floyd Little, Austin "Goose" Gonsoulin, Rich Jackson, and Lionel Taylor. Hall of Famers John Elway, Shannon Sharpe, and Gary Zimmerman are also honored. Some of the greatest defenders in team history, such as Randy Gradishar, Tom Jackson, Karl Mecklenburg, and Billy Thompson are included as well.

Who decides on the Ring of Famers? From the start, Bowlen has had a panel of voters, including himself, to pick the Ring of Famers. The media was originally involved in those decisions, but the Broncos have gone away from utilizing the media. Today, the four-person committee includes Bowlen, former general manager John Beake, former defensive coordinator Joe Collier, and former Broncos radio announcer Larry Zimmer. Jim Saccomano, the team's vice president of corporate communications, helps the group with statistics and historical information.

Each year, the committee meets to talk about possible candidates. The main qualifications are that the player must have spent at least four years in a Broncos uniform and he must be retired for at least five years. The one exception to the rule was John Elway. The five-year retirement rule was waived for him, and he was inducted into the Ring of Fame in 1999—just a few months after finishing his career.

For the current players, the Ring of Fame is a reminder of the Broncos greats of the past. "Yeah, you've got to respect the guys that come before you," Dumervil said. "They were very good players and brought a good tradition here."

John Beake

Nowadays, John Beake plays a significant role with the Broncos as one of the men on the Ring of Fame committee. For years, he was a key figure in the team's front office. Beake joined the Broncos in 1979 and became assistant general manager in 1984. In 1985, he got the general manager position and held that post for 14 seasons, helping the Broncos to five Super Bowls. In 1999, he was made the team's vice president of administration, and then from 2002 to 2009 he was the vice president of football operations for the NFL. His career included two years as an assistant at Penn State University, one year as the offensive coordinator at Colorado State University (1975), and several years as an assistant coach for the Kansas City Chiefs and New Orleans Saints.

Greek

Former Broncos linebacker Karl Mecklenburg has had 16 football-related surgeries, including nine on his knees. "I've spent a lot of time with Greek," Mecklenburg said. "He would get me back on the field. He would get me ready to go."

"Greek" is Steve Antonopulos, who joined the Broncos as an assistant athletic trainer in 1976. He later became the head trainer and finished his 40th season with the club in 2015.

"He's kind of like Greeley," Mecklenburg joked, in reference to the Broncos' former training camp site. "Great memories don't come back when you see him, but he was necessary."

Mecklenburg was kidding, of course. While seeing Greek does remind players of past or current injuries, he's been an enjoyable member of the Broncos family for decades. "I think he could relate to people," Sammy Winder said. "He wasn't just all about his job. He did a good job of conversing with everybody."

Antonopulos is well known as one of the NFL's top trainers and may be one of the best in all of professional sports. Mecklenburg, for one, credits Antonopulos for helping him last 12 years in the NFL. "I wouldn't have had the length of a career and I wouldn't have had the opportunities to get out there and do what I was able to do if we didn't have the training staff and the doctors that we had," said Mecklenburg, who played in Denver from 1983 to 1994. "To be able to be committed to that organization for as long as Steve has, he's dealt personally with every single guy that's come through there since he started, and that was long before I got there. He's a teammate. He's somebody that his number one priority is getting the Broncos to win."

He sure did that. Maybe it's just a coincidence, but prior to his arrival, the Broncos had never even been to the playoffs. They got there for the first time in his second season, and during his tenure, the Broncos have been to the playoffs 18 times and reached the Super Bowl six times. "That staff on any team is critical, but for being there as long as he has, I don't know how you put it into words," said Billy Thompson, who added Greek was the only trainer he would allow to tape his ankles. "He's a part of those years that I was there. I don't know what we would have done without him. He was key and has been a key for a zillion years. He got you ready to play."

90 Sacco

Jim Saccomano hasn't worked for the Broncos forever. It only seems that way. Formerly the vice president of corporate communications, Saccomano joined the Broncos' public-relations department in 1978 and worked in various roles through his retirement in 2014.

A native of Denver, he is a graduate of Metro State College of Denver and earned a master's degree from the University of Colorado. Keeping with his Colorado roots, Saccomano was director of public relations for the Denver Bears baseball team and then spent three years in broadcasting before joining the Broncos. Since becoming a part of the Broncos, Saccomano has carved out a reputation for being one of the elite public-relations and media-relations personalities in the NFL, if not all of sports. "He's so highly respected in the NFL, and not only by the publicity people, but [by] the media," said former Broncos radio announcer Larry

Zimmer, who worked closely with Saccomano for several years. "They don't come any better than Jim."

During his tenure, Saccomano saw the Broncos go to six Super Bowls, winning two of them. He has also been a part of the NFL's public-relations team for 20 other Super Bowls. Saccomano was on hand when the Broncos traded for John Elway. He handled media relations when head coaches Dan Reeves, Wade Phillips, Mike Shanahan, and Josh McDaniels were all hired.

While he didn't join the Broncos until 1978, you'd be hard-pressed to stump him on any aspect of Broncos history. "You want to know anything about the Broncos or Denver, that's who you ask," Thompson said. "Jimmy Saccomano, he knows any stat. He told me stuff about me I didn't know. You want to know something, that's who you call in this organization."

Saccomano's deep well of knowledge is only part of what makes him so popular among the media that has covered the team for years. He's also extremely loyal—to the Broncos, to Denver, to his family (he has a wife, two children, and grandchildren), and his beloved New York Yankees. "I think he's got great loyalty on both sides," Zimmer said. "I think he's got loyalty to his team and to his owners and to the head coach, and also to the media. He's an honest man and he's got a great work ethic."

In recent years, his role has changed and taken him further away from the media-relations aspect of his job. As he has let the staff that he trained handle the majority of those duties, though, he's not far away. "The influence of Saccomano is definitely there," Zimmer said.

91 John Lynch

John Lynch was already 32 years old and 11 years into his NFL career before he became a Bronco in 2004.

During the next four seasons, from 2004 to 2007, he was a leader in the Broncos secondary and a pillar in the Denver community. "He had four excellent years and four Pro Bowls," Mike Shanahan told DenverBroncos.com. "I have never been around a guy that was more of a pro than John."

Prior to his arrival in Denver, Lynch played 11 seasons with the Tampa Bay Buccaneers, earning five trips to the Pro Bowl and helping the Bucs win their only Super Bowl, in 2002. He played a pivotal role in a Tampa Bay defense that is still revered as one of the top units in NFL history.

In 2003, Lynch suffered a stinger in his neck and played most of the year in pain. Considering his age and his injury, Tampa Bay let him go in free agency. Several teams tried to woo Lynch, but he picked Denver. Although Lynch had his prime years in a Tampa Bay uniform, he was an exceptional addition to the Broncos, bringing his hard-hitting style to a defense that needed more toughness.

He registered 76 tackles and forced three fumbles in his first season as a Bronco. He followed that up in 2005 with 69 tackles, four forced fumbles, and a career-high four sacks. He was in on 97 tackles in 2006. Despite another neck injury, which limited him to 13 games, Lynch had 62 more tackles in 2007. Time finally caught up to Lynch, though. Shanahan told him before the 2008 season that his role would be reduced. Lynch came to training camp anyway but quickly realized he didn't like his role. He asked for his release, was granted it, and pursued other opportunities. He signed with the New England Patriots but didn't make the team. Later that fall, he announced his retirement.

Whether it was stopping the run, breaking up a pass, or delivering a big interception or sack, Lynch was one of the more versatile safeties of his era. "That's the thing I always loved about the position—at times you were asked to be a defensive lineman and at times you were asked to be a linebacker and other times you were asked to cover like a cornerback," Lynch told DenverBroncos.com upon his retirement in 2008. "They asked a lot, but I always loved that challenge."

Perhaps more than his play on the field, Lynch brought to the Broncos a level of veteran leadership that they needed during those years. "He was like a coach around the locker room, and you don't come around players like him very often," Shanahan said.

Lynch gave it all he had on the field, but that's only part of what endeared him to Denver fans during his short time with the team. Lynch was also a stand-up player in front of the media, the type of player who would talk after a loss just as easily as he would after a win. When he did talk to reporters, he was genuine and passionate. That, too, made him popular—not only among the media, but among the fans. He also became quite connected with the Denver community through his charity work, most notably by helping numerous youths through the John Lynch Foundation.

Lynch didn't have his best years in Denver, but his time with the team was memorable, and he left a lasting impression on the Broncos and their fans. In 2016, the Broncos elected him to their Ring of Fame. "I can tell my kids when they grow up that I had a chance to play with John Lynch," former Broncos cornerback Dre Bly told DenverBroncos.com.

92 Clinton Portis

During the 2002 and 2003 seasons, Clinton Portis was, without question, one of the elite running backs in the National Football League.

If there was ever a doubt about that, all you had to do was ask Portis. He'd tell you. "You don't know of no great player without confidence," he said. "You think of the greatest people of all time. You look at Muhammad Ali, you look at Michael Jordan, Wayne Gretzky—they all had confidence. All of them. You've got to have confidence to become that clutch guy when it's on the line."

Portis only played for the Broncos for two years, but his tenure was significant both on and off the field.

On the field, he was a brilliant player who often came through in the clutch. His greatness as a player, however, is what helped Denver acquire one of its best players of all time.

Denver went into the 2002 NFL Draft still seeking a star running back to replace Terrell Davis, whose career was derailed by knee trouble. In the second round of the draft, Denver selected Portis, a brash and confident back from the University of Miami, which is well known for brash and confident players. For all his flamboyance, Portis was as good as advertised, if not better, on the field. He was the NFL's Offensive Rookie of the Year that season, rushing for 1,508 yards—a franchise rookie record—and 15 touchdowns. In 2003, Portis was even better, gaining 1,591 yards and scoring 14 touchdowns, helping the Broncos finish 10–6 and reach the postseason. Becoming the third player in NFL history to gain 1,500 yards in each of his first two seasons, Portis was selected for the Pro Bowl that season.

Portis' most memorable moment in a Broncos uniform came on December 7, 2003, at home against the Kansas City Chiefs. That afternoon, he gained 218 yards and scored five touchdowns in a 45–27 rout of the Chiefs. Somehow, he had a pro wrestling–style championship belt on the sideline and put it on at game's end. Denver fans were thrilled to have their franchise running back, and Portis was pleased to prove to everyone how great he was.

The problem, for Portis, was that he wasn't paid like an elite player. At the end of the 2003 season, he still had two years to go on his rookie contract, which would pay him less than $900,000 combined for those two seasons. Portis wanted more money. Broncos coach Mike Shanahan, who had built a reputation for growing star running backs, wasn't about to break the bank for Portis, however. That impasse led to one of the most significant trades in team history. Shanahan dealt Portis to the Washington Redskins for Pro Bowl cornerback Champ Bailey and a second-round draft choice.

Portis couldn't have been happier, especially because the trade included a new eight-year, $50.5 million dollar contract that made him the NFL's highest-paid running back. "No one would have ever imagined me getting out of Denver anytime soon," he said at the time. "Coach Shanahan called me and basically said, 'Thank you for what you have done for this organization. But I cannot pay you what you're worth. You deserve to be paid as one of the top players in the NFL.' He gave me the opportunity to talk with the Redskins. And they made it happen."

Portis, as usual, had big things in mind when he went to Washington, including a trip to the Super Bowl. The Redskins made the playoffs twice in his seven seasons, winning just one postseason game. Portis' results were mixed. He had four great seasons but also three injury-plagued years before finishing his career after the 2010 season with 9,923 yards.

As for the Broncos, well, they made out just fine. Shanahan was always confident he could find a capable replacement for Portis.

"I've never worried about it because we're going to have a guy who steps up who's a good back for us," Shanahan said before the 2004 season. That year, Reuben Droughns ran for 1,240 yards. The second-round pick the Broncos got in the deal turned out to be running back Tatum Bell, who wasn't great but did rush for 2,342 yards in three seasons before being traded to Detroit.

The key to the deal, however, was Bailey. Denver immediately signed him to a seven-year, $63 million deal, and he proved well worth the investment.

93 South Park

Every once in a while, the Broncos make cameo appearances in television shows and the movies.

In the opening scene of *Back to the Future*, a Denver Broncos clock can be seen in Doc Brown's garage. John Elway has an episode of *Home Improvement* and the 2007 film *Resurrecting the Champ* among his acting credits. *The Simpsons* has poked fun at the Broncos a few of times, most notably in an episode where Homer dreams of owning the Dallas Cowboys and expresses his disappointment when he's given the Broncos instead.

Nowhere have the Broncos been more prominently featured than in Comedy Central's *South Park*, an irreverent animated series known for pushing the limits of censorship. Creators of the popular series, Trey Parker and Matt Stone, both grew up in Denver, as Broncos fans. The series, which debuted in 1997, features a group of kids who live in the Colorado mountain town of South Park. Like the show's creators, the kids are Broncos fans; subsequently, the Broncos, including former quarterbacks John Elway and Jay Cutler, have been a part of several episodes.

Cutler was good-natured about his appearance, in which he meets two of the show's kids during a party. One of the kids, Stan, tells Cutler, "You kinda suck, but my dad said you might be good someday." That drew a laugh from the real-life Cutler. "It was cool. I thought it was funny," Cutler said. "They can make fun of me if they want to."

That's what Parker and Stone are famous for doing—making fun of anything and anyone. Yet for Parker and Stone, the inclusion of the Broncos into their show stems from their passion for their favorite team. In fact, the two appeared together, wearing Broncos uniforms, in a commercial for the NFL Network.

In the commercial, Parker and Stone mention growing up and seeing the Broncos go to, and lose, four Super Bowls—all before South Park went on the air. "Energized by our success on television, the Broncos went to the Super Bowl once again, and won," Stone quips during the commercial. Added Parker: "That was the greatest day of our lives."

94 Not So Classy in San Diego

Broncos history is full of great moments and memorable games, but it also contains a few moments that fans and players would love to forget.

December 28, 2008, will forever be remembered as one of the more embarrassing days in team history.

At the start of the 2008 season, Mike Shanahan, in his 14th season as Broncos head coach, declared on a local radio station that his team would make the playoffs. The Broncos had missed the playoffs in 2006 and 2007. They hadn't gone three consecutive years without a postseason berth since 1980 to 1982.

Despite several bumps along the way—including injuries to more than a handful of running backs and embarrassing losses to the New England Patriots and Oakland Raiders—the Broncos put themselves in position to end their playoff drought. Following a 24–17 win against Kansas City on December 7, the Broncos were 8–5. They led the AFC West division by three games, with three to play. All the Broncos needed in the last three weeks was one more win or one more San Diego loss. So few panicked when the Broncos lost at Carolina the next week—even though San Diego won to close the gap to two games.

On December 21, the Broncos figured to close out the division against the 6–8 Buffalo Bills at Invesco Field at Mile High. After taking a 13–0 lead, the Broncos were well on their way. It was the Broncos who ended up needing to rally late in the game, though. Down 30–23 with less than nine minutes to play, quarterback Jay Cutler and the Broncos had two more chances. The talented young quarterback led Denver to the Bills 15-yard line with 5:42 to go, but his next pass was intercepted. On his next opportunity, Cutler led the team down the field, once again to the Bills 15. After back-to-back incompletions, the last one on fourth down with 32 seconds left, the Broncos walked off the field with a stunning 30–23 loss. Meanwhile, down in Tampa, Florida, San Diego routed the Buccaneers for their third straight win. Denver's three-game lead shrank to one.

Now, the entire season was down to one game—in San Diego, against the red-hot Chargers. The winner would be the division champ; the loser would go home. Motivated and on a roll, San Diego embarrassed the Broncos in the season finale. Chargers quarterback Philip Rivers threw for 207 yards and two touchdowns, LaDainian Tomlinson scored three touchdowns, and the Chargers routed Denver 52–21. The game was every bit as ugly as the score indicates. The Broncos lost their cool at various times of the game and looked like no match for the Chargers. "A complete disaster, probably the worst loss of my career," Broncos Pro Bowl cornerback Champ Bailey told the *Denver Post* the next fall. "There was so much on the line and we didn't even show up. That was the worst."

Denver made NFL history that day. The league began divisional play in 1967, and no team had ever missed the playoffs after holding a three-game lead with three games to play. It was the second time in three years that the Broncos went into the final game of the season needing a win to get into the playoffs and failed to get it. The massacre in San Diego was different, however. That loss changed the whole direction of the franchise.

In the wake of that loss, Shanahan was fired. His replacement, Josh McDaniels, traded Cutler in the spring of 2009. The Broncos would never be the same again. "That's not my place to say what happened and why, but who knows if we would have won, what would have happened all around?" linebacker D.J. Williams said to the *Denver Post* during the 2009 season. "You get to the playoffs, anything can happen. But we dropped the ball in that one. We had a prime-time game, win or go home. We lost and we went home."

95 Cookie

When the gold Cadillac pulled up to training camp in 1965, everybody knew who was inside.

Carlton Chester Gilchrist, known as "Cookie" throughout his playing days, was one of the most unique individuals ever to suit up for the Denver Broncos.

A bruising fullback who stood 6'3" and weighed in at about 250 pounds, Gilchrist made his mark—albeit not always a good one—everywhere he went, even during his first season as a Bronco. Every team he played for during his 14 seasons of professional football loved his talent. Yet all of them grew frustrated by his antics off the field. "People think I'm an oddball because I'm a Negro who speaks up," he said in 1964, while a member of the Buffalo Bills. "But I have a lot on my mind. It's an internal disease, and it'll eat me alive if I don't get out of my system what I think about things."

No, Cookie was not quiet. That's how he got that Cadillac in the first place. After being traded from Buffalo to Denver in 1965, he became the highest-paid player in the AFL. "When he first got there, they had to buy him a Cadillac," former Broncos safety Goose Gonsoulin said. It wasn't just any Cadillac, though. Gilchrist made sure people knew when he was around. On the side of his car, he painted Lookie, lookie, here comes Cookie.

Asked how he got his nickname, Gilchrist once said, "My mother called me 'Cupcake,' my father called me 'Doughnut,' and the family settled on 'Cookie.'" You just never knew what Gilchrist would say or do next, yet when he was focused on the field, he had few peers.

Gilchrist was the first running back in AFL history to rush for 1,000 yards when he ran for 1,096 yards for Buffalo in 1962, winning the league MVP honors. Gilchrist never went to college, instead choosing to sign with the NFL's Cleveland Browns right out of high school, in 1954. He was cut by the Browns but spent eight years playing in Canada before joining the Bills in 1962. He wore out his welcome in Canada and in Buffalo with his antics off the field—and on. Frustrated over his role on the Bills offense, he actually quit during a game in 1964. Head coach Lou Saban decided to cut Gilchrist, but team members voted to bring him back, so Saban did.

Cookie Gilchrist gets some hard yards against the Houston Oilers during a 1965 game. Photo courtesy of Getty Images

Saban, who later coached the Broncos, traded his powerful fullback to Denver before the 1965 season. He was an instant hit in Denver, and he made an impression on Gonsoulin right away. "When he first came to Denver, we had a party," Gonsoulin said. "He had it upstairs in his suite. We go up to it, and there's Sonny Liston. Him and Sonny Liston are standing side by side and Cookie is bigger than Sonny Liston. I said, 'Put you all's fists up,' and Cookie had bigger fists than him." Liston, one of the great boxers of all time, didn't measure up to Gilchrist physically and probably

One-Year Wonders

Several players have come through Denver and produced one great year before falling off the map. Following are some of the most memorable:

Mike Croel, LB, 1991: A first-round draft choice, he had 10 sacks and was named the NFL's Defensive Rookie of the Year. In six more NFL seasons, he netted a total of 14.

Reuben Droughns, RB, 2004: In three previous NFL seasons, Droughns ran the ball 40 times for 97 yards. In 2004, he led the Broncos with 1,240 yards and six touchdowns. After the season, he demanded more money, but the Broncos traded him to Cleveland.

Olandis Gary, RB, 1999: As a rookie in 1999, Gary rushed for 1,159 yards and seven touchdowns. During the next three seasons combined he had 455 yards and two touchdowns.

Brandon Lloyd, WR, 2010: After barely playing in 2009, Lloyd caught 77 passes for an NFL-best 1,448 yards and 11 touchdowns, making the Pro Bowl in 2010. The next season, he caught 19 passes for 283 yards before being traded midseason.

Phil Nugent, DB, 1961: In his only AFL season, he intercepted seven passes.

Javon Walker, WR, 2006: That season, he caught 69 passes for 1,084 yards with eight touchdowns. The next season, he got hurt and caught just 26 passes for 287 yards and then got released.

appreciated the fullback's fighting mentality. "His character was that he was a great player and he would kind of let you know it and then challenge you to prove that he's not," Gonsoulin said. "He was just a tough guy. He was a big guy. Good, hard runner."

Gilchrist ran for 954 yards and six touchdowns in 1965 with the Broncos. He was a star, and he acted like it. "The owners had to treat him different," Gonsoulin said. "They had to let him do certain things. We would go out there and the coach would say, 'Okay, everybody run five 100-yard sprints,' and they'd leave it up to us. Cookie would say, 'I ain't running those sprints,' and he'd just walk in. He'd do whatever he wanted to. He had special privileges, I guess."

Despite his antics, he was popular among his teammates. "He was a gentleman, and I really liked Cookie," Gonsoulin said. "We really liked being around him. He was a winner."

Conflicts with Broncos head coach Mac Speedie led to Gilchrist being traded to Miami during training camp in 1966. He came back in 1967, ironically with Saban as head coach, but that stint was even shorter. He ran for 21 yards on 10 carries in the season opener and broke his leg. That was the last game of his brilliant yet controversial career.

96 Mr. Versatility

Of all the players in the Broncos' Ring of Fame, Gene Mingo may have been the least likely to ever get there.

Mingo came to Denver in 1960 to try out for the Broncos, who were a first-year team in the first-year AFL. A native of Akron, Ohio, Mingo was a mischievous kid who left elementary school to help take care of his sick mother. Later, he dropped out of high school and joined the Navy. While in the Navy, he was sent to Little Creek Amphibious Base in Norfolk, Virginia. The base had a football team, comprised of former college players, as well as a few former pros.

"Playing in the service, when you go against the Marines, Army, or even another Navy team, it was almost like playing against the Raiders or the Chiefs," Mingo said. "That's where I got most of my experience, playing service ball against Quantico, Camp Lejeune, Fort Belmar, Fort Dix."

Mingo left the Navy early in 1959 and returned to Akron to work at a Goodyear tire plant, but the itch to play football was still there. He began writing letters, and sent one to Broncos general manager Dean Griffing, who gave Mingo him a shot, signing him to a $6,500 contract.

During that first training camp, the Broncos had well over 100 men trying to earn a spot on the roster. Mingo was talented, but he needed something to stand out from the crowd, and luckily for him, he did get noticed. Trainer Fred Posey told Mingo, "They were going to cut you this weekend and you kicking field goals saved you a job."

With that, Mingo earned a spot and became the first black field goal kicker in pro football. In fact, there's only been a few since. "I didn't know that I was a pioneer. I knew that the man upstairs gave me an opportunity to kick field goals and I took advantage of it. I did whatever the Broncos asked me to do," said Mingo, who also played halfback.

If Mingo had just been a field goal kicker, that might have been enough to earn a spot in Broncos history. He was much more than just a kicker, though. Mingo may have been the most versatile player in team history, and put his skills on display right away. In the Broncos' first-ever regular season game, on September 9, 1960, they played an away game against the Boston Patriots and Mingo rushed for 66 yards, kicked an extra point, and returned a punt 76 yards for what turned out to be the winning touchdown in a 13–10 victory.

In 1960, Mingo led the AFL in field goals (18) and total points (123), and in 1962, he led the league in both categories again (27 field goals, 137 points). He played five seasons with the Broncos and in that time he kicked 72 field goals and scored 408 total points. He also gained 777 yards and eight touchdowns as a runner, caught 47 passes for 399 yards and three touchdowns as a receiver, and even threw two touchdown passes.

During the 1964 season, the Broncos traded him to the Raiders. Mingo kept playing until 1970, suiting up for the Raiders, Miami Dolphins, Washington Redskins, and Pittsburgh Steelers. Nothing could ever replace his time in Denver, though. He wasn't just an original Bronco; he was a devoted Bronco. Mingo was one of several players in 1961 who went door-to-door to help gain support for the team and keep them in Denver. "This is my team, this is my state now even though I'm from Ohio.... I will do anything I can for the Broncos."

After football, Mingo's life unraveled for a while as he became addicted to drugs. That led to an incident when he was arrested after accidentally shooting his wife. "I made a mistake in '86, but that mistake turned me into a much, much better person," he said.

With his wife by his side, Mingo turned his life around. At 50 years old, he earned his GED high school equivalency degree and in the late 1980s he became a drug and alcohol counselor. "I don't like to see people hurting, and I enjoy being a counselor," he said. "I will help anyone that needs help."

For what Mingo did as a Bronco, he probably should have been in the Ring of Fame long ago, but his off-the-field troubles likely kept him out for years. Finally, in 2014, the Broncos honored him with a spot in the Ring of Fame. He became the fourth original

Bronco to be honored, along with Goose Gonsoulin, Lionel Taylor, and Frank Tripucka.

"I didn't think I would ever get in," he said. "It means a lot to me. The Broncos gave me a start. They gave me my chance and I took advantage of it."

97 To Do: Buffalo Bill Museum and Grave

Since 1960, the Broncos have been one of the main attractions in Denver. Perhaps the first great entertainer in Colorado history, however, was William F. "Buffalo Bill" Cody.

One of the great showmen of the Wild West, Buffalo Bill is immortalized at the Buffalo Bill Museum and Grave at Lookout Mountain, about 15 miles west of Denver in the town of Golden. A true cowboy, Buffalo Bill spent much of his early years as a fur trapper and gold miner. He also joined the Pony Express and served in the United States Army. He gained his nickname from his success as a hunter.

Later, Buffalo Bill went into show business, starting up the Buffalo Bill Combination, which featured a variety of plays and a Wild West show. Buffalo Bill aimed to entertain and educate with his shows, which included hundreds of performers in addition to live animals, including buffalo. Among those who performed with Buffalo Bill were "Texas Jack" Omohundro, "Wild Bill" Hickok, and Annie Oakley. Cody's show, Buffalo Bill's Wild West Show, became a popular attraction around the United States and in Europe. He used real cowboys, cowgirls, and American Indians in his shows.

Buffalo Bill took his show on the road but had strong ties to Colorado. He first came to Colorado in 1859, and from 1886 to 1916, he performed in Colorado 35 times. He died in Denver in 1917 and was buried on Lookout Mountain, which was his dying wish, according to his wife and close friends.

Lookout Mountain is a popular destination for Denverites, as it provides spectacular views of the Rocky Mountains and the Mile High City. The museum itself opened in 1921 and is a treasure trove of western history. It features several exhibits about Buffalo Bill's life and artifacts from the Old West. Tourists can also visit Buffalo Bill's grave.

While the museum has several permanent exhibits, it also features temporary exhibits that change yearly and special events throughout each year. The museum is also a great spot for kids, with several interactive and educational activities offered. Located about 30 minutes from Denver, it is still one of the most popular attractions for locals and visitors. It's a must-see for anybody who appreciates and admires the Old West.

98 The Toughest Bronco?

It would be difficult to determine the toughest player in Broncos history. Yet any discussion of that honor would be incomplete without mention of Lewis "Bud" McFadin.

A true cowboy from Rankin, Texas, McFadin was an original Bronco and starred on their defensive line from 1960 to 1963. Although he had been away from football for nearly four years, the Broncos could tell immediately that McFadin would be an important part of their defense. McFadin's biography in the Broncos'

1960 media guide read: "Destined to be a defensive great in the American Football League. Terrific size and crushing strength, all man in every respect."

Had McFadin not taken a bullet to the stomach four years earlier, he might never have played in Denver.

In 1956, McFadin wrapped up his fifth season with the NFL's Los Angeles Rams, where he was a two-time Pro Bowl player. During his off-seasons, McFadin worked at a country club near Houston that he and his wife owned. Following the 1956 season, McFadin got into a dispute with a patron on the country club's golf course. "He told a guy to leave, and the guy wouldn't leave," said Goose Gonsoulin, who was McFadin's roommate when they played together in Denver. "Bud told him, 'I'm coming out there this afternoon and I want you to be gone.' When he did, the guy had a gun and Bud reached over and grabbed it and pulled it toward him and it went off and hit him in the stomach. Bud went in and called a cab and went to the hospital." McFadin recovered, but it appeared his playing career was over. After 1956, he never played for the Rams again.

With the birth of the AFL and the Broncos in 1960, McFadin was lured out of retirement by Broncos assistant coach Jimmy Cason—who was a teammate of McFadin's in Los Angeles. With a ragtag roster in 1960, the Broncos had little talent and fewer leaders. McFadin and quarterback Frank Tripucka commanded respect. "They were the two older guys," Gonsoulin said. "Whatever they said, they were like our bosses."

McFadin played in the AFL All-Star Game three times with the Broncos (1961–63). By 1963, the Broncos' media guide read that McFadin was the "most respected player in professional football for ability and personal habits."

Although the Broncos weren't very good during those years, McFadin put genuine fear into opponents—and teammates. He was a tough son of a gun. McFadin went to the University of

Texas, located more than 280 miles from his high school in Iraan, Texas. Once there, he became homesick for his horse. He nearly left school because of it, but school officials made arrangements to bring McFadin's horse to Austin. He stayed and went on to earn All-American accolades in 1949 and 1950. McFadin was also a champion in boxing and wrestling.

Years later, Gonsoulin spent time with McFadin in Houston. "Bud had cows and horses and all that crap," Gonsoulin said. "Those horses were scared of him."

McFadin's time in Denver was short. Following the 1963 season, he was traded to the Houston Oilers. He played two seasons with the Oilers before retiring and coaching the Oilers' defensive line for five seasons.

After football, he became a rancher on a full-time basis. He passed away in 2006. "He was a strong man—as far as physically, as far as his constitution and his personality," said Mark McFadin, Bud's son, following his father's passing. "He was very strong but very kind and gentle at the same time. Very mellow, very easygoing. Just pretty much an old cowboy."

That old cowboy may have been the toughest man to ever wear a Broncos uniform.

"Strongest guy I ever met," Gonsoulin said.

99 Denver Gold

Many football fans would argue that the worst part of the NFL is that it stops play for six months a year.

Several wealthy businessmen agreed, and in the spring of 1982 they announced the start of a new 12-team professional football league—the United States Football League. David Dixon, who had helped bring the NFL's Saints to New Orleans in the 1960s, cooked up the idea of the "other season," meaning the USFL would play its games in the spring and summer, when the NFL was resting. Other pro leagues, most notably the World Football League in the mid-1970s, had tried and failed. USFL owners felt they had the right formula: in addition to the other season, the USFL aimed to play in NFL cities and in NFL stadiums. Ten of the 12 teams during the inaugural season of 1983 played in NFL cities, including the Denver Gold.

Hungry for more football, fans in many cities, including Denver, turned out in droves—just as the team owners predicted. The Gold drew more than 45,000 fans to Mile High Stadium for their first game, on March 6, 1983, against the Philadelphia Stars. Gold owner Ron Blanding added a twist to the game: he offered fans a refund if they didn't like the product. Hardly anybody wanted one. "The Denver crowd was incredible," said Harry Sydney, who starred at running back for two seasons with the Gold. "They accepted that football. Maybe because it was that time of year, but it was awesome."

Red Miller—six years after guiding the Broncos to the Super Bowl and more than two years after being fired by the Broncos—was hired as the first head coach of the Gold. Another ex-Broncos coach, John Ralston, was the head coach of the Oakland Invaders. "It was great playing for Red, because you had a proven winner," Sydney said. "Here's a guy that knew what he was doing. He had the passion for the game, so it was awesome."

Miller didn't last long, though. He and Blanding didn't see eye to eye, and Miller was fired 11 games into the season. His replacement was none other than Craig Morton, the Broncos' quarterback during the 1977 Super Bowl season. Morton had finished his playing career just a few months earlier but wasn't quite the field general the Gold needed. "Craig Morton was different," Sydney said. "Craig was a guy that was really more of a face. You respected both of them, but in different ways. Red you respected because he took a lot of other people to greatness. Craig, you respected him because he had been there."

On the field, the Gold weren't a great team. They finished 7–11 that first year. But they were the only team in the league that didn't lose money. The Gold roster also featured some familiar faces for Broncos fans, including former backup quarterbacks Jeff Knapple and Craig Penrose. Because of the popularity of the game in Denver, the first USFL Championship Game was played at Mile High Stadium, with the Michigan Panthers defeating the Philadelphia Stars 24–22.

Although the Gold improved to 9–9 in 1984, big changes occurred before the 1985 season. Doug Spedding bought the team and Darrell "Mouse" Davis took over as head coach. Davis brought his high-powered "run and shoot" offense to the Gold. They racked up big-time stats and finished 11–7 to qualify for the playoffs. That was it for the Gold, though. Following the 1985 season, the Gold merged with the team in Jacksonville, Florida, and planned to play in Jacksonville. That never happened, as the 1985 season was the last for the USFL.

Arena League

The Broncos and Denver Gold weren't the only pro football teams to have come through Denver. The Mile High City has twice been home to Arena Football League teams. In 1987, the Denver Dynamite was a charter franchise of the Arena League and won the ArenaBowl title. They suspended operations in 1988, but returned to play three more seasons before folding in 1991. Arena football returned to Denver in 2003 with the expansion Colorado Crush, owned by Pat Bowlen and John Elway. The Crush won the 2005 ArenaBowl title. They played six seasons, from 2003 to 2008 before the AFL suspended operations. When the AFL returned, the Crush did not.

Some USFL owners, including Donald Trump of the New Jersey Generals, convinced others to ditch the plan of the "other season" and take the NFL head-on with a fall season. Trump and others figured that would eventually lead to the two leagues merging—much like the AFL and NFL did in 1970—with some USFL teams becoming NFL teams. That would have filled the pockets of some USFL owners. Instead, the two leagues ended up in court. The USFL sued the NFL, accusing the NFL of monopolizing professional football and controlling television coverage on the major networks. The $1.32 billion antitrust case lasted three months. In the end, the USFL won, yet instead of getting hundreds of millions of dollars in damages, the jury awarded the league $1. Antitrust law automatically tripled that to $3. For USFL owners, who had lost tens of millions of dollars, that judgment signaled the end of their run.

"It was an alternative, and it was a good alternative," Sydney said of the USFL. "The prices were reasonable. They tried to make it fan-friendly. Even the players were more accessible. It was a great league at the right time. Unfortunately, some of the powers that be didn't recognize how good it was at that time. They wanted to make it more."

The league did have a lasting impact, however. With a desire to showcase star players, the USFL had lured big names to the league. That eventually led to the NFL paying its players more money in an effort to keep them. USFL stars such as Jim Kelly, Steve Young, and Reggie White went on to have Hall of Fame careers in the NFL. Gary Zimmerman, a Hall of Fame offensive lineman for the Broncos from 1993 to 1997, spent two seasons in the USFL, as well. Doug Flutie, Bobby Hebert, Scott Norwood, and Herschel Walker also went on to good NFL careers. "There's a lot of guys that got their feet wet in the USFL," Sydney said.

Sydney was one of them. After three seasons in the USFL—he played for the Memphis Showboats in 1985—he spent five seasons with the NFL's San Francisco 49ers and one with the Green Bay Packers. He later worked as an assistant coach for the Packers for six seasons. After winning two Super Bowl rings with the 49ers, he won another as a Packers coach. Cut by the Cincinnati Bengals and Seattle Seahawks before joining the USFL, Sydney made a name for himself in Denver, rushing for 1,762 yards in two seasons. "The Denver Gold gave me the ability to keep my dream alive," he said. "If I never had those numbers and that success, [playing in the NFL] never would have happened for me."

Sydney, who founded My Brothers Keeper, a nonprofit organization in Green Bay that mentors boys and men, is a proud USFL alum—and still cherishes the time he spent as a member of the Denver Gold. "It was awesome, man," he said. "The fans, they just loved football. It's a football town."

100 Before T.D. There Was...T.D.

Tony Dorsett was done. That's what the Dallas Cowboys thought, anyway.

After 11 brilliant years as a running back for the Cowboys, Dorsett was shipped to Denver in 1988.

That's right, nearly a decade before Terrell Davis carved out a sensational career as a Broncos running back, another famous T.D. played the position in Denver.

From 1977 to 1987, Tony Dorsett was a star with America's Team. After a remarkable collegiate career at Pittsburgh, where he won the Heisman Trophy, Dorsett helped the Cowboys win Super Bowl XII—against the Broncos—in his rookie season. That was the first of five straight 1,000-yard seasons for the runner. In fact, from

1977 to 1985, he had eight 1,000-yard seasons, falling short only in strike-shortened 1982.

By 1987, however, Dorsett was no longer the man in the Dallas backfield. Although he was the fourth-leading rusher in NFL history by the end of 1987, he was number two on the Dallas depth chart. The emergence of Herschel Walker made Dorsett expendable. The Broncos had won two straight AFC championships and felt Dorsett could help bring them their first Super Bowl title. They shipped a future fifth-round draft choice to Dallas for the 34-year-old running back. "He's going to help us tremendously," John Elway said at the time of the deal. "We're going to try to feature him and give him the football and let him run with it. We need a big-play back."

Dorsett had some good moments with the Broncos, but he certainly wasn't the player he was early in his career. He never made the impact the Broncos hoped he would. In 1988, Dorsett led the team with 703 rushing yards. He passed Franco Harris and Jim Brown to become the second-leading rusher in league history, with 12,739 yards. He had two 100-yard games, but 404 of his yards came in just four games. Nine times he failed to gain even 40 yards.

While Dorsett struggled, so did the Broncos. They went 8–8 and failed to reach the playoffs. Dorsett also didn't help himself in the eyes of Broncos head coach Dan Reeves. During the season,

Willie Brown

Tony Dorsett is one of two Hall of Famers who had brief stints in Denver. Cornerback Willie Brown played four seasons with the Broncos (1963–66), making the AFL All-Star team twice and intercepting 15 passes as a Bronco. He had nine interceptions in 1964. After the 1966 season, Brown was traded to Oakland. He played 12 seasons with the Raiders, making the AFL All-Star game three times and the Pro Bowl four times, reaching the Super Bowl twice and winning it once. He was inducted into the Hall of Fame as a Raider in 1984.

Dorsett was arrested for driving under the influence of alcohol. In another game, Reeves kept Dorsett on the bench for all but one play—and Dorsett didn't touch the ball on that play. It was the only game he ever played in the NFL in which he didn't touch the ball.

Reeves was also unhappy about Dorsett's lack of production in the passing game. He told the veteran to work on catching Elway's passes before the 1989 season. When Dorsett stayed home in Dallas during the summer of 1989 and failed to show up for voluntary workouts, Reeves wasn't thrilled. "I don't know how you can learn to catch a guy's passes if he's in Denver and you're in Dallas," Reeves said. "I'm disappointed because he said he was going to be here."

Dorsett did show up for training camp, but his career took another disappointing turn at that point. During a non-contact drill in camp, he tore up his left knee. He never played again. "I don't think anybody wants to go out in this fashion," he said at the time. "We all want to go out in a blaze of glory, but that's life in the big leagues."

As of 2012, Dorsett ranked eighth in NFL history in rushing yards and was one of just six players in the Pro Football Hall of Fame to have worn a Broncos uniform. While his one season in Denver wasn't the most memorable year of his career, it did leave a lasting impression on one of his teammates—fellow running back Sammy Winder. "That was like a dream come true," Winder, who gained 543 yards in 1988, said of playing with Dorsett. "Tony was in the league while I was still in college, and I idolized his play. To get the opportunity to line up in the same backfield with him, that was tremendous."

Trivia

Q: Which two current NFC teams were once AFC West rivals of the Broncos?
A: The expansion Tampa Bay Buccaneers played in the AFC West in their inaugural year of 1976. In 1977, Tampa Bay moved to the NFC Central and the Seattle Seahawks joined the AFC West. Seattle remained in the AFC West through 2001 before moving to the NFC West when the NFL expanded to eight divisions.

Q: Which former Broncos head coach set the record for the longest pass play in NFL history?
A: Frank Filchock, who was the Broncos' first head coach, was playing for the Washington Redskins on October 15, 1939, when he threw a 99-yard pass to Andy Farkas against the Pittsburgh Steelers. Until 1963, when the mark was duplicated, it stood as the only 99-yard pass in league history. It has since been repeated numerous times.

Q: Only one quarterback in Broncos history has gone through an entire season without having anyone else on the team throw at least one pass. Who is that quarterback?
A: Jake Plummer threw all 521 of the Broncos' passes in 2004. In every other season in Broncos history, at least two different players have thrown a pass.

Q: Through the 2015 season, four Heisman Trophy winners have suited up for the Broncos since their inaugural season of 1960. Who are those four?
A: Steve Spurrier, who won the 1966 Heisman Trophy, was with the Broncos during training camp in 1977 but didn't make the

team. Tony Dorsett, the 1976 winner, was the Broncos' leading rusher in his only season in Denver, 1988. Ron Dayne, the 1999 winner, played in Denver in 2005. Finally, 2007 winner Tim Tebow played in Denver during the 2010 and 2011 seasons.

Q: Who were the three future Pro Bowlers who spent at least part of the 1994 season on the Broncos practice squad?
A: Tight end Dwayne Carswell, center Tom Nalen, and wide receiver Rod Smith all went from being on the Broncos practice squad in 1994 to becoming future Pro Bowlers. Since the NFL began using practice squads in 1989, Carswell, Nalen, and Smith are still the only players in team history to go from the practice squad to the Pro Bowl.

Q: On September 21, 1969, Steve O'Neal of the New York Jets kicked a 98-yard punt at Mile High Stadium—still the longest punt in pro football history. Which Broncos Ring of Famer was back deep to try to field that punt?
A: Billy Thompson was the punt returner on the day Steve O'Neal kicked his record 98-yard punt. "The ball hit right on the nose when it came down and bounced and it was just rolling," Thompson said. "It was the most incredible punt I'd ever seen."

Q: Of the 41 players who caught touchdown passes from John Elway, who caught the most?
A: Shannon Sharpe caught 42 touchdown passes from John Elway, more than any other receiver. Vance Johnson was second, with 35, but Johnson caught more postseason touchdowns from Elway (4) than anybody else.

Q: Which legendary NFL receiver finished his career as a Denver Bronco?
A: Jerry Rice, the NFL's all-time leader in receptions, receiving yards, and total touchdowns, competed for a roster spot with the Broncos during training camp in 2005. After playing in all four preseason games, he decided to retire rather than play a 21st season.

Q: Going into 2015, which college has sent more players to the Broncos than any other school?
A: The University of Colorado had 32 players go on to play for the Broncos heading into 2015. The University of Florida was second on the list with 30.

Q: Through the 2015 season, who were the only two quarterbacks to win their first playoff game with the Broncos?
A: Craig Morton (1977) and Tim Tebow (2011) are the only two quarterbacks to win their Broncos playoff debut. John Elway (1983), Gus Frerotte (2000), Jake Plummer (2003), and Peyton Manning (2012) all lost their initial postseason games in Broncos uniforms.

Q: When the Broncos went to the Super Bowl after the 2015 season, they tied the NFL record with eight Super Bowls appearances. Which teams reached their eighth Super Bowl before the Broncos?
A: The Dallas Cowboys set an NFL record with their eighth Super Bowl appearance in 1995. In 2010, the Pittsburgh Steelers got to their eighth Super Bowl, and in 2014, the New England Patriots tied the mark. The Broncos joined that list in 2015.

Q: Who are the two Broncos that have been named the Associated Press Offensive Rookie of the Year?
A: Running back Mike Anderson was the Associated Press Offensive Rookie of the Year in 2000, and running back Clinton Portis earned the award in 2002.

Q: Going into 2016, which player had scored the most touchdowns in Broncos history?
A: Rod Smith had a team-record 71 career touchdowns going into the 2016 season. Terrell Davis was second with 65.

Q: In 2010, the Broncos roster included quarterback Brady Quinn and tight end Richard Quinn. Who is the only other player in team history with a last name beginning with *Q*?
A: Aside from the two Quinns, backup running back Frank Quayle (1969) was the only player in team history with a last name beginning with *Q*.

Q: Who was the only Bronco to ever wear No. 18 from 1960 to 2011?
A: Frank Tripucka, the team's first quarterback, from 1960 to 1963, was the only player to wear No. 18. His number is one of three retired by the Broncos—including John Elway's No. 7 and Floyd Little's No. 44. However, after the Broncos signed quarterback Peyton Manning in the spring of 2012, Tripucka gave permission for Manning to wear No. 18. Manning wore No. 18 during his four seasons in Denver.

Bibliography

Books

2015 Denver Broncos media guide (as well as past editions of the media guide).

Dater, Adrian. *The Good, The Bad & The Ugly: Denver Broncos.* Chicago: Triumph Books, 2007.

Frei, Terry. *'77: Denver, the Broncos, and a Coming of Age.* Lanham, MD: Taylor Trade Publishing, 2008.

Howsam, Robert Lee. *My Life in Sports.* Unpublished, 2009.

Little, Floyd with Tom Mackie. *Floyd Little's Tales From the Broncos Sideline.* Champaign, IL: Sports Publishing, LLC, 2006.

Morton, Craig with Adrian Dater. *"Then Morton Said to Elway..."* Chicago: Triumph Books, 2008.

Romanowski, Bill with Adam Schefter and Phil Towle. *Romo, My Life on the Edge: Living Dreams and Slaying Dragons.* New York: HarperCollins, 2005.

Saccomano, Jim. *Denver Broncos: The Complete Illustrated History.* Minneapolis: MBI Publishing Company, 2009.

Saccomano, Jim. *Game of My Life Denver Broncos: Memorable Stories of Broncos Football.* Champaign, IL: Sports Publishing LLC, 2007.

Shanahan, Mike with Adam Schefter. *Think Like a Champion.* New York: HarperCollins, 1999.

Zimmer, Larry. *Stadium Stories: Denver Broncos.* Guilford, CT: The Globe Pequot Press, 2004.

Magazine and Newspaper Articles

Alzado, Lyle, "I'm Sick and I'm Scared," *Sports Illustrated,* July 8, 1991.

Associated Press, "It's fourth and long for Denver's Dorsett," *The Capital*, August 11, 1989.

Associated Press, "Upchurch ends pro career," *Gettysburg Times*, May 24, 1984.

Associated Press, "Griese's play continues to draw rave reviews," *Santa Fe New Mexican*, November 7, 2000.

Associated Press, "From backup to boss," *New York Times*, February 7, 1995.

Associated Press, "Cowboys deal Dorsett to Broncos," *Pacific Stars and Stripes*, June 6, 1988.

Associated Press, "Newspaper suggests Bronco take polygraph test," *Santa Fe New Mexican*, July 21, 1983.

Armstrong, Jim, "Armstrong sustained by attitude and spirit," *Denver Post*, September 2, 2007.

Brohard, Mike, "Griffith runs into fame," *Longmont Times-Call*, February 1, 1999.

Graham, Pat (Associated Press), "Broncos launch new era as Cutler succeeds Plummer," *Indiana Gazette*, November 28, 2006.

Hoffer, Richard, "Happy Days," *Sports Illustrated*, August 2, 1993.

Jekins, Chris, "The old man pulls his load with TD," *Colorado Springs Gazette-Trail*, October 17, 1977.

Johnson, William Oscar, "Whole new league, whole new season," *Sports Illustrated*, May 24, 1982.

Klis, Mike, "Zimmerman gets in Hall of Fame," *Denver Post*, February 3, 2008.

Lake, Thomas, "Bad nights in the NFL," *Sports Illustrated*, April 11, 2011.

Lewis, Al, "Shoes on, Karlis' kick is still good," *Denver Post*, March 16, 2007.

Lieber, Jill, "He bares his sole," *Sports Illustrated*, November 12, 1984.

Looney, Douglas S., "In Denver, delirium is spelled E-l-w-a-y," *Sports Illustrated*, August 15, 1983.

Lowe, Peggy and Julia C. Martinez, "Voters agree to back new Broncos stadium," *Denver Post*, November 4, 1998. (http://football.ballparks.com/NFL/DenverBroncos/articles.htm)

Madison Capital Times, "Upchurch cleans up act," July 18, 1983.

Montville, Leigh, "Mama's boy," *Sports Illustrated*, September 28, 1998.

Murphy, Austin, "Late bloomer," *Sports Illustrated*, October. 28, 1996.

Murphy, Austin, "You gotta love Tim Tebow," *Sports Illustrated*, July 27, 2009.

Neff, Craig, "The award was only token," *Sports Illustrated*, August 11, 1986.

Reilly, Rick, "Ultimate losses, ultimate victory," *Sports Illustrated*, February 2, 1998.

Sanko, John, "NFL backs Bowlen's play for new Broncos stadium," *Rocky Mountain News*, May 15, 1997. (http://football.ballparks.com/NFL/DenverBroncos/articles.htm)

Shrake, Edwin, "A love affair with a loser," *Sports Illustrated*, March 29, 1965.

Shrake, Edwin, "Tough cookie marches to his own drummer," *Sports Illustrated*, December 14, 1964.

Silver, Michael, "Little big men," *Sports Illustrated*, January 26, 1998.

Silver, Michael, "Seven up," *Sports Illustrated*, February 2, 1998.

Silver, Michael, "The magnificent 7," *Sports Illustrated*, February 8, 1999.

Sports Illustrated, "Scorecard," May 26, 1986.

Telander, Rick, "Getting there the hard way," *Sports Illustrated*, January 19, 1987.

Underwood, John, "Mile-high hopes in high old Denver," *Sports Illustrated*, October 22, 1962.

Wiley, Ralph, "Would he rather be a Unitas or a Mantle?" *Sports Illustrated*, August 11, 1983.

Williamson, Bill, "Broncos release Al Wilson," *Denver Post*, April 14, 2007.

Willis, Paul, "An original Bronco, 'Bud' McFadin, 77, stayed true to team," *Rocky Mountain News*, February 16, 2006.

Zimmerman, Paul, "Football," *Sports Illustrated*, October 27, 1992.

Internet

www.1043thefan.com, "The Drive with Big Al and D-Mac," http://www.1043thefan.com/podcasts/Episodes.aspx?PID=1623

Associated Press. "All-Pro LB Wilson released by Broncos," sports.espn.go.com, April 14, 2007, http://sports.espn.go.com/nfl/news/story?id=2836410

Associated Press. "Broncos turn out to pay respects to Darrent Williams," sports.espn.go.com, January 7, 2007, http://sports.espn.go.com/nfl/news/story?id=2722245

Associated Press. "Cutler has 'little' chip on his shoulder from draft," sports.espn.go.com, November 14, 2007, http://sports.espn.go.com/espn/wire?section=nfl&id=3111100

Associated Press. "John Fox hired to coach Broncos," sports.espn.go.com, January 13, 2011, http://sports.espn.go.com/nfl/news/story?id=6019160

Associated Press. "Texans hire Alex Gibbs, promote Kyle Shanahan," sports.espn.go.com, January 9, 2008, http://sports.espn.go.com/nfl/news/story?id=3189246

Associated Press. "This time, Zimmerman follows Elway's block…into Hall," www.usatoday.com, August 1, 2008, http://www.usatoday.com/sports/football/nfl/2008-07-30-gary-zimmerman_N.htm

Baseball-Reference.com, "John Elway," http://www.baseball-reference.com/minors/ player.cgi?id=elway-001joh

Bickley, Dan. "Kurt Warner to Tim Tebow: Let your actions be your words," www.azcentral.com, November 26, 2011, http://www.azcentral.com/sports/cardinals/articles/2011/11/26/20111126nfl-kurt-warner-tim-tebow-advice.html

Blevins, Jason. "Red Rocks celebrates a century of road shows," www.denverpost.com, May 13, 2011, http://www.denverpost.com/ci_18046255?source=rssdp

Caldwell, Gray. "Greek Honored," www.denverbroncos.com, March 1, 2011, http://blog.denverbroncos.com/denverbroncos/greek-honored/

Caldwell, Gray. "Leaving a Legacy," www.denverbroncos.com, Nov. 17, 2008, http://www.denverbroncos.com/ news-and-blogs/article-1/Leaving-a-Legacy/d3dfccbc-7892-11df-ba56-acc8e62813e9

Caldwell, Gray, "Rod Smith Transcript," www.denverbroncos.com, July 24, 2008, http://www.denverbroncos.com/news-and-blogs/article-1/Rod-Smith-Transcript/d6e68df6-7892-11df-ba56-acc8e62813e9

Cardona, Felisa and Lindsay H. Jones, "Willie Clark guilty of killing Bronco Darrent Williams," www.denverpost.com, March 12, 2010, http://www.denverpost.com/ci_14660167

CBC Sports, "Broncos swap Portis for Bailey," www.cbc.ca, March 5, 2004, http://www.cbc.ca/sports/story/2004/03/04/broncos-redskins040304.html

CBC Sports, "Terrell Davis retires from NFL," www.cbc.ca, August 20, 2002, http://www.cbc.ca/sports/story/2002/08/19/davis020819.html

CBSSports.com wire reports, "Broncos slip up against Bills, fail to lock up AFC West," www.cbssports.com, December 21, 2008, http://www.cbssports.com/nfl/gametracker/recap/NFL_20081221_BUF@DEN

CBSSports.com wire reports, "Chargers (8–8) rout Broncos for third straight AFC West title," www.cbssports.com, December 28, 2008, http://www.cbssports.com/nfl/gametracker/recap/NFL_20081228_DEN@SD

Clayton, John. "Broncos bolster defensive corps," sports.espn.go.com, March 1, 2009, http://sports.espn.go.com/nfl/news/story?id=3942161

Clayton, John. "Wilson, Broncos' first-round draft pick in '99, retires," sports.espn.go.com, September 10, 2008, http://sports.espn.go.com/nfl/news/story?id=3579956

Collegefootball.org, "Bud McFadin," http://www.collegefootball.org/ famer_selected.php?id=40103

Coloradosports.org, "Joe Collier," http://www.coloradosports.org/inducteeprofile.cfm?id=2

Davis, Nate. "Plummer likes Tebow's game, wishes he'd curb Jesus references," www.usatoday.com, November 21, 2011, http://content.usatoday.com/communities/thehuddle/post/2011/11/former-broncos-qb-jake-plummer-on-tim-tebow-ill-like-him-a-little-better-when-he-stops-talking-about-jesus/1#.T0L9JHmwXcA

DowntownDenver.com, "16th Street Plan," http://downtownden-ver.com/Business/DevelopmentandPlanning/ 16thStreetPlan/tabid/174/Default.aspx

ESPN.com news services. "Texans to hire Denver O-coordinator Kubiak as coach," sports.espn.go.com, January 23, 2006, http://sports.espn.go.com/nfl/news/story?id=2302213

Forbes.com, "#12 Denver Broncos," http://www.forbes.com/lists/2011/30/nfl-valuations-11_Denver-Broncos_308211.html

Greenberg, Steve. "Jay Cutler: 'I have a stronger arm' than Elway," aol.sportingnews.com, October 9, 2008, http://aol.sportingnews.com/nfl/story/2008-10-09/jay-cutler-i-have-stronger-arm-elway

Klis, Mike. "Broncos trade Cutler to Bears," www.denverpost.com, April 3, 2009, http://www.denverpost.com/broncos/ci_12056941

Legwold, Jeff. "Broncos return to scene of 2008 disaster: San Diego," www.denverpost.com, October 16, 2009, http://www.denverpost.com/premium/broncos/ci_13573098

MacMahon, Tim. "Wade Phillips learned from his mistakes," sports.espn.go.com, October 2, 2009, http://sports.espn.go.com/dallas/columns/story?id=4524768

Marshall, John. "Broncos' Portis darts past the three backs drafted ahead of him," community.seattletimes.nwsource.com, December 14, 2003, http://community.seattletimes.nwsource.com/archive/?date=20031214&slug=nflfeature14

Marvel.com, "Wolverine (James Howlett)," http://marvel.com/universe/Wolverine_%28James_Howlett%29

Mason, Andrew. "Dumervil Already a Man of Many Positions," www.denverbroncos.com, June 2, 2006, http://www.denverbroncos.com/news-and-blogs/article-1/Dumervil-Already-a-Man-of-Many-Positions/eb09182c-7892-11df-ba56-acc8e62813e9

NMHU-HClub.com, "Lionel Taylor," http://www.nmhu-hclub.com/ index.php?option=com_content&view=article&id=96:lionel-taylor-&catid=52:2001&Itemid=151

Oakes, Courtney. "15 Minutes: Ex-Broncos Wright can't stay away from football," www.aurorasentinel.com, July 14, 2011, http://www.aurorasentinel.com/sports/ article_76cbb0ae-ae69-11e0-a49b-001cc4c03286.html

Prisco, Pete. "Top corner or star back? Bailey makes it clear," www.cbssports.com, June 8, 2004, http://www.cbssports.com/ nfl/story/7403302

Saccomano, Jim. "Remember When…Alzado vs. Ali," www.denverbroncos.com, July 14, 2011, http://blog.denverbroncos.com/jsaccomano/remember-when-alzado-vs-ali/

Saunders, Dusty. "Long orange line leads to Logan," www.denverpost.com, August 3, 2009, http://www.denverpost.com/broncos/ci_12980052

SportsIllustrated.com, "They Said It," January 20, 1964. http://sportsillustrated.cnn.com/vault/article/magazine/MAG1075566/index.htm

SportsLine.com wire reports, "Broncos not worried about finding Portis' replacement," www. Cbssports.com, May 8, 2004, http://www.cbssports.com/nfl/story/7314747

Stapleton, Arnie. "Randy Gradishar hopes to join John Elway in Hall of Fame," www.usatoday.com, January 31, 2008, http://www.usatoday.com/sports/football/ 2008-01-31-230500230_x.htm

Ward, Randy. "A Breakdown of the History of the 3-4 Defense," www.nflgridirongab.com, June 26, 2009, http://www.nflgridirongab.com/2009/06/26/a-breakdown-of-the-history-of-the-3-4-defense/

YouTube.com, "Brian Dawkins History-Weapon X," http://www.youtube.com/watch?v=JPN0jOaWlsE

YouTube.com, "Denver's Three Amigos," http://www.youtube.com/ watch?v=Z15HGEuzXU0

YouTube.com, "The Magician: Marlin Briscoe," http://www.youtube.com/watch?v=zwtPPS8PLlw

Other Internet Sources

http://www.14ers.com/

http://www.buffalobill.org/

http://www.cherrycricket.com/

http://www.coloradoski.com/

www.DenverBroncos.com

http://www.gilpinhistory.org/

http://www.nationalwestern.com

www.profootballhof.com

www.pro-football-reference.com
http://www.redrocksonline.com/
http://www.usfl.info/gold/
http://www.usatoday.com/story/sports/nfl/broncos/2016/01/29/pat-bowlen-owner-denver-super-bowl-50-john-elway/79537700/
http://media.denverbroncos.com/
http://www.nfl.com/liveupdate/gamecenter/56831/DEN_Gamebook.pdf
http://www.legacy.com/obituaries/beaumontenterprise/obituary.aspx?pid=172433591
http://www.denverpost.com/broncos/ci_27650532/peyton-manning-passes-physical-makes-return-broncos-official
https://www.youtube.com/watch?v=2mfw21aJKn0
http://www.nfl.com/videos/nfl-films-sound-efx/0ap3000000635823/Sound-FX-Broncos-get-the-best-of-the-Panthers
http://www.pro-football-reference.com/players/M/MingGe20.htm
http://www.denverpost.com/broncos/ci_25726273/better-late-than-never-ring-welcomes-mingo
http://gazette.com/nfls-first-black-kicker-has-turned-life-around/article/63366

Interviews

Steve Atwater
Champ Bailey
Marlin Briscoe
David Bruton
Sandy Clough
Eric Decker
Elvis Dumervil
Terry Frei

Austin "Goose" Gonsoulin
Robert Howsam
Tom Jackson
Charley Johnson
Floyd Little
Karl Mecklenburg
Craig Morton
Dan Reeves
Shannon Sharpe
Harry Sydney
Billy Thompson
Alfred Williams
Sammy Winder
Larry Zimmer